OXFORD
G N V Q

C000185554

Advanced
LEISURE & RECREATION

CAMBRIDGE
TRAINING AND
CTAD
DEVELOPMENT
LTD

OXFORD
UNIVERSITY PRESS

OXFORD
UNIVERSITY PRESS

Oxford University Press is a department of the University of Oxford.
It furthers the University's objective of excellence in research, scholarship,
and education by publishing worldwide in

Oxford New York

Athens Auckland Bangkok Bogotá Buenos Aires Calcutta
Cape Town Chennai Dar es Salaam Delhi Florence Hong Kong Istanbul
Karachi Kuala Lumpur Madrid Melbourne Mexico City Mumbai
Nairobi Paris São Paulo Singapore Taipei Tokyo Toronto Warsaw

with associated companies in Berlin Ibadan

Oxford is a registered trade mark of Oxford University Press
in the UK and in certain other countries

British Library Cataloguing in Publication Data

Data available

ISBN 019-8328281-X

Designed by Design Study, Bury St Edmunds and Chris Lord Information Design,
Brighton, East Sussex.
Typeset by The Write Idea, Cambridge.

Printed and bound by G. Canale & C., Italy

Contributors include:

Jim Johnson, Michael Bourke, Doug Morrison, Julia Macintosh, Gillian Dale

Thanks for permission to reproduce
photographs/extracts go to:

Advertising Standards Authority (Logo p. 229);
Age Concern (web p. 13); Allsport UK Ltd.
(Tennis tournament p. 336, tournament p. 148,
150, Athletics tournament p. 120); Brighton
Borough Council (Deserted beach p. 73,
Crowded beach p. 68, 73); British Telecom
(Swimathon p. 318, 325); Bromley Leisure and
Community Services (Golf course p. 30, 162,
168); Bury Bowl (Bowling Alley p. 266); Bury St.
Edmunds Leisure Services (Fete p. 329, 350,
356); Cambridge City Council (p. 222, 223);
Cambridge Hi-tech Recruitment (advert p. 43);

Doncaster Leisure Park (The Dome p. 124);
English Tourist Board (Disabled criteria p. 72, 20
tips for visitors p. 73); Financial Times (Internet
p. 136); Forte Hotel Group (Gym instructors p.
144, Lobby Manager p. 250, 282, Receptionist
p. 267, Employee talking to one person p. 48,
52, 204, 213, Employee talking to a group p.
262, Fitness Instructor p. 36, 40, 139); Health
and Safety Commission (Logo p. 77, 87); Health
and Safety Executive (Advice booklet p. 81, Logo
p. 87); ILAM (Logo p. 210); Independent
Television Commission (Logo p. 229); Ipswich
Tourist Information (Booking form p. 331);
McDonalds (p. 256, 258, 300); MINTEL
(sponsorship p. 133); National Trust, The (Logo

p. 29); Observer (sponsorship p. 133); Office for
National Statistics (Social Trends 30 p. 8, 9, 10,
33, 34, 145); Racing Line (Front cover p. 164);
Radio Authority (Logo p. 229); Ragdale Hall Healt
Hydro (leisure centre p. 132); Ramblers'
Association, The (Ramblers group p. 6, 12, 140);
Reed Exhibition Companies UK (Trade exhibition
p. 235); RSPB (Brochure p. 18, 29); Snowdonia
Tourist Services (p. 227, 320); Sports Council
(table p. 145); St. Edmundsbury Borough Council
(Leisure services department structure p. 24,
Advert p. 226, Skating p. 340); Stepstone (web
p. 44); Warwick Arts Centre (Arts Centre p. 331)

Contents

ABOUT THE BOOK

This book contains the information you need to complete the six mandatory units of your Advanced Leisure and Recreation GNVQ.

How it's organised

This book is organised in units and sections, like the GNVQ, so it's easy to find the information you need at any point in your course. Each section is divided into chapters. They cover all the topics in the section, using the same headings as the GNVQ specifications. At the end of each section there are some key questions, so you can check your knowledge and prepare for the unit tests. At the end of the unit, there are suggestions for an assignment, which will help you produce the evidence you need for your portfolio. There are also key skills signposted at the end of each unit to help you identify the vocational requirements that your portfolio evidence can fulfil.

What's in it

The book presents information in several diff e rent ways so it's interesting to read and easy to understand. Some information is given in the words of people who actually work in travel or tourism jobs – for example, a travel consultant in a travel agency, a development officer on a tourist board or the manager of a hotel in a seaside resort. There are definitions of important words like 'tourism' or 'seasonality'. There are illustrations, maps and diagrams, and examples of brochures and leaflets, case studies which go into the details of a range of leisure and recreation organisations, and photographs of facilities and people working in them.

How to use the book

Decide which part you want to read. For example, you can go straight to any section and read through the relevant chapters. You can find the information about any topic by looking at the list of contents at the front of the book and deciding which chapter looks most useful. Or you can use the index at the back to find the page reference for a specific topic or organisation.

As well as information, the book has suggestions for things you can do to help you learn about leisure and recreation in a practical way. Discussion points suggest topics that you can think about and discuss with other people – other students on your course, your tutor or teacher, friends, family, people who work in leisure and recreation. Activity boxes ask you to do things like write a press release for a promotional campaign, roleplay customer service situations, visit facilities to collect information, and so on. They will help you to get a real-life picture of leisure and recreation organisations and what it's like to work in them.

When you've finished a section, try answering the key questions at the end.

You may want to make notes of your answers and use them when you're preparing for the unit tests. The assignment at the end of each section suggests what you can do to produce evidence for your portfolio. You might want to make an action plan for each assignment to help you plan and carry out the work.

Other resources

By itself this book is an important and valuable source of information for your GNVQ studies. It should also help you use other resources effectively. For example, it suggests that you should find out more information about some topics, which you could find in a local library, from the Internet, or from other books about leisure and recreation. It also asks you to investigate facilities yourself by visiting them or reading about them.

Over to you

It's your GNVQ and your job to make the best of the opportunity to learn about leisure and recreation. Use this book in whatever way helps you most. For example, you could:
- look at the contents page to give you the whole picture
- use the index to find out specific bits of information
- read a chapter at a time to help you understand a topic
- look at the assignment before starting a section so you know what you have to do
- turn things on their head and start with the key questions to see how much previous knowledge you have about a section.

It's over to you now. Good luck.

UNIT **1**

Section 1.1
The development of the leisure and recreation industry

Section 1.2
The structure and scale of the leisure and recreation industry

Section 1.3
Working in the leisure and recreation industry

Section 1.4
Pursuing your own progression aims

Investigating leisure and recreation

About this unit

This unit offers an introduction to the dynamic and very diverse leisure and recreation industry in the UK. You will investigate the factors that contributed to its rapid growth since the 1960s. You will research the structure and scale of today's leisure and recreation industry and learn that it is made up of many public, private and voluntary organisations that interact to supply an enormous range of products and services to consumers.

You will also investigate the wide range of careers available in leisure and recreation so that you can identify possible employment opportunities that match your aspirations, skills and abilities.

SECTION **1.1**

The development of the leisure and recreation industry

There is a huge consumer demand for leisure and recreation products and services. This section will help you to understand the many different factors that contribute to this demand. These factors include socio-economic and technological developments and changing consumer needs which have combined to produce the rapid growth in the leisure and recreation industry which has taken place since the 1960s.

66 *The leisure industry has taken off in the last 20 years. It's a massive business now. Lots of our shows are doing well because people have more money to spend on entertainments. It's the same for other venues. There's a great deal of activity going on all over the country – probably more than there has ever been in the past.* 99

press and publicity officer at an entertainments venue

66 *There's been a huge growth in this area in small businesses involved in the leisure and recreation industry. It's not just fitness and golf clubs! The number of restaurants and take-aways has doubled in five years. We've even got three cyber-cafés in the town and I can't count the number of pubs which have turned themselves into café-bars in the last two years. They even have bouncers on the doors at weekends!* 99

chief executive, chamber of commerce

66 *People work hard today and they want to enjoy their leisure time. There's a large and growing industry devoted to making sure that they do.* 99

manager of a multi-screen cinema complex

1.1.1 Defining leisure and recreation

Defining leisure is difficult, because it's easier to talk about what it doesn't mean than what it does mean. It's all the things you do that are not about work, essential chores or natural imperatives like sleeping, or anything else you don't do for pleasure or entertainment. The boundary is not always clear – for example, gardening may be leisure to some and a chore to others.

Recreation describes the activities that you do in your leisure time. The list is huge and perhaps limitless. When completing the parts of application forms that ask for leisure pursuits, many people used to put in the things they thought would sound respectable, such as reading, sports, walking and going to the theatre. Would you put in playing computer games, surfing the Net, clubbing, watching quiz shows on TV? It probably depends on the kind of place you are applying to: modern employers often prefer people with modern habits!

The leisure and recreation industry embraces the entire range of activities that people do in their spare time. The range of activities, products and services that it supplies is vast and multifaceted. It's one of the biggest and fastest-growing service industries in the UK.

The main distinctions between the types of leisure activity are:
- active (e.g. playing sport, walking) or passive (e.g. reading, watching television)
- home-based (e.g. listening to music or playing cards at home) or away from home (e.g. going to the pub or the cinema).

Home-based leisure is one of the fastest-growing sectors. It manufactures and sells music centres, games consoles and computer games, books, gardening tools, bulbs and seeds, and many other things besides, so that people can enjoy their leisure time without having to leave home.

Leisure is the opportunity and time outside working hours to choose and take part in activities or experiences which are expected to be personally satisfying.

Recreation is what people do in their leisure time. It may be active, like taking part in a sport, or it may be passive, like watching the TV or reading a book or magazine.

Leisure and recreation activities

- arts and entertainment – theatres, concert halls, galleries, art centres, museums, bingo halls, race tracks, theme parks, home-based entertainment
- sports and physical activities – sports centres, leisure centres, running tracks, sports stadiums, gyms, fitness centres, swimming pools
- play – playing fields, parks, adventure playgrounds, play schemes
- outdoor activities – natural spaces for walking and climbing, campsites, open-air swimming pools, botanical gardens, nature trails, garden centres, activity centres
- heritage – historic sites, industrial attractions, working museums
- catering and accommodation – food and drink services in hotels, hostels, campsites etc.; facilities such as meeting rooms

1.1.2 Increase in leisure time

The way people use their leisure and recreation time has changed enormously during this century. Most people now:

- have more time available for leisure activities because of social and economic developments which have changed working hours and patterns
- have more personal disposable income – money which does not have to be spent on necessities like housing, heating, food and clothing
- are more mobile – more people own cars, and the public transport system allows them to travel much more widely
- have different needs and expectations – for example, they may be more aware of the importance of health and fitness and of the need to balance work and leisure
- want more access to the countryside.

In the Nineteenth Century it was possible to talk about a 'leisured class'. It included landowners, politicians and wealthy industrialists – people who didn't have to spend all their time working for a living and who could afford to pay for their leisure activities. Most other people, including children, had to work long hours and had no time or money to enjoy any leisure.

Since the Second World War, most people in the UK have had time for leisure and do use it. In 1998, the average weekly working hours for full-time employees were: male 45.7, female 40.7.

Reasons for increased leisure

- the hours people work each week – since the end of the Second World War in 1945 the working week has become much shorter
- the way people work – there's more job sharing and flexitime, part-time and short-term contracts, home-working and self-employment
- new groups of consumers with disposable income, e.g. single people and couples in full-time work
- changes in trading laws – Sunday is no longer an official day of rest so all kinds of entertainment are available.

Average hours usually worked per week by full-time employees: by gender, EU comparison, 1998

	Hours	
	Males	Females
United Kingdom	45.7	40.7
Portugal	42.1	39.6
Greece	41.7	39.3
Spain	41.2	39.6
Germany	40.4	39.3
France	40.3	38.7
Sweden	40.2	40.0
Italy	39.7	36.3
Denmark	39.3	37.7

Source: Labour Force Surveys, Eurostat.
'Social Trends 30', Office for National Statistics © Crown Copyright 2000

1.1.3 Growth in personal disposable incomes

Disposable income is the amount of money left after all essential expenses such as housing, heating and basic food or clothes.

Some people have higher levels of disposable income than others:

- students living on grants and earnings from holiday jobs tend to have a very low level
- single professionals or couples with jobs and no children tend to have quite a high level.

Disposable income is money that people can use however they wish. They can choose to save, give to charity, invest in high fashion items, pay for home gyms, eat and drink with friends, go to parties, travel all over the world, go to the theatre or cinema, watch or participate in sporting activities, go to evening classes – the list is endless.

Expenditure of working age couple households with children and without children: by type of household, 1998-99

United Kingdom	Percentages	
	Without children	With children
Housing	17	18
Food	14	18
Leisure goods and services	17	17
Motoring and fares	19	16
Household goods and services	14	14
Clothing and footwear	6	6
Alcohol	4	3
Fuel, light and power	3	3
Tobacco	1	2
Other goods and services	4	4
All household expenditure (=100%)(£ per week)	441	465

Source: Family Expenditure Survey, Office for National Statistics
'Social Trends 30', Office for National Statistics © Crown Copyright 2000

Household expenditure by economic activity status of head of household, 1998–99

United Kingdom

	In Employment	Self-employed	Un-employed	Retired	Un-occupied	All
			Percentages			
Motoring and fares	18	19	17	13	15	17
Leisure goods and services	17	17	14	19	17	17
Food	16	17	20	19	20	17
Housing	18	15	12	14	12	16
Household goods & services	14	14	12	15	14	14
Clothing and footwear	6	7	7	5	7	6
Alcohol	4	4	5	3	4	4
Fuel, light and power	3	3	4	5	5	3
Tobacco	1	1	4	1	3	2
Other goods and services	4	4	4	5	4	4
All household expenditure (=100%)(£ per week)	450	485	239	194	244	352
Expenditure per person (£ per week)	169	164	91	125	101	149

Source: Family Expenditure Survey, Office for National Statistics
'Social Trends 30', Office for National Statistics © Crown Copyright 2000

DISCUSSION POINT

Expenditure on housing and staple food is essential. In your own household, what else do you think is a necessity?

And what are your main luxuries?

If your household has cars, are they essential or a luxury?

An economist working in a local authority interprets the information in the table:

66 *Figures like these give an idea of spending patterns. As with most surveys, the picture is broad. You can see that the amount of money spent on leisure is high. But there are many members of society who cannot enjoy expensive leisure facilities because they are short of money – such as the unemployed, single parents, some of the elderly, people in low-paid jobs, and some students. Although they have little disposable income, they are potentially a good market because they have more disposable time. The challenge is to develop low-cost products and services that will attract this group and potentially improve their lifestyle.* 99

DISCUSSION POINT

Can you think of low-cost leisure activities, products and services for people on low incomes, or in particular groups such as the elderly in residential care?

1.1.4 **Improved mobility**

The transport options now available – car, train, coach, bus – allow people to travel quite long distances to take part in leisure activities. They can:

- drive to remote countryside for a day of climbing or walking
- take a train to London to visit major exhibitions like the Millennium Dome or the Motor Show
- organise coach trips to the seaside for the elderly or the young
- follow their team wherever it goes in the world
- travel to Newcastle or London for a night's clubbing.

The countryside has long been seen as a place where you can 'get away from it all'. As working lives have centred themselves in towns and cities, people increasingly see the countryside as a resource for leisure and recreation. Developments in rail and road transport, especially the big increase in car ownership, have made getting to rural areas easier.

As well as providing traditional pursuits like walking, wildlife, bird-watching and riding, the countryside is also the place to go for:

- water sports and boating on lakes, rivers and reservoirs
- climbing hills, mountains, cliffs and rocks
- farm holidays – now a major income source for many farmers
- green or eco-tourism, where people actively seek countryside activities that support the environment
- orienteering, trekking, mountain biking and survival games in the wilder areas like fells and moors.

In response to the increased demand, governments have passed laws aimed at making rural areas accessible to the public and protecting them from damaging developments. For example:

- ten National Parks and 33 Areas of Outstanding Beauty have been established as a result of the National Parks and Countryside Act (1949)
- the Countryside Act (1968) gave local authorities power to establish local parks and protect local areas of rural interest.

On the other hand, Sites of Special Scientific Interest (SSSIs) – areas that have special characteristics that are of interest to scientists, such as meadows with rare wildflowers or butterflies – have been steadily eroded. More and more of the countryside is being developed and getting less attractive; a 1999 survey showed that, between the early 1960s and the early 1990s, the area of tranquillity in England reduced by 21%; the percentage of England that is tranquil (i.e. has a low level of noise and light pollution) reduced from 70% to 56%; and the average size of tranquil areas went down from 193 sq. km to 52 sq. km, a fall of 73%. If things don't change, argues the Council for the Protection of Rural England (CPRE), there will be little countryside left to enjoy by the end of the Twenty-first Century.

DISCUSSION POINT

What effect do you think developments of transport had on leisure and recreational facilities:

- in seaside towns in Britain?
- elsewhere in Britain?

There are many useful web sites that address this issue. Visit the Council for the Protection of Rural England (*http://www.cpre.org.uk*), the Joint Nature Conservation Committee (*http://www.jncc.gov.uk*) and the many press releases from the Countryside Commission (*http://www.coi.gov.uk/coi/ depts/GCM/GCM.html*). That should get you started!

DISCUSSION POINT

How would your leisure and recreation activities be restricted if you did not have access to a car or public transport?

ACTIVITY

Make three lists and put down four or five activities in your area that:

- are easier by car – for example, visiting a theme park
- can be attended by anyone with access to public transport – for example, a rock concert at a sports centre in town
- require some form of transport – for example, a day trip to France organised by the local coach company.

Then list leisure and recreation activities which don't need any form of transport.

1.1.5 Demographic changes

Demography is the study of the way populations change, using statistics. It includes factors such as births, deaths, income, the incidence of disease and the proportion of people of different ages.

Demographic statistics can help policy makers decide things such as how many schools or old peoples' homes will be needed in the future. Here's an example.

The number of people over pensionable age is projected to increase from 10.7 million in 1996 to 11.8 million in 2011.

Allowing for the women's retirement age change (to 65), the population of pensionable age will rise to 12.0 million by 2021.

These and other statistics about older people are available at *http://www.ageconcern.org.uk*

Source: National Population Projection, Office for National Satistics

By and large, the major UK trends that are widely recognised are:

- an increase in the number and percentage of older people in the UK
- an increase in the disposable income of younger people
- an increase in the number and percentage of working parents, which also stimulates an increase in services such as childminding and domestic work.

People are living longer and there is a comparatively low birth rate, so the population is said to be ageing. The leisure and recreation business needs to take note of trends like that and develop appropriate new products and services. Here are some more interesting figures from the Age Concern web site:

Living alone

In Great Britain in 1996:

- in the 65–74 age group, 21% of men and 39% of women lived alone
- 31% of men and 58% of women aged 75 and over lived alone.

In 1996, of people

aged 65 to 74	75 and over	
74%	62%	of men were married
53%	28%	of women were married
13%	29%	of men were widowed
35%	62%	of women were widowed

In 1997/8, amongst pensioners who were mainly dependent on state pensions and living alone:

- 81% had central heating, compared to 89% of all households
- 14% had a car, compared to 69.8% of all households
- 91% had a telephone, compared to 94% of all households
- 62% had a washing machine, compared to 91% of all households.

Social changes can lead to changes in personal needs and expectations. A journalist on a leisure magazine explains how the increasing numbers of elderly people in society has affected the leisure and recreation industry:

66 *We're seeing an increase in recreational services for the elderly. This generation doesn't want to end its days in a geriatric ward or a dreary old people's home staring at the wall all day. Old people's recreation often has to be more organised, as they don't tend to have cars, so it may involve group excursions to places of interest, from the seaside to an art gallery or a concert or cabaret. There are some interesting educational initiatives like the University of the Third Age, encouraging them to come back to study. And there are now some initiatives where older people are being encouraged to learn computing and get on the World Wide Web. Watch this space!* 99

DISCUSSION POINT

What kind of recreational activities do you know of for the over 65s? Do you think the recreation industry is providing them with the services and products they need? Think of two or three examples.

ACTIVITY

What recreational services and products are available in your area for elderly people? Check out with the library and your local authority, look in the *Yellow Pages*, or contact an old people's home and ask the management what recreational activities the residents use. Make a 'top ten' listing of their favourites.

1.1.6 **Fashions and trends**

People's needs and expectations change all the time, so the market must change with them and the industry has to develop new products and services. This may mean creating entirely new activities using technology or targeting new or emerging groups of people. Examples include:

- the development in the 1990s of computer games – before then the computer was mainly a work tool
- the growth of cybercafés (pubs and even barbers)
- the development in the 1990s of the All Bar One style of trendy drink and food venues which appealed to upwardly mobile young people who wanted a place to go after work; there are many other similarly branded venues throughout towns in the UK
- the growth of lesbian and gay pubs, clubs and restaurants
- the merging of different pop music cultures such as bangla music
- the popularity of raves in the 80s and early 90s
- the salsa phenomenon – hitting all the age groups in different ways
- surfing the Web, chatting, conferencing, gaming, gambling and shopping on line.

New products get developed or new sectors get identified through marketing research.

Needs and expectations reflect economic and social aspirations, trends and fashions. The health and fitness industry changed completely in a generation: the rather grim and puritanical sweat boxes of yesterday have been replaced by a whole array of high-tech machinery, fitness programmes, personal trainers, designer clothing and designer bodies. There's a hunger for information on getting and staying fit and healthy which sits strangely alongside the persistent popularity of smoking and drinking.

People have more information about health and fitness now than they used to. As a result the demand for sports and fitness facilities has increased but the demand has also been fuelled by the increase in leisure time and disposable incomes. People expect facilities to offer a wider range of products and services. For example, big fitness centres now offer bar and restaurant facilities and shops for 'designer brand' leisure-wear.

ACTIVITY

Carry out a mini-survey of two people who are over 55 years old. Ask each of them what they think the biggest change has been in the way they take their leisure and how they think it's changed for their generation. Then try to predict what your kids will be doing for their leisure when they reach 16.

15

1.1.7 **Technological developments**

Changes in working hours and methods are not the only reason for the increase in leisure time. There are more things to do, because of technological advances like the invention of electricity, changes in transport, the development of the World Wide Web.

Look at this table, which shows the standard of living up to 1997.

	1981	1994	1995	1996	1997
Average earnings (GB only)(£ per week)(April)(Jan 1990=100)	124.9	325.7	336.3	351.5	384.5
retail prices (Jan 1987=100)	74.8	144.1	149.1	152.7	157.5

It's pretty normal to have washing machines, refrigerators and deep-freezes, and more and more households are centrally heated. In the past a lot of time would have been spent washing and repairing clothes, and making and maintaining fires to keep the home warm.

Technological development has had a profound effect on the way in which people are able to spend leisure time in their own homes: radio and television, computers, games machines, video, DVD and CD players provide flexible alternatives to the facilities offered by, for example, cinemas, pubs, and fitness and sports centres. And new things keep appearing: digital TVs let you view football games from different angles, choose your own instant replay and go shopping. Shopping itself (or some kinds of shopping) has turned into a leisure pursuit which can involve the whole family. The Mall of America in Minneapolis has a full-sized Ferris wheel and a series of rides right at its heart. Half of what goes on in theme parks is shopping; Gateshead's Metro Centre tries to be a fun place to be in as well as to go shopping.

ACTIVITY

Go to a local newspaper office or library and ask to look at a newspaper printed about 100 years ago. Make a list of any news items or advertisements illustrating different kinds of leisure activities or facilities available for leisure activities. Do the same with a recent copy of a local newspaper. How has the range of activities changed?

ACTIVITY

There's a lot of information about this kind of thing on the World Wide Web – use it if you want to. Look at newspaper sites, museums, or just try some searches.

Key questions

1 What are some of the reasons that leisure time has increased since the Second World War?

2 How has increased mobility affected the leisure industry?

3 What is disposable income and how does it affect leisure?

4 What impact do changing social expectations and fashions have on the leisure and recreation industry? Consider two examples from your own experience.

5 What affect will the ageing population have upon the leisure industry?

SECTION **1.2**

The structure and scale of the leisure and recreation industry

The recreation industry is huge and very diverse. This section aims to stimulate you to find out the range and variety of facilities, products and services that it offers. Also, you need to understand the way things are organised and the different stakeholders that affect the industry's development.

There are huge players in the leisure and recreation industry – Rank, AOL-TimeWarner, Disneyland, Virgin. There are many many more small actors providing local services which meet local demand. Who drives the industry?

economist

There is a wide range of leisure activities available today – probably greater than ever before. A lot of companies employ huge numbers of people to meet the demand and competition is fierce. That is good news for the customer.

manager of a multiscreen cinema complex

We've launched our first set of virtual museums, with lots of activities for young people to try out on line. It's been a revelation to the whole team to discover what's possible.

team leader, museum on-line development team

1.2.1 The structure of the leisure and recreation industry

Recreation is divided into three distinct sectors:

- the private sector – profit-making businesses such as private health clubs, fairs, bingo halls and Web-based casinos
- the public sector – facilities and services provided by local authorities or central government, such as council leisure centres or recreational fitness classes for the elderly
- the voluntary sector – organisations that are 'not for profit', often aiming to promote a good cause; they may be large, like the Youth Hostels Association (*http://www.YHA.org.uk*) or the Scouts (*http://www.Scouts.com*), or small, local ventures organising outings for the elderly or riding for disabled people.

You need to know which sector an organisation is in, and how this affects the way it works. For example, if it's in the private sector it will be trying to create products and services that are designed for the interests and price range of the target market sector. If they are in the public sector, they will need to think about the best way to show the funders that they are getting value for money. In the voluntary sector, fund-raising is a constant issue.

Six key components

Because the industry is so diverse it's been divided up into six major components. This makes it easier to think about the very wide range of what there is. The components are:

- arts and entertainment
- sports and physical recreation
- heritage
- catering
- countryside recreation
- home-based leisure.

You need to know about the main types of organisations, facilities, products and services within these six components. All of them exist in the private, public and voluntary sectors.

ACTIVITY

Use a wordprocessor to create a table like this one:

Sector	Private	Public	Voluntary
Arts and entertainment			
Sports and physical recreation			
Heritage			
Catering			
Countryside recreation			
Home-based leisure			

Put down at least one and at most two examples of each key component under each sector that you know of in your area.

The private sector

> **Private sector** organisations are owned by shareholders (even if there's only one). These may include individuals, companies or institutions. They aim to make a profit so that they can reward their investors through dividends, their customers through improved quality and their employees through improved conditions.

Private sector businesses range from those owned by one person to big multinationals with thousands of shareholders worldwide (for example, TimeWarner).

Because they aim to make a profit and because their investors want to see a good return on their investment, they tend to operate in areas of the industry where there are large numbers of potential customers. Smaller businesses may also specialise in particular market segments, as this taxi driver does:

66 *I specialise in taking some of the old ladies down to the Temple to have tea and discussions with their friends. They don't like to travel with just anyone in a cab – they prefer someone they know and trust, who understands them. I've upgraded to a minibus because I'm getting known in the area. It's a good little business for me.* **99**

Facilities

Examples of facilities provided by the private sector are:

- sports and recreation – sports clubs, water sports, snooker halls, bowling alleys, ice skating, fitness clubs, golf courses, tennis courts, football clubs
- arts and entertainment – cinemas, galleries, theatres, concert halls, rock concerts, night clubs, arts centres, race tracks, home-based video and computer entertainment, theme parks, bingo halls, amusement arcades
- catering and accommodation – pubs and cafés, hotels, hostels, boarding houses, bed and breakfast accommodation, self-catering accommodation, restaurants.

Managing facilities

Private sector organisations also manage facilities on behalf of the public sector. This happens because the Local Government Act (Competition in Sports and Leisure Facilities) 1988 states that local authorities must put the running of their sports and leisure facilities out to tender. This has given the private sector opportunities to bid for contracts from local authorities for facility management and service provision which was previously carried out by the public sector alone. They have to do it cost-effectively and make their profit within a fixed budget.

DISCUSSION POINT

Do you think that using private sector companies to manage facilities owned by the public sector is a good thing?

What benefits are there to people using the facilities?

What disadvantages are there?

Finance and investment

Private sector organisations can get the money they need to invest in their businesses from several different sources:

ACTIVITY

The aim here is to get you thinking about price and value for money. Ask six people you know about the money they spend on their recreation. Find out:

■ what they spend most on

■ why they do it – what's the main benefit they get?

■ how they decide whether they are getting value for money

■ what kind of thing would make them stop spending that kind of money.

Put down two or three sentences of good advice for the owners of one of the recreation businesses your sample liked.

DISCUSSION POINT

Think of two or three more examples of risk ventures yourself. Are they successful? How is their success measured?

■ personal savings – owners of organisations provide money themselves

■ loans – banks, building societies, insurance companies and pension companies all lend money to the private sector

■ private shares – a private limited company can sell shares in the business to private individuals such as employees or to companies who are connected to the business in some way

■ public shares – a public limited company can sell shares to the public anywhere in the world through the Stock Exchange

■ venture capital – venture capitalists are banks and companies who specialise in financing new business ventures

■ government grants – the Government may award grants if it thinks that the organisation will make a significant contribution to the local economy.

All investors in the private sector expect to earn money from their investment. Lenders earn money from the interest they charge on loans; shareholders earn shares in the profits, known as dividends, and also make money from selling their shares when the share price increases.

Risk ventures

Sometimes private companies can raise money for schemes that would not be suitable for public sector organisations, which have to be more cautious because they are spending public funds. Private individuals and lenders may be prepared to invest their capital on a venture that may give them a good return. But it may not, which is why it is a risk.

Examples of successful risk ventures in leisure and recreation are:

■ Richard Branson's 'Virgin' label – a brand covering airlines, the music recording business and soft drinks

■ pub groups such as Wetherspoon's

■ PlayStation and Nintendo games consoles

■ active holiday centres like Center Parcs

■ theme parks such as Alton Towers.

Joint provision

In the 1990s, the public and private sectors became more intermingled, with an increase in facilities and services provided jointly. The marketing officer for an inner-city music venue explains the benefits:

66 *We would never have got off the ground without the council. They helped us put together our grant application to the regional arts board and they provide funding for some of our educational work. We discuss our programmes with them and often do joint marketing – when people come here they also find out what's going on in other city venues.* 99

1.2.3 The public sector

Public sector organisations are normally funded by national government or local authorities. Examples are tourist boards, arts centres and tourist information offices.

National provision

In the UK the Government doesn't often get directly involved in providing leisure and recreation facilities. Instead it provides financial assistance through government agencies which make grants available to local authorities and voluntary organisations. The agencies are managed by the Department of Culture, Media and Sport which has strategic responsibility for leisure and recreation.

The Department gets an annual budget from the Treasury. Since 1994, much of the money available to the agencies which support leisure and recreation comes from the National Lottery.

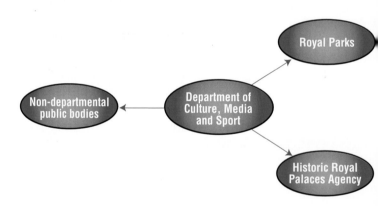

Other government departments which provide funds for recreational activities are:
- the Department of the Environment – supports the Countryside Commission and English Nature
- the Department of Agriculture – supports the Forestry Commission
- the Department for Education and Employment – supports some recreational activities through education budgets
- the Welsh Office – funds the Wales Tourist Board and CADW (Welsh Heritage).

THE SPORTS COUNCILS

There are four Sports Councils in the UK – one each for England, Wales, Scotland and Northern Ireland. The English council now uses the brand name Sport England.

Sources of funding:

- national government
- commercial activities
- sponsorship from the private sector for specific activities.

Aims:

- to increase participation in sport and physical recreation
- to increase the quantity and quality of sports facilities
- to raise standards of performance
- to provide information for and about sport.

Activities:

- make grants and loans to local authorities to fund community facilities and projects
- provide funds to national sports governing bodies for improving administration, participation, coaching and training standards
- run national publicity campaigns
- run the National Sports Centres
- administer and distribute sports and recreation grants from National Lottery funds.

Charitable trusts

Greenwich Leisure Limited is a good example of the charitable trusts that are becoming significant in the leisure and recreation sector. There are now six local authorities across the country using the Greenwich Leisure Limited model for the delivery of their leisure centre services.

In July 1993, because of the necessity of reducing spending, Greenwich Council was faced with the prospect of closing two or three of its seven leisure centres.

As an alternative to closure, a new company was formed as a not-for-profit industrial and provident society for the benefit of the community and with charitable aims. This solution attracted discretionary rate relief of £400,000 and all staff retained their jobs. A share issue of one share per employee, at £25 per share, was used to raise the cash needed for the legal registration of Greenwich Leisure Limited. The local authority agreed to let the centres to the company for a peppercorn (i.e. nominal or very low) rent for seven years.

Greenwich Leisure Limited has been successful in reducing costs to the council while increasing income and concessionary access. Two additional centres have been added to the management portfolio.

Local provision

Most local authority leisure and recreation services are financed by local taxes from:

- businesses – they pay a tax known as the Uniform Business Rate
- residents – they pay a Council Tax related to the value of their homes.

These taxes pay for a wide range of services, including education, housing and social services. So there isn't usually a lot left over for leisure. Local authorities have a legal duty to provide some amenities, such as public libraries. But in general the provision of leisure and recreation services is discretionary. These services are usually provided through leisure and recreation departments.

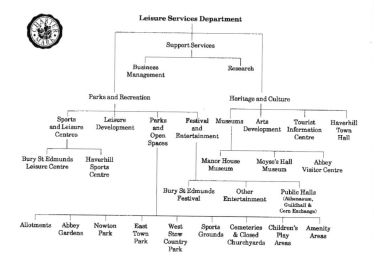

Local authorities often see their role as to provide facilities for people who live in the area, rather than people who come from outside. The chairperson of the leisure and recreation committee on a town council explains why:

❝ *We are elected by the people of this town to provide a service to them. That means our priorities on this committee are to provide the services people living here want. For example, we subsidise the sports centre and swimming pool very heavily. Recently we sold some land in the centre to a developer on the condition that the firm built a new swimming pool. Over the last five or six years there's been a rolling programme to improve the parks and public spaces. New children's play areas have been put up and we've built a pavilion on the main green by the river to provide refreshments. Last month I asked officers to do a survey of residents to find out what they would most like us to do next – it will probably be a long list!* ❞

DISCUSSION POINT

How might the leisure and recreational policies of an inner city area differ from those of a rural area?

Policy

Like other public sector organisations, leisure and recreation facilities follow strategies and policies decided by their governing bodies. Policies are set at two levels:
- at national level by the Government
- at a local level by local authorities.

Local authorities are responsible for carrying out as well as setting policies. They have to make sure that their provision of leisure and recreation funds and facilities conforms to government policies and regulations. They also have to take into account the needs and expectations of the local people and the policies of the political parties elected to local council seats.

Contract management

The Local Government (Competition in Sport and Leisure Facilities Order) Act 1988 requires local authorities to put the running of its sports and leisure facilities out to tender. This means that local authority departments have to compete with other businesses for contracts to run these facilities. Sometimes they win the contracts, but not always. So some of the facilities once run by the authority are now run by private sector companies. Local authorities still control important aspects such as pricing, programmes and opening hours.

The Labour Government which came into office in 1997 developed Best Value (BV) as a key element in its programme for modernising local government. The intention of Best Value is to put the customers first and provide them with quality services at affordable costs. There is more about Best Value in section 3.1.3, pages 127–128.

Funding

Money for spending on public sector leisure and recreation activities and facilities comes from the public – particularly money raised by taxation and lottery grants.

The Government raises its money from taxation. There are two types:
- direct taxation like income tax
- indirect taxation like VAT which is included in the price of many goods and services you buy.

The Treasury allocates amounts of money to the government departments which are responsible for the various aspects of public spending. The government departments responsible for leisure and recreation allocate money in the form of grants to national and regional organisations like the Sports Councils. They in turn make grants to leisure and recreation organisations and facilities at a local level.

Local government raises its money through the Uniform Business Rate and the Council Tax.

The diagram below shows the flow of money to and from central and local government:

WHERE THE MONEY COMES FROM

ACTIVITY

When you visit local leisure and recreation organisations and facilities, look out for signs of public funding. Examples are:

- exhibitions sponsored by the local authority
- printed acknowledgements of funds received in programmes for theatres or sporting events
- National Tourist Board or Sports Council logos on posters.

Make a note of them – collect examples of programmes etc. and take photographs of notices in facilities.

Joint provision

Sometimes, public and private sector organisations get together to provide facilities. This sort of partnership is getting more common. A local councillor who sits on the leisure and amenities committee explains:

66 *We can't afford to incur big capital costs ourselves. So we work with others – for example, we put in applications to the National Lottery for grants where the matching amount of money is put up by private business. We are represented on the Board of the local theatre trust as well and recently helped them get a substantial grant from the Lottery for renovating their buildings. Quite often we have partnerships with much smaller organisations. For example, the café on one of our public parks is franchised out to a young couple who run it very successfully throughout the year, winter and summer. We wouldn't be able to do that ourselves.* 99

1.2.4 The voluntary sector

> The **voluntary sector** consists of not-for-profit organisations like charitable trusts and registered charities.

Organisations in this sector get their income from donations, legacies, grants, membership fees, admission fees and trading activities. The National Lottery also provides funds. The revenue raised by voluntary sector organisations is always invested back into their facilities and services.

The voluntary sector is an important part of the UK leisure and recreation industry. Many smaller facilities are completely or partly run by volunteers – small, local concerns like local sports clubs, social clubs, conservation groups and youth clubs as well as large nationwide organisations like the National Trust. Volunteers often carry out the managerial, administrative and operational work, sometimes with paid staff and sometimes on their own.

Influencing national policy

Many organisations in the voluntary sector exist to promote special causes, issues and interests. They lobby government at national and local levels to support, protect and encourage the sector's aims, activities and interests. Two well-known examples in the leisure sector are Wildlife Trusts and the Ramblers Association.

THE NATIONAL TRUST

http://www.nationaltrust.org.uk

The National Trust, founded in 1895, is the largest voluntary organisation in the UK. It is the third largest landowner in the UK, after the Crown and the Forestry Commission. Its aim is to protect the countryside and properties of national and  historical interest. Coastline, countryside, ancient monuments, nature reserves, waterways, buildings – the Trust protects and maintains a great variety of places of historic interest and natural beauty.

The Trust is a registered charity which depends on the voluntary support of the public and its members. Its income is from membership fees, admission fees and trading activities like gift shops and tea-shops, as well as donations, grants and legacies. It uses its income to preserve the land and properties it owns and to buy land and property which would otherwise decline or be destroyed by commercial redevelopment.

As well as headquarters in London, the Trust has regional offices throughout the UK. Members can join voluntary associations, formed and run by Trust members themselves. The Associations enable them to share common interests – activities include lectures, visits to properties and involvement as volunteers in the work of the Trust.

Organising national interest

Many large voluntary organisations attract national interest in their activities by raising people's awareness of concerns and issues through campaigns and promotions. They put a lot of money into promotions, sponsorship, educational projects, radio and television features and interviews, newspaper and magazine adverts, articles and features, brochures and flyers, and direct mailing. Many of them have magazines and information services for their members. They may also offer advice to national government and their members may take part in government committees.

Developing facilities

The voluntary sector may provide facilities that the public sector can't afford or that won't raise a high enough or quick enough return for private sector interest. All these facilities still have to be run on a commercial basis. To attract customers, facilities need to provide what the customers want by offering ease of access, value for money, services like food and drink, information and customer care.

The voluntary sector also develops facilities in parts of the industry that are too small or too specialised to attract funding from the public or private sector. For example, many local and amateur sports facilities are set up, managed and maintained by volunteers.

Managing facilities

The voluntary sector manages facilities using paid and unpaid staff. Many organisations are run by committees or boards of trustees. Large-scale operations like the national galleries and museums, city theatres, sporting bodies and heritage buildings have a core of full-time paid staff members, but they may also rely on volunteers. Small-scale, local operations rely entirely on volunteers.

Organising local interest

Much of the voluntary sector operates at a local, 'grass roots' level. People join local groups, take part in activities in the area and campaign for better local facilities.

Providing for a common interest

Many organisations in the voluntary sector started because people with a common interest organised themselves into groups which could provide the facilities and services they wanted. Saga Holidays, which is now one of the largest holiday companies in the UK and specialises in holidays for older people, started as a voluntary organisation. Thomas Cook, who ended up with a travel agency of worldwide coverage which still flourishes today, started his career by organising a day trip for members of the local Temperance Society.

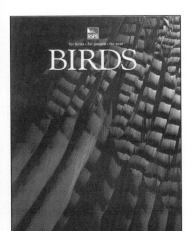

Some organisations started as a result of concerns like conservation and preservation – for example, the National Trust or the Royal Society for the Protection of Birds (RSPB). Others are a result of shared interests in sporting or leisure activities like the Wildfowlers' Trust and the Ramblers' Association.

Raising funds

Being able to finance what they want to do is as much an issue for the voluntary sector as it is for the public and private sectors. Funding comes from trusts, donations, legacies, grants, membership fees, admission fees and any trading activities like gift shops. Organisations have staff responsible for fundraising activities like gaining sponsorships and grants and increasing membership. Fundraising is often part of marketing.

ACTIVITY

Look through the recruitment pages of the local, national and trade press for advertisements for jobs in the voluntary sector. They are often advertised in the media and marketing section of the recruitment pages of national newspapers as well as voluntary sector sections.

What sort of organisations are advertising for staff?

What do the adverts tell you about them?

1.2.5 # Relationships between the sectors

DISCUSSION POINT

As you read through the case studies, ask yourself what the relationship is between organisations in the three sectors – public, private and voluntary. Are they about:

■ the dual use of facilities?

■ joint provision of facilities?

■ partnerships?

■ contracting?

■ cooperative ventures?

All three sectors – public, private and voluntary – have a role in providing leisure and recreation services. The case studies on these two pages show that the three sectors can provide similar facilities in leisure and recreation.

THE GOLF BUSINESSES

There are around 2,000 golf courses in the UK and 5 million players. The industry is worth around £3 billion per year and is still growing. In 1989 a report estimated that 700 new courses would be needed by the year 2000. Recently, many of the prime site courses in the UK have been bought by Japanese investors. Golf courses are run in three main ways: as private courses, municipal courses and as voluntary sector clubs (sometimes known as private membership clubs).

Private clubs are run as businesses and aim to make a profit for the owners. They are managed by employees of the company. Income is mainly from membership fees, green fees (payments made by non-members who play the course), tuition and retail sales of golf equipment, clothes and accessories. Many private clubs also provide other leisure and recreation facilities such as bars, restaurants, conference facilities, fitness suites and squash courts. Some diversify more widely into hotels and timeshare or second home developments.

Municipal courses aim to provide a service to the local community. They are publicly owned and managed by employees of the local authority. Income is mainly from 'pay as you play' fees, although some municipal courses have members as well. Extra income comes from tuition, catering and retail sales. Fewer than 20 per cent of golf courses in the UK are currently publicly owned.

Voluntary sector clubs are owned by their members. They aim to satisfy the needs and wants of members, and to break even (in other words, they don't have to make profits for owners). They are run by a committee of members and usually employ a steward to manage the facility. Their main sources of income are membership and green fees. Non-members pay a temporary membership allowing them to play the course for a limited time, such as a day.

THE MUSEUMS BUSINESS

The English Tourism Council lists over 900 museums in the UK. To qualify for their listing, the museum has to attract more than 5,000 visitors a year. Over a quarter of the museums listed attract more than 50,000 visitors a year. In the last 25 years, over 500 new museums have opened. Who owns them?

The government owns at least 32 major museums. Twenty-one of them are classified as national museums. They include the British Museum, the Victoria and Albert Museum, the Science Museum and the Natural History Museum. These museums are grant funded through the Department of Culture, Media and Sport and also rely on sponsorship to fund major exhibitions. In recent years the Government has introduced admission charges to most of its museums.

Local authorities own and run around 100 of the larger museums. Although mainly staffed by local authority employees, they have on average 20 per cent of volunteer staff as well. Some, though not all, local authority museums charge admission. But they are often not profitable, so they still rely on grants from the authority.

Independent companies or voluntary organisations own and run the rest. Over 70 per cent of the new museums are run by the private sector. Fifty per cent of all staff are volunteers. Like other museums, the independents charge admission fees. They also rely on the provision of other facilities like shops and cafés to reach a level of income at which they can survive.

Although the number of museums has increased in the last 20 years, the number of visits is declining. Museums are facing growing competition from heritage attractions like the Jorvik Centre in York. Except for museums in big cities, attendance is seasonal – bad weather is good news for museums!

ACTIVITY

Choose one type of service in leisure and recreation. Find out how the three sectors work together to provide the service. Look out for examples of:

■ dual use of facilities – e.g. the local authority hiring a privately owned swimming pool for school classes

■ joint provision of facilities and cooperative ventures

■ contracting by one sector to another.

1.2.6 The scale of the leisure and recreation industry

Consumer spending

You can measure the scale of the leisure and recreation industry in the UK by looking at:

- how many people work in the industry
- how much money it makes for the economy.

There are several sources of information for these figures and you will need to develop your picture of this lively and rapidly growing industry from a number of these sources:

- government statistics – such as *Social Trends,* the *General Household Survey* and the *Employment Gazette,* compiled and published by Her Majesty's Stationery Office (HMSO)
- industry organisations
- organisations such as Learning and Skills Councils, Regional Development Agencies or the economic development departments of local authorities, which keep track of labour market information in their areas.

When you use these sources, remember that the figures may be approximate rather than exact.

The Key Note Leisure and Recreation (UK) 1997 Report says that consumer spending on leisure activities and products rose by 27.7% between 1992 and 1996, reaching a total of £122.2m.

Consumer spending on non-essential goods and services has grown significantly in the last 20 years as retail prices for both essential and non-essential goods have fallen. Lifestyles are changing and consumers have a wider choice. For example, the expansion in home-based leisure has been driven by media and technology developments, such as the arrival of Channel 5, cable, satellite and digital television and has created an expanding industry in home entertainment goods. The average expenditure on television, video and audio equipment was approximately £3 per household per week in the late 1970s compared to nearly £8 in 1998/9.

As well as the spending by people living in the UK on leisure and recreation, most of the money tourist spend when they visit the UK is on leisure, recreation, transport and hospitality. So pubs, restaurants, hotels, museums and leisure attractions all benefit from tourism.

Employment statistics

For up-to-date and reliable information on employment statistics and trends the best sources of information are national training organisations (NTOs) as they often maintain labour market information on their sector. A list of the main NTOs operating in the leisure and recreation industry is given opposite. Their reports and publications are available in careers and public libraries. Growth sectors include catering and hospitality, sports and fitness, leisure activities.

ACTIVITY

Contact your local authority and Chamber of Commerce or Trade. Find out how any restaurants and take-aways operated in your area in 1995 and in 1998. What are the main reasons for the change in the number of businesses?

Choose one sector in the leisure and recreation industry which particulary interests you and contact the relevant NTO. Find out what it forecasts for numbers employed and market size over the next five years. Is this sector growing. If so, by how much? What are the key factors behind its expected growth and what will the new jobs be?

The leisure industry is sometimes described as a 'Mickey Mouse' industry because it creates relatively few full-time, permanent jobs. What statistics would you use to disprove this? Collect two or three sets of figures from the sources listed on this page, and any others you know of. Write a paragraph or two explaining:

■ what the figures show

■ what they tell you about the patterns of employment in the industry.

OR

Find out how many people are employed by Disney in their theme parks world-wide. Look at the Disney web site (*http://disney.go.com/ disneycareers/index.html*) and see whether they think there's anything wrong with being 'Mickey Mouse'.

The main NTOs for the leisure and recreation industry are:

■ The National Training Organisation for Sport, Recreation, and Allied Occupation (*http://www.sprito.org.uk*)

■ Hospitality Training Foundation (*http://www.htf.org.uk*)

■ Hotel and Catering Institutional Management Association (*http://hcima.org.uk*)

■ National Training Organisation for the Arts and Entertainment Industries (*http://metier.org.uk*)

■ Cultural Heritage National Training Organisation (*http://www.chnto.org.uk*)

Participation trends

Look at the tables below and on the next page from *Social Trends*. It shows some important changes in the leisure and recreation business.

Carry out a small survey with your family and friends and families and see if you can establish different age profiles for two kinds of day visits. For example, do males under 20 years spend more time visiting friends than those over 25? Give an interpretation of what you find.

Attendance at cultural events

Great Britain	Percentages		
	1987–88	1991–92	1997–98
Cinema	34	44	54
Plays	24	23	23
Art galleries/ exhibitions	21	21	22
Classical Music	12	12	12
Ballet	6	6	6
Opera	5	6	6
Contemporary dance	4	3	4

Source: Target Group Index, BMRB International

'Social Trends 30', Office for National Statistics © Crown Copyright 2000

DISCUSSION POINT

Television is already installed in nearly all homes in the UK. There has been a dramatic rise in the number of home-computers. In 2000 a number of organisations including AltaVista and ntl began to provide free access to the Internet and free telephony. Discuss with your fellow students, what you think the impact on the home-based leisure sector will be over the next five years.

Participation in home-based leisure activities: by gender

Great Britain

	Percentages		
	1977	1987	1996–97
Males			
Watching TV	97	99	99
Visiting/entertaining friends or relations	89	94	95
Listening to radio	87	89	90
Listening to records/tapes/CDs	64	76	79
Reading books	52	54	58
DIY	51	58	58
Gardening	49	49	52
Dressmaking/needlework/knitting	2	3	3
Females			
Watching TV	97	99	99
Visiting/entertaining friends or relations	93	96	97
Listening to radio	87	86	87
Listening to records/tapes/CDs	60	71	77
Reading books	57	65	71
DIY	22	30	30
Gardening	35	43	45
Dressmaking/needlework/knitting	51	47	37

Source: General Household Survey, Office for National Statistics
'Social Trends 30', Office for National Statistics © Crown Copyright 2000

Key questions

1 What are the six components of the leisure and recreation industry?

2 How does the Government provide support for leisure and recreation?

3 What sort of leisure and recreation facilities do local authorities provide?

4 How do organisations in the private sector attract funds to provide leisure and recreation products and services?

5 What role do voluntary organisations play in the UK leisure and recreation industry?

6 What are the five ways in which the three sectors – private, public, and voluntary – can relate to each other? Give examples of each.

7 What are three ways that the scale of the leisure industry can be measured?

SECTION **1.3**

Working in the leisure and recreation industry

There is a wide variety of jobs in the recreation industry and many types of employer. This section will increase your knowledge of job opportunities in leisure and recreation and will help you to identify the skills that you have to offer. It will help you to analyse your own strengths, weaknesses and interests. You will also learn about how employers recruit people to work for them.

66 *To work in leisure and recreation you sometimes need to be a Jack-of-all-trades. I work for a national heritage organisation. My job involves overseeing the day-to-day running of the property, opening it to the public, ensuring security and maintaining the property and the contents of the house. A marketing background is helpful, as is some knowledge of art history, and I need managerial skills for dealing with staff. What I most enjoy about my work is the variety.* **99**

administrator of a National Trust property

66 *All staff have annual appraisals where they can look at how things have gone in the previous year with their manager. This is a chance to discuss every aspect of their jobs. Staff are told what they are doing well and about areas where they might be able to improve. It is also an opportunity for them to talk about areas in which they would like some more training.* **99**

press and publicity officer at an entertainments venue

1.3.1 The range of jobs

Recreation needs people to carry out the whole range of tasks and roles that there are. Some are common to all businesses – managers, marketers, accountants, administrators, secretaries, IT support, finance, health and safety, and so on.

Others are specific to each of the different sectors and key components. Here are some examples:

- arts and entertainment – entertainers, box office, customer service, information providers, ticketing and booking, maintenance, retail
- sports and physical recreation – specific sports skills, customer service, teaching, maintenance, health and safety, security
- heritage – customer service, guides, horticulture, security
- catering – in all the others via fast-food, sales, waiting, buffets
- countryside recreation – tour guides, specific skills such as climbing, fell-walking, bird or wildlife watching
- home-based leisure – sales and customer service, handling complaints, supporting help calls.

Recreation is a growing business and it's international: you may find yourself anywhere in the world. It's often seasonal, so travel makes a lot of sense – you can live in perpetual summer if you play your cards right. The kind of jobs you'll find may be:

- full-time – management, marketing, administration, ground maintenance
- part-time – working evenings, mornings, afternoons on specific projects or events, teaching keep fit classes for the elderly, aerobics for the ambitious and t'ai-chi for the terrified; running kids' parties at fast food restaurants
- temporary – helping to build or change attractions, or deal with large numbers at peak times of the year
- seasonal – working mainly in the summer, getting people in and out of boats on a lake, selling ice cream on the beach, commentating on the bus tour.

DISCUSSION POINT

This seasonal and fluctuating nature of the work has its good and bad points. From your point of view, what are they? Note down some positive things about seasonal work, and some negative ones. How you feel about those issues has a lot to do with how you'll plan your career.

1.3.2 **Nature of employment**

Like all modern employment, you can't rely on a job in the leisure and recreation industry lasting for a lifetime. All that stopped in the 1980s and 1990s. And in this industry, work has always been seasonal for obvious reasons. Some jobs will need you to have undergone training first, others will encourage you to do on-the-job training. All employers will be impressed if you have already had work experience in the holidays or at weekends.

Is there a common theme in all this diversity? A manager of a major theme park says:

66 *A passion for people, that's what we want to see. We exist to give others a good time. I like to say to new staff that in this business there are only three things that count. The first is our customers. The second is our customers. And the third is our customers. If we want them to come back to us, they have to like what they got and are getting. And if something goes wrong, we put it right if we possibly can. Remember – every complaint can lead to a new sale if you can make the person feel that you listened, understood and took action.* 99

Many jobs in the leisure industry operate during 'unsociable hours.' In other words, you may find yourself working evenings and night shifts as well as weekends. For example, cinemas, theatres will require evening staff, and restaurants may have late evening hours. Some jobs require that you work in shifts of several days at a stretch. For instance, camp guides and outdoor sporting instructors may work in remote locations with customers who are on holiday.

Another aspect of the leisure industry is that it's a 'people business'. A great majority of the jobs will have direct dealings with the public. So any training or experience in customer service will be advantageous when you seek work.

1.3.3 Personal and technical skills

The skills that make up a successful employee are a mixture of personal and technical. Both are important, although the weighting may vary for different jobs.

There are some personal skills that apply across the board, for example the ability to cooperate with other people and be a good team player.

Technical skills are specific to the job area you choose. For example, the ability to swim is obviously a technical skill that must be mastered by a lifeguard.

Look at the list of key components on page 19. Each of them implies different technical skills. And each of them will have national and local organisations that can advise you on the best way to develop those skills.

ACTIVITY

Go to the college or local library, or your careers advisers and get the latest edition of Occupations from the Careers and Occupations Advisory Centre. Make a table with two columns in a wordprocessor or spreadsheet. Put the six components down on one side and some of the technical skills and qualifications on the other. Don't put more than one or two per component.
OR
Surf the Web looking for national organisations in each key component. A search engine such as UK Max, Google, or Yahoo! will find the sites for you. Go to the parts of their site that describe jobs, and paste any useful information you find into your document. Make some notes about the technical skills and qualifications routes that are described.

Look at the case studies on the next page to see that it is often necessary to employ both personal and technical skills in a given situation.

DISCUSSION POINT

These case studies show an interesting mix of personal and technical skills at work. Working with one or two others, note the personal skills and technical skills being shown by the two people. Which are more important to the business? What are the things they say that an employer would really appreciate from the point of view of what the business really needs?

“ *I see myself as very organised and precise. I love sports but I also love working on business models and planning things out. I guess my main weakness is that I find it quite hard to be patient with people who seem to be wasting my time. Not a good idea in this business – not something you should admit to at the interview. So when that question came along, I said I thought I would like to develop my interpersonal skills and my people management skills, to complement the analytical and planning side.* ”

“ *I love helping people to make themselves feel better. Nothing gives me more pleasure than seeing a person who has been ill starting to get their fitness back. Last year I had to teach a lady of almost 60 to swim. She had been scared of water all her life and wanted to get over the fear. It took a long time – several weeks. I just had to wait for her to accept that she was safe with me. You should have heard the whoop when she finally took off. But I have to admit, I find the form-filling and reports you have to do a lot harder. I'd much rather spend the time with the clients. I came clean on that at the interview. I said, you are not getting someone who loves to write, but you are getting someone who loves to work with people. And of course I will do all the work to the best of my ability, even the writing bits. As long as you help me master the systems you have.* ”

1.3.4 **Your strengths, weaknesses and interests**

You need to have a good idea of what these are. It's also what potential employers will be looking for in you. Of course, strengths are better than weaknesses, but often strengths carry some weaknesses with them.

It's good to have a way of talking about yourself that shows you have thought about this. Look again at the two case studies on the opposite page where successful applicants describe the way they dealt with difficult questions about their strengths and weaknesses. Then have a go at putting down yours.

ACTIVITY

Consider the following questions as you examine your strengths, weaknesses and interests. Make a few notes about all these points.

1   What are your main interests? What are your favourite activities – academic work, sports, entertainment, reading, computer work, social work?
2   Think about experiences you have enjoyed. What kind of school, social, or sports activities do you like? Make a list of ten activities you have really enjoyed in the last four years.
3   What relevance do they have to the kind of career you would like?
4   What did you have to learn so as to enjoy them? What skills do you still need to learn to go on getting better at them?
5   Put down any school, work or voluntary activities you are involved in that would say positive things about you.
6   Make a list of clubs or other organisations you have joined.

ACTIVITY

List the sectors of the industry which are available to you as a job option. For example, if you live in a tiny village in the country you won't be seeking a job as a museum guide (unless you plan to move). If you want to live and work in London, you won't be seeking a job as a mountaineering instructor.

ACTIVITY

List what sorts of jobs are available to you in the short term and in the long term. For example, in the short term you could probably find temporary work waiting tables or serving at a pub. In the long term, with appropriate training and experience, you could become a restaurant manager or pub owner.

1.3.5 **How employers recruit people**

Prepare a job description summarising the tasks, activities and responsibilities the job entails

Prepare a person specification describing the skills, qualifications, experience and personal qualities the job-holder should have

Advertise the job

Evaluate the applications

Short list the suitable applicants to interview

Interview the applicants

Decide which of the interviewees is the best candidate

Offer the job to the best candidate

It's very useful for you to appreciate the process of recruitment from the other side. If you can understand what the employer is looking for, you'll have a much better chance of preparing yourself and showing the aspects of your skills and personality that will give the right signals and get you that job.

Recruitment and selection procedures

Organisations invest a great deal of time and money in recruiting and selecting staff. Leisure and recreation organisations rely on keeping their customers happy, and to do this they need staff who are:

- hardworking
- cheerful, enthusiastic and motivated
- skilled and experienced, or willing to learn.

> **Recruitment** is the process of attracting possible candidates for a job.
> **Selection** is the process for assessing and choosing the most suitable candidate.

Once an organisation is sure about:

- the job they need someone to do
- the type of person they are looking for
- the conditions of service (hours, salary, leave entitlement, etc.)

it can start the search for suitable candidates.

Advertising vacancies

Job vacancies can be advertised both within the organisation, to allow existing staff to apply, and externally.

> Places to advertise include:
> - in national or local press
> - in trade publications and professional journals
> - on radio and television
> - through recruitment agencies
> - via the World Wide Web.

National press

All national newspapers sell advertising space on their recruitment pages. They often have certain days for jobs in particular skills areas – for example, media and marketing on Mondays, education on Tuesdays, computer technology on Wednesdays and so on. Local newspapers have jobs pages, too. Newspapers – and their jobs pages – are also published on the World Wide Web. That's often a good way of looking back to get a sense of what has been on offer for some time.

THE SWANSDOWN HOTEL

Part-Time Staff
required for lunchtime waiting.
Experience preferred
but training is given.
Applicants must be over 18.

Please contact J Foster
on 01284 231 231

SICKLESMERE SPORTS & LEISURE CENTRE

Position available for
LIFEGUARD

Appropriate qualifications for
children's and main pool essential

Applicants to contact: Kate Wilkins 01787 598348

Hunters Retreat

*The following positions are available
in our Traditional Country Hotel*

BREAKFAST CHEF
FULL-TIME RESTAURANT STAFF
PART-TIME BAR STAFF
KITCHEN PORTER
COMPETITIVE WAGES
SPLIT SHIFTS
EXPERIENCE NOT ESSENTIAL

Contact R Malik, Manager, by telephone
01287 359081

Trade press

All commercial areas have their own specialised publications aimed at people working in those areas.

ACTIVITY

Find out what trade journals there are for the sector of the leisure and recreation industry you'd most like to work in.

CAMBRIDGE
HI-TECH
RECRUITMENT

RECRUITMENT CONSULTANTS

**Technical Specialists
for the Software I.T.,
Telecoms, Electronics,
Computer and High
Technology Industries**

Tel (01223) 467724
Fax (01223) 321273

Radio and television services

Radio and television stations offer advertising services for job vacancies. Information services like Teletext are also used to advertise job vacancies.

Recruitment agencies

Recruitment agencies are private businesses which help organisations to fill vacancies. People looking for work give their details to the agencies and the agencies match them against details organisations give them of vacancies. Many agencies specialise in recruitment for particular skills, like secretarial skills, or particular industry areas, like the catering industry.

ACTIVITY

Use the *Yellow Pages* to find out how many recruitment agencies there are in your area. Contact a few and ask about the sort of jobs they deal with. Keep a note of any agencies you think might be useful to you when you're looking for work in the future.

If you are connected to the Internet, try using the on-line version of the *Yellow Pages* (you can find it at *http://www.yell.com*). And if you are looking for organisations in specific areas, try *http://www.scoot.co.uk*, which also finds things by town, postcode and business type.

ACTIVITY

Look through newspapers, magazines, journals and web sites, and collect different examples of advertisements for jobs in leisure and recreation, keeping a record of where you found them. From your research, where do you think you are most likely to find advertisements for your first job in leisure and recreation?

In the public sector, the Department for Education and Employment runs Jobcentres where local vacancies are advertised. Jobcentre staff are trained to give advice on careers and to put people in touch with employers advertising relevant vacancies. They also provide free leaflets which give advice on jobsearch and interviewing skills.

The World Wide Web

There are a lot of recruitment web sites, offering to match up jobseekers to employers. And many employers include a careers section on their web site which tells you the jobs they have and the skills they are looking for. Some organisations even give detailed advice on how to submit your CV so that it can be read automatically by an optical character reader and scanned by intelligent software to find the skills you are offering. Newspapers have excellent web sites that include job vacancies. And professional and trade organisations also have web sites with lots of information on careers in their sectors. There's a list at the end of this unit. Try putting your target job or job area into several search engines. Interesting things may appear.

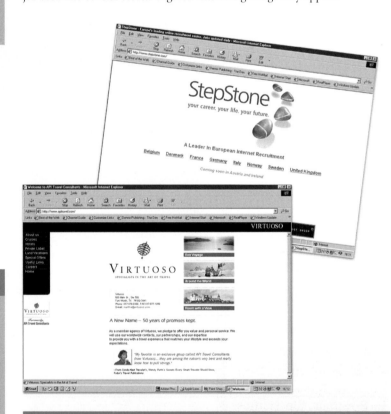

DISCUSSION POINT

What are the pros and cons of each of the recruitment advertising means given here?

A **job description** summarises what a job involves – day-to-day tasks, responsibilities, location, and so on. It gives applicants a useful overview of a job, and is often included in the successful applicant's contract of employment.

A **person specification** summarises what type of person the organisation is looking for to do the job – skills, experience and qualifications needed, personal qualities which would be helpful, and so on.

Job descriptions

When organisations produce a job description, it gives them a chance to really think about the tasks and responsibilities involved in the job they are advertising.

Contents of a job description

- job title – for example, 'senior sales adviser', 'promotions supervisor', 'bookings assistant'
- reporting structure – who reports to the job-holder and who the job-holder reports to; for example, 'responsible for a team of two people', 'reporting to the section manager'
- job responsibilities – for example, 'establishing and maintaining a client database', 'writing copy for mailshot brochures', 'selling European holidays to customers'

Job Description

Organisation: Purcell's Garden Centre
Job title: Assistant manager - tools and equipment
Reporting to: General manager
Job description:
- Oversee general layout and running of tools and equipment department
- Supervise department sales staff
- Meet with product sales representatives on a regular basis to maintain backstock levels
- Organise in-store product demonstrations
- Assist general manager with standard sales and administration duties

---

The recruiting officer in a public sector entertainments venue describes how job descriptions help him when he's looking for new staff:

66 *The job description makes it clear what is expected from the job-holder. It defines what tasks they have to do, how much authority they have and who is in charge of them. When I'm considering applicants, the job description tells me what sort of experience the job-holder should have and what sort of things they need to be able to do.* 99

DISCUSSION POINT

How effective would the recruitment and selection procedure be without a job description for the vacant post?

Person specifications

A person specification gives a picture of the ideal applicant, and is often used by leisure and recreation organisations to show clearly the type of person most likely to fit into their team.

As the personnel manager for a large hotel chain explains, preparing both job descriptions and person specifications is a very important part of the recruitment process:

66 *Before I advertise a vacancy I always check the job description and person specification I used last time I recruited, just to make sure that there haven't been any changes. For instance, I need to make sure that the job itself hasn't changed, and I also need to make sure that we are still looking for the same type of person we looked for when we last advertised. For example, last time we recruited a conference manager we needed someone with considerable knowledge of the catering trade and with experience of managing staff. The job itself has now changed because the organisational structure of the organisation has changed. Now, a conference manager working for us needs to be multilingual and computer literate. This is because we are doing a lot of conferences for foreign trade fairs, so languages are important, and we've installed a complete new IT system. In the case of the conference manager I needed to change the job description and the person specification to make sure that they realistically described the job we were offering and the person we were looking for.* **99**

A person specification usually includes the following information:

- personal qualities (e.g. must be capable of creative thought, outgoing, enthusiastic, capable of leading and motivating a team)
- personal achievements (e.g. must have at least two years' experience running a similar department)
- vocational qualifications (e.g. GNVQ in Leisure & Recreation)
- academic qualifications (e.g. GCSEs, A levels)
- competence (e.g. experience of preparing successful fund-raising proposals).

Person Specification

Job title	Assistant manager – garden tools and equipment
Qualifications	Academic GCSE Maths and English
	Vocational GNVQ Leisure and Recreation (Advanced)
	or
	NVQ Retail Operations Level 3
	A business management qualification would be desirable
Experience	Minimum two years' experience in retail setting

Personal attributes and qualities
- good communication and administration skills
- selling skills
- stock purchasing skills
- able to work on own initiative
- lively and friendly person
- effective team skills

Evaluating job descriptions and person specifications

Effective job descriptions and person specifications are useful tools in the recruitment and selection process. If they've been properly thought out, they should help an organisation to:

- match applicants to vacancies
- minimise the possibility of inappropriate appointments
- match business objectives to jobs
- plan training and development needs of job-holders.

Matching applicants to vacancies

Clearly defining the types of tasks the job-holder will be doing and the aptitudes and qualifications the job-holder will need creates standards applicants must match. For example, if you know that the job requires a teamworker, you can look for evidence of teamwork or an aptitude for teamwork in the applicants' letters and CVs.

Minimising the possibility of inappropriate appointments

The job description and person specification should provide a good guide to what a job entails and the sorts of skills and aptitudes needed by the job-holder. Having a clear picture of the job helps to create a clear picture of the appropriate person for that job.

Matching business objectives to jobs

All jobs within an organisation should relate to its business objectives. The job description and person specification should make clear how the job contributes to the business objectives.

A team leader at an outdoor activity centre explains how the jobs of the instructors in his team relate to the centre's business objectives:

66 *The centre's key objectives are to provide outdoor activities for all age ranges, comply with all health, safety and security rules – those set by law and our own guidelines – and have happy customers.*

My team are all qualified instructors with experience of working with different age groups. The nature of the work demands a high level of physical fitness. They are all trained in first aid and we regularly update their skills and knowledge in health, safety and security practices and procedures.

All the team members are energetic, outgoing people who believe that life should be fun. In addition to the right qualifications, they also need strong interpersonal skills. These help them to be good team workers and to deal well with the customers. 99

Training and developing job holders

Most people expect their jobs to develop in terms of skills and responsibilities. Job descriptions and person specifications can be useful for training and development in three ways:

- they identify existing skills and aptitudes which may be developed
- they identify skills and aptitudes people can acquire in order to move into the job
- they provide a measure of how far the job-holder has developed.

Short listing applicants

An advertisement for a job vacancy will bring in many applications. Short listing is the process for picking out the ones which match most closely the type of skills and experience the vacancy demands. They will go on the short list as people to interview. The key tools in this process are the job description and the person specification. Any applicant who matches them is someone to interview. People with skills and experience outside the industry are also worth interviewing if their skills or experience would be useful to the job.

Dealing with references

References are comments and appraisals given by people (referees) who know or have worked with the applicant. They are used by the recruiting organisation to check on the information the applicant has given them and to find out more about what the applicant is like as a person and a worker. Most people choose the following to act as their referees:

- their current employer or manager
- a previous employer or manager
- a teacher or tutor.

Interviews

Interviews are the opportunity to meet the applicant and discuss in detail what the job involves. The key to an effective interview is careful preparation. The interviewer and interviewee must prepare all the information that the other might need and questions that will help bring out the right sort of information.

Here's how the personnel officer for a cinema complex prepares for interviews:

❝ I read the interviewees' CVs very thoroughly and make notes on any aspects I want to know more about. I also prepare a list of questions I want to ask all the interviewees to find out about their reasons for wanting the job, their background, experience and achievements and so on. I use the job description and person specification to prepare questions that give the interviewees a chance to talk about their suitability for the job. An interview is a two-way process, so I think about the information the interviewees will need from me – information about the organisation, the job, the opportunities and so on. There's also a practical side – I prepare an interview room, tell all staff that interviews will be going on and make sure that there won't be any interruptions during any interview. ❞

Assessing applicants

Interviewers will assess applicants during the interview and also spend some time after the interview reviewing their assessment. They'll consider the answers the applicants gave and the questions they asked, what sort of personality traits they showed, how they came over and so on. The interviewers will use their observations to assess the applicants further against the job description and person specification.

Some organisations also use assessment techniques like job skill tests and aptitude tests.

The leader of a team of fitness instructors explains what she does to assess potential recruits to the team:

❝ We do a three-part assessment: an interview, a mock class and a written test. At the interview, the candidate is interviewed by me and a team colleague. We have a form we've prepared with questions to ask and space for notes on the candidate's responses. The form also includes boxes we tick on personal qualities we pick up on through asking questions and observing the candidate – things like personal appearance, confidence, communication skills, levels of knowledge demonstrated and so on. During the mock class, myself and a colleague act as observers and other team members act as class participants. Again, we have a form to help us note down our observations and after the class we add notes on the feedback from the team members who took part in the class while the candidate does the written test. The written test is made up of questions on health and safety, good instruction practice, putting together and running fitness classes and so on. We then go through all the information we've collected from the assessment and decide which of the candidates best matches the job we're offering. ❞

Confirming employment

Once the interviewers have made their choice, they will contact the person to offer them the job. Usually, job offers are made in writing.

17th May 1999

Janice O'Rourke
12 New Close
Bilbourne
Buckinghamshire
MK41 3PT

LIFESTYLE
LEISURE LIMITED
29 Market Hill
Bilbourne
Buckinghamshire
MK41 1WB
Tel: (01296) 346838
Fax: (01296) 346839

Dear Janice

Fitness Instructor

Following your interview last week, I'm pleased to offer you the post of Fitness Instructor.
I'm enclosing two of the copies of a draft contract which sets out the terms and conditions for the post.
If you wish to accept the offer you should sign one and return it to me as soon as possible.
Please feel free to call me if you have any further questions.
I look forward to hearing from you.
Yours sincerely

B. Lubienski

Bruno Lubienski (Programmes Manager)

17th May 1999

Martin Crewe
51 Meadowcroft
Bilbourne
Buckinghamshire
MK41 8AP

LIFESTYLE
LEISURE LIMITED
29 Market Hill
Bilbourne
Buckinghamshire
MK41 1WB
Tel: (01296) 346838
Fax: (01296) 346839

Dear Martin

Fitness Instructor

I'm sorry to tell you that your application for the post of Fitness Instructor has not been successful.
You were a strong candidate and we were very impressed with your performance at the interview.
I will keep your details on file in case a suitable vacancy arises in the future and I wish you every success in your applications elsewhere.
Yours sincerely

B. Lubienski

Bruno Lubienski (Programmes Manager)

Notifying rejections

Once the successful candidate has accepted the job, the next stage is to notify all the others that their applications have been unsuccessful. The personnel officer who works for a sports complex financed by a local authority explains how he approaches rejection letters:

66 *Being told you haven't got a job you wanted can be a painful experience, so it is important that letters bringing this news are as kind as possible. It's best to get the bad news over with first. It's also helps to pay a compliment like 'you were a very strong candidate and we were impressed by your knowledge of our facilities' and to wish them success in future applications.* **99**

Key questions

1 What are the differences between personal skills and technical skills?

2 How will analysing your strengths, weaknesses and interests help you in your career planning?

3 What would you expect to find in a) a job description and b) a person specification?

4 Name three places you would find advertisements for job vacancies in the leisure and recreation industry.

5 What are the key tools used to compile a short list for a job vacancy?

6 How would you find out how many recruitment agencies operate in your area?

SECTION **1.4**

Pursuing your own progression aims

This section will help you to plan your own career in the industry. You will learn how to obtain the information and advice which will help you to select from the wide range of employment, training and education opportunities which are open to you. There is information on the important practical steps, such as producing a curriculum vitae (CV), processing a typical employment, training, or education application, and preparing yourself for an interview.

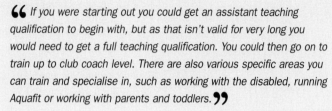

66 If you were starting out you could get an assistant teaching qualification to begin with, but as that isn't valid for very long you would need to get a full teaching qualification. You could then go on to train up to club coach level. There are also various specific areas you can train and specialise in, such as working with the disabled, running Aquafit or working with parents and toddlers. 99

swimming pool manager

66 Posts in our organisation are usually advertised in the creative and media sections in national papers, and we also advertise in the local paper. Another way for people to get into the field is as students gaining work experience. In my particular job you need press or public relations experience – working on a newspaper gives you a sense of what makes news and what would be good photocalls. People often get involved in student papers – that's another good way to get experience. We have someone working in our box office who is doing a course in arts administration. She has also gained invaluable experience by working as a volunteer doing publicity for a theatre going to the Edinburgh Festival. 99

press and publicity officer at an entertainments venue

1.4.1 How to plan your own career development

You need a career development plan. Not because you can predict everything that will happen in your career, because you can't. But a career plan will help you to be clear about the process of jobsearch and recruitment, and will help you think about the steps that follow your first job.

A career goal – for now!

If you did the activity on page 41 you have already started making a career development plan. The next thing you need is a career goal.

A career goal helps you focus on what you want to do for a living. It may be a specific job you want, like a fitness instructor, facility manager or retail food outlet manager. The goal doesn't have to stretch far into the future, although it can if you are that kind of person. It'll probably change.

Start from the general area you want to work in. Look again at those six components and the three main sectors. Which are for you? Which sound interesting? A career goal might start with the phrase 'I'd like to work in . . .' then 'in the area of . . .' then 'maybe as a . . .' and finally 'or maybe as a . . .'

That's just as good as being able to say 'I want to be the managing director of Alton Towers by the time I'm 23 years old.'

Rather than limiting your future, a career goal may help you discover possibilities you might not have thought about. You'll be taking more control of your life, rather than just drifting into a job.

And once you have a career goal, a career plan is the next step. That's where you start to plan your route in.

A career plan

A career plan sets down your skills and interests, and helps you focus on the career that best suits your talents. After that you look at the skills and training you need and the opportunities there are, and the advice and help you need to make it all happen.

Career Plan

Career goal:

To become a Fitness Centre Manager. To help build up and expand the business by helping people in the area to make the most of their lives by keeping fit.

Requirements:

Qualifications in health and fitness.

Ability to:

■ work as part of a team and lead

■ relate to people and motivate them to do more

■ use the measurements from the fitness equipment to give advice

■ deal with complaints

■ write letters on the computer

■ use a spreadsheet

■ do basic accounts

■ know basic anatomy and physiology.

Current skills and interests:

■ holiday work at local fitness centre

■ learnt how to use spreadsheets and database; ran a mailmerge for a promotion

■ worked as part of a team

■ helped with school physical education classes for younger students.

Plan to reach career goal:

■ get a traineeship – ideally a Modern Apprenticeship – in a fitness centre

■ get my NVQ level 3 in Coaching, Teaching and Instruction

■ work hard and get recognised as someone who is willing to give it all they've got

■ leave there after four years if I haven't got promotion – get a better job

■ go on from there.

Other career plans could be much more detailed and specific.

There are many resources on the World Wide Web that will help you construct a career plan. Examples include:

■ *http://www.mapping-your-future.org/planning/careersa.htm*

■ *http://www.nsn.k12.nv.us/nvdoe/nvdoe_teams/siwe/smp/edplan.html*

■ *http://www.umf.maine.edu/~chd/careerplan.html*

■ *http://www.careers-gateway.co.uk/mainpage.htm.*

1.4.2 The range of opportunities

You may be aiming to identify the job you want and then go for it. Or you may be more interested in matching your particular skills and strengths to various jobs in the industry as a whole and finding the best fit. For managerial or professional positions it's possible to range more widely, as roles such as management and marketing have common features across many components and all sectors.

The range is very wide. Here are some good ways of getting a sense of what there is.

NTOs:

- identify skill shortages and training needs in their sector
- give advice on education and careers guidance provision
- develop occupational standards, including S/NVQs, and advise on the naional qualifications structure
- give advice on training arrangements and solutions.

1.4.3 Getting the right information and advice

Where do you go for quality help and advice? The best places are:

- careers companies
- professional bodies
- employers in your target area
- the World Wide Web.

Careers companies

Every area has its careers company. They are usually voluntary agencies that have to win the contract through competitive tendering. They have professional staff, large libraries of resources and many computer-based resources. They will also have access to the Internet. Many now provide on-line support for jobseekers and career planners. There's a list of them at *http://www.careerworld.net*.

Professional bodies

Browse the web site of the most appropriate NTO for your intended career (see the list on page 55), and paste any information that looks useful into your wordprocessed career plan file.

The NTOs are all responsible for setting up Modern Apprenticeships (MAs) in their component part of the industry. Modern Apprenticeships and work-based learning routes are a very good way of getting straight into work after you finish school or college. It's the practical way in. MAs offer a framework of training in a vocational subject, usually lasting for three years, for young people between 16 and 25. They are designed to meet the needs of employers, so people who complete them are well equipped for their work in the industry. This industry wants people who will make it succeed, and practical experience counts as much as educational attainment.

Employers in your target area

If you know the kind of employer you want to work for, now is the time to make contact. The best first move is to telephone and ask who to write or e-mail. Then do it. Send your CV. If you feel confident, send an e-mail with your CV attached. If you have a web-based CV, give them the URL. But send a paper copy as well.

Ask them to advise you about the opportunities that they have and see if they will let you come in to see them for a discussion. Give them a clear idea of what you want to do and why, and if you can fit it in, offer to come and help out for free, to show them how keen you are.

Most employers like you to be interested in them and are keen to encourage new entrants into their business. But a few are unfriendly and unhelpful. It's just human nature – don't be put off if you get brushed off. Just go somewhere else.

1.4.4 CVs and job applications

UNIT

1

SECTION **1.4**

CV is short for **curriculum vitae**, which is Latin for 'course of life'. The aim of a CV is to give employers enough information about your qualifications, skills and experience to enable them to decide whether to interview you for a job. In the USA and Canada they call this a *resumé* – the French for a summary of your life. It's the same as a CV.

The two most common ways to apply for jobs in leisure and recreation are:
- through application forms
- with a CV and letter of application.

Employers usually specify on job advertisements how they want people to apply, and it is important that applicants follow their instructions. If they want people to fill in an application form, they won't be impressed by a CV and covering letter.

Content of CVs

A CV should include enough information about experience and qualifications to show the person's suitability for a job. Too much information can be as bad as too little. A CV should be no more than two pages long – any longer, and the employer may not bother reading it.

The layout and presentation of a CV is very important. It should be typed or wordprocessed, printed out clearly, and checked carefully for mistakes in spelling and grammar. Photocopied, creased, misspelled and otherwise untidy documents often go straight in the bin.

The example below shows one standard approach to laying out a CV.

Information to include in a CV:
- name, address and telephone number
- education and training – giving details of schools and colleges attended
- vocational qualifications (e.g. GNVQs, NVQs)
- academic qualifications (e.g. GCSEs, A levels)
- employment record (details of jobs done to date including part-time and relevant casual work)
- skills including personal skills (e.g. driving licence, foreign languages spoken)
- other achievements
- interests and hobbies.

```
Name:           Trevor Marshall
Address:        29 Lindwell Court
                Walthamstow
                London E173JH
Telephone:      0181 576 3481


Employment to date
1999 to present Manchester Arts Centre
I joined the organisation in March 1992 in the capacity of box
office manager. I am currently responsible for managing the booking
arrangements in a multi-complex, busy centre. I am responsible for
staffing resources and for dealing with all the verbal and written
complaints which the organisation receives. In 1995 I began working
towards my NVQ in Customer Care and so far have achieved units 2
and 3.

1995 to 1999 Littlehurst Community Centre
I joined the centre in the capacity of telephone booking clerk,
taking bookings from customers for events at the centre. In 1992 I
was promoted to section leader and was given responsibility for two
junior members of staff. My duties included dealing with customer
queries and complaints and handling all the associated paperwork.

Personal qualities
I believe that I am a good communicator. I enjoy working with
customers and helping to solve problems. I enjoy working alone and am
able to use my initiative and take decisions on my own. I also enjoy
teamwork and like to be part of an effective and energetic team.

Qualifications
Units 3 and 4 of the NVQ in Customer Care
GCSE passes in English, French, German, Maths, Geography, Art,
Religious Studies

Interests and hobbies
I enjoy walking, travelling and listening to music. I am the drummer
in a local band and I am an active member of the local amateur
dramatic society and the football club.
```

CVs on the web

More and more colleges encourage you to post your CV on their web site (or you may have your own anyway). This is a good way of showing that you are multiskilled and computer literate. You could include some multimedia showing your achievements with photos, sound or video. Go for it.

Content of letters of application

Unless the organisation states otherwise in the advert, it is usual to send a letter of application with a CV. You can use the letter to explain why you are interested in the job and why you feel you should be considered for the job.

Quality of presentation of letters of application

Letters of application should follow a standard letter format. They should be on good-quality paper and preferably typewritten or wordprocessed. The content should be concise and to the point. Spelling and grammar should be accurate and the tone of the letter should be polite yet friendly.

```
                                              Andrew Forster
                                             82 Breacon Drive
                                                 Crawley Park
                                                     Ampthill
                                                     MK20 2BE
                                            17th January 1999

Mrs Lynne Wentworth
Personnel Manager
Devon Hotel
Parkway
York YO2 7UY

Dear Mrs Wentworth

Hotel Receptionist - 'York News' 15th January, 1999

Following your recent advertisement in the 'York News',
I am enclosing my Curriculum Vitae for your
consideration.

As you will see I have an Advanced GNVQ in Leisure &
Recreation and have worked part-time, during my school
holidays, as a receptionist at the Hunter's House Hotel
in Stafford.

I am very keen to work in York and am available to come
for interview at any time which is convenient for you.

I hope that this application is of interest to you, and
look forward to hearing from you.

Yours sincerely



Andrew Forster
```

1.4.5 Interviews

Job interviews have two aims:

■ to assess whether an applicant is suitable for the job

■ to give the applicant a chance to get more information about the job.

In the leisure and recreation industry, depending on the organisation's procedures, interviews may be conducted by:

■ the owner of the business

■ a director

■ a manager

■ a team leader or supervisor

■ a personnel manager.

Sometimes there may be an interview panel made up of two or more people.

An interview is your opportunity to show prospective employers what you're like as a person. Your CV and letter of application will have convinced them of your possible suitability. The interview gives:

■ them a chance to find out more about you

■ you a chance to find out more about them.

Because an interview is a face-to-face meeting, your appearance and your communication skills play an important part.

Preparation

Careful preparation for an interview is crucial. A personnel manager explains how she looks for evidence of preparation by the interviewee:

66 *There are certain things I always look for in an applicant – I expect them to arrive on time, and to look neat and tidy. I am impressed if they bring a portfolio of work as evidence of what they've put about their skills and aptitudes in their CV. I like candidates to know something about our company – it shows they've taken the time and the trouble to find out about us. And I expect someone who is serious about working here to ask relevant questions. Not just 'How much holiday will I get?', but sensible questions about opportunities for training and promotion, and the people they are likely to be working with. I always give serious consideration to anyone who shows that they have prepared carefully for the interview and thought about what they want to say.* 99

ACTIVITY

Have a look at the interview tips that Microsoft give people on their web site (*http://www.microsoft.com/college/apply.htm*).

Before an interview:

■ find out as much as possible about the organisation

■ ring up and confirm the address and directions for getting there, and the name and job title of the interviewer

■ re-read the advertisement, job description and person specification, and try to 'match' your skills and experience with what is required

■ prepare and practise answers to the questions most likely to be asked

■ prepare any questions you want to ask

■ decide what you're going to wear.

Personal presentation

People can't help making judgements based on their first impression. Once an impression is made, it's difficult to shift. So it is important that the first impression you make on an interviewer is a positive one.

Body language

> **Body language** means the non-verbal messages you give out through your posture, facial expressions, gestures and eye-contact.

Body language works in two ways:
- it can support your verbal messages
- it can undermine your verbal messages.

DISCUSSION POINT

What is your immediate impression of the person shown in the three illustrations? What is it about each illustration that triggers your response?

ACTIVITY

Get together with a partner. Sit facing each other as if you were the interviewee and your partner the interviewer. Fold your arms, cross your legs and look at the floor, then stay in that posture while you tell your partner about something that interests you – for example, a hobby, a sport or the sort of music you like. Then tell them again, but this time sit up straight, with your hands clasped loosely and resting on your lap and your shoulders relaxed.

Change roles and repeat the exercise.

Discuss with your partner the effects body language had in each case.

Make notes on what you've learnt from the exercise and how you can use it to help your performance at interviews.

ACTIVITY

Make a checklist of things to consider about personal appearance that will help you when you're preparing for an interview.

Asking and answering questions

An interview is an opportunity to give and get information. Your performance at an interview will be improved if you think beforehand about the sort of questions you might be asked and the sort questions you want to ask the interviewer. Listen carefully to questions you are asked and answers you are given. Don't be afraid to give yourself time to think before you answer or to say if you don't understand the question.

> **Interview questions to be ready for**
> - Why do you want this job?
> - What personal qualities do you have to offer?
> - What ambitions do you have?
> - Why did you leave your previous job? or Why do you want to leave your present job?
> - What can you offer this organisation?
> - What do you do in your spare time? What are your hobbies and interests?
> - What is your greatest achievement?
> - Do you have any questions?

Confidence

Interviews can be nerve-racking. But you can help yourself feel more confident by careful preparation. On the day, you can use your body language to present a confident appearance.

UNIT

1

SECTION **1.4**

Presenting a confident image

- Calm your nerves with a few deep breaths.
- Stand up or sit up straight.
- Look at the interviewer while you are talking and listening.
- Smile.
- Speak clearly and positively.
- Remember that the interviewer wants you to be there because you're a good candidate for the job.

The facilities manager for a heritage site made this point on confidence:

66 *Being asked to come for an interview should give you confidence in itself. It means that your letter and CV were amongst the few that stood out from all the others. You've been picked out as someone interesting, someone with potential.* 99

Demonstrating and evaluating interview techniques

To perform well in an interview means having confidence in your communication skills. As with all skills, they can be improved with practice and feedback. Recruitment experts recommend that people get the help of friends they can rely on to give them honest, constructive criticism and helpful advice.

ACTIVITY

Get together with a couple of friends. Go through the recruitment pages of the local, national or trade press and pick a job in the leisure and recreation industry you would like to apply for. You can all choose the same job or you can each choose a different one. Contact the organisation and ask for the job description and person specification for the job you've picked. Prepare a CV and a letter of application for the job. Prepare to be interviewed and prepare to interview your friends for the jobs they've chosen. Carry out the interviews and give each other feedback on your performance as interviewee and interviewer. You might find it useful to make a video recording of each interview so you can see for yourselves how well you did. Make a list of any skills you want to improve and arrange with your friends to help you practise them further.

Key questions

1   What kind of information might you include in a career plan?

2   Why do organisations ask for a letter of application?

3   What information should be included in a CV?

4   How does personal presentation affect an interview?

5   How should an interviewee prepare for an interview?

Assignment

Part 1

Produce a report on the UK leisure and recreation industry. The report could be in the form of:

- a 'feature' article for a magazine
- a radio-type programme, recorded on cassette
- the script and storyboard (a storyboard is a sequence of images which show the main story) for a TV programme.

The report should give the historical background of the industry and should also describe the industry as it operates today. The report should include:

- reasons for the rapid development of the industry since the 1960s
- its scale and significance
- its structure and key components
- the range of public, private and voluntary sector organisations within each component.

Use examples of leisure and recreation facilities in your area to support your investigation.

If you're writing a feature article, use illustrations such as photographs, graphs and charts. If you're recording a radio-type feature, get two or three different people to record the examples to give some variety. If you're doing a TV programme, write a script for the presenter and keep the storyboard short; twelve images in all should be enough. You might like to get help from students on media and communication courses.

Part 2

Get together with two or three friends. Investigate the employment opportunities of the leisure and recreation industry by reviewing the jobs listed in the recruitment pages of local, national or trade press. Pick two leisure or recreation jobs from the current listings. Obtain the job descriptions and person specifications for each of the jobs. Discuss them with your friends and make notes on your evaluation of them.

Prepare your CV and letters of application for each job and give them to your friends to evaluate. Evaluate their CVs and letters. Give each other feedback and note down your evaluations.

Roleplay interviews for each job with your friends. Arrange to have the roleplays recorded on video and ask your tutor to act as an observer. Review your own and each other's performance and give each other feedback. Ask your tutor for an evaluation. Make notes on the comments you make and receive and evaluate your own performance as interviewer and interviewee.

Use all the notes you've made to write a brief account of what you did for the assignment and summarise the evaluations you made on each aspect.

KEY SKILLS

You can use the work you are doing for this part of your GNVQ to collect and develop evidence for the following key skills at level 3:

when you	**you can collect evidence for**
	communication
investigate the development, scale and structure of the UK leisure and recreation industry	key skill C3.2 read and synthesise information from two extended documents about a complex subject; one of these documents should include at least one image
	key skill C3.3 write two different types of documents about complex subjects; one piece of writing should be an extended document and include at least one image
	working with others
carry out your investigation into the UK leisure and recreation industry	key skill WO3.1 agree realistic objectives and the action and resources needed to achieve them; provide information, based on appropriate evidence, to help agree responsibilities; agree suitable working arrangements with those involved
	key skill WO3.2 organise and carry out tasks in ways that help you to be effective and efficient in meeting your responsibilities; seek to establish and maintain cooperative working relationships, agreeing ways to overcome any difficulties; exchange accurate information on the extent to which work is meeting expected timescales and quality, agreeing changes where necessary to achieve objectives
	key skill WO3.3 agree the extent to which the objectives have been met; identify factors that have influenced the outcome; agree ways the activity could have been done differently to enhance work with others
	improving own learning and performance
carry out your investigation into the UK leisure and recreation industry and/or carry out your investigation into employment opportunities in the industry	key skill LP3.1 seek information on ways to achieve what you want to do, and identify factors that might affect your plans; use this information to agree realistic targets with appropriate others; plan how you will manage your time to meet targets, including alternative action for overcoming possible problems and use of support from others
	key skill LP3.2 prioritise and manage your time effectively to complete tasks, making revisions to your plan as necessary; seek and actively use feedback and support from relevant sources to help you meet your targets; use different approaches to learning, drawing on learning from other tasks and adapting methods to meet new demands
	key skill LP3.3 provide information on quality of your learning and performance, identifying factors that have affected the outcome; identify targets you have met, seeking information from relevant sources to establish evidence of your achievements; exchange views with appropriate others to agree action for improving your performance

UNIT **2**

**Safe working
practices in
the leisure
and recreation
industry**

65

About this unit

All organisations, whether large or small, must ensure that they provide a safe environment for both staff and customers. This is both a legal requirement and essential commercial sense.

In this unit, you will become aware of the laws and regulations that all leisure and recreation organisations have to follow. Within this broad context, you will investigate how:

- hazards can be kept to a minimum
- leisure and recreation organisations tackle their health, safety and security responsibilities
- managers plan carefully to ensure a safe and secure environment for staff and visitors, through regular inspections, following correct procedures and staff training.

You will find out how risk assessments must be carried out and the important part they play in health and safety management.

This unit links well with:

- unit 5 Customer service
- unit 6 Leisure and recreation in action.

This unit is externally assessed.

SECTION 2.1

Working within the law

By their nature, leisure and recreation organisations deal with a lot of people. Whenever there are people around, it is important to protect their health, safety and security and there is a range of laws whose purpose is to safeguard customers and staff. There are additional laws to safeguard the environment. In this section you will discover that not only do organisations have a legal and ethical obligation to obey these laws, but that it is sound commercial sense to do so.

> ❝ We are affected by health and safety legislation, particularly on the technical side – the stage and lighting. Also we have to observe the fire regulations which can be extremely rigorous. We maintain security through alarms and close-circuit TVs, as well as by extensive locking. ❞
>
> *press and publicity officer of an entertainments venue*

> ❝ We have a health and safety officer and adhere to all the rules concerning things like fire exits, putting bright tape onto things so people don't trip over them, ensuring electrical equipment works and having first-aid procedures. We also have a designated first-aider on the premises all the time. ❞
>
> *manager of a nightclub*

2.1.1 **Introduction**

The best way to understand the importance of health, safety and security issues in the leisure and recreation industry is to think about what could happen if they are ignored.

These may be extreme incidents, but they show that health, safety and security problems can seriously affect customers using leisure and recreation services, as well as staff and organisations.

The leisure and recreation industry is very conscious of health, safety and security. In fact, it has an excellent record. Most visitor attractions and facilities like fairgrounds and sports stadiums are generally safe, serious hazards are rare, the number of accidents per passenger mile on public transport systems is low, and violent incidents at football grounds are the exception.

Health, safety and security issues aren't just the ones that make the headlines when things go wrong. The vast majority are simple, everyday things requiring common sense, sensible precautions and consideration for others.

Health, safety and security are important to:
- the organisation
- individual employees
- staff as a whole
- customers
- customer care
- public relations
- the environment.

2.1.2 **Safe working practices**

UNIT

2

SECTION **2.1**

The organisation

Legal considerations aside, no organisation wants to have a reputation for bad health, safety or security practices. Apart from the ethical issues, it can lead to serious, or even complete, loss of business. For example:

- a facility with a poor reputation for security will quickly lose customers and could face insurance problems
- a restaurant repeatedly prosecuted by environmental health officers for low hygiene standards will find it hard to shake off the image of being an unsavoury or risky place to eat
- owners and directors may have to pay large sums in compensation to injured parties which may lead to financial ruin.

DISCUSSION POINT

Think of two or three different incidents in leisure and recreation where the health of customers was harmed or their safety or security affected in some way. For each one, discuss:

- how far the organisations providing the service should be held responsible for the harm done to customers
- what steps the organisation could have taken to avoid the incident or minimise the risk of it.

A health and safety expert who advises leisure and recreation facilities comments:

66 *No organisation offering a service can be absolutely sure that all possible risks are removed. Some are outside their control. Some problems may be the result of customers' mistakes. But customers should expect organisations to do everything they reasonably can to reduce the risk of incidents. Measures to ensure the health, safety and security of customers and employees should be a high priority in the organisation's management plan.* 99

Health, safety and security affect all aspects of an organisation. The programmes director of an outside activity centre explains why health, safety and security issues are an integral part of everything the organisation does:

66 *Whatever we do has a health, safety or security aspect. For example, the facilities we offer have to be inspected and maintained. So we have to have staff to do that and we have to ensure that they're properly trained. They need tools, equipment and in some cases protective clothing. All of these are costs which have to be built into our budgets. We can't just bolt on the health, safety and security aspects. We have to think them through, cost them out, resource them and work them into our systems and procedures.* 99

ACTIVITY

Any leisure or recreation activity will require these components:

- land and premises
- materials, equipment and/or machinery
- staff
- activities involved in providing products and/or services
- customers.

For each component listed, ask yourself these questions:

- What health, safety and security issues might affect this?
- What could happen if the issues were ignored?

Note down your ideas.

Staff

Individuals working in leisure and recreation have a right to expect that, while at work, their personal needs for health, safety and security will be met by their employer.

Rights imply duties, and employees also have a duty to take reasonable measures to protect their own health, safety and security. They must observe all health, safety and security measures laid down by the organisation. They must also avoid placing others at risk, including both customers and fellow workers.

Health and Safety Policy

The board of directors wishes to pursue a policy to promote health and safety at work and seeks the cooperation of all staff members, trainees and visitors for that purpose. The company will provide working conditions which comply with the statutory requirements of the Health and Safety at Work, etc., Act 1974, and other approved codes of practice as appropriate. These standards are intended to provide adequate or more than adequate standards of health and safety.

We have concern for company staff members, and also for the many freelance contractors, temporary staff and visitors who use these premises. It is considered vitally important that this policy and all health and safety facilities and procedures, are in operation and adhered to; that they are monitored and reviewed regularly; and that everything possible is done to maintain an environment where full consideration is given to health and safety in all the company's activities.

1   The employer ensures, as far as reasonably practicable in the current state of knowledge, the health, safety and welfare at work of all staff members, trainees, clients and visitors to the premises. This is achieved by:
   • providing adequate working conditions with facilities and procedures intended to safeguard health and safety
   • providing information, instruction, training and supervision to create a safe and healthy environment for all employees and visitors.
2   The employer encourages staff members to cooperate with management in all health and safety matters.

Extract from Health and Safety Policy

Customers

Customers expect certain standards from the organisations where they buy products and services. They expect that:

■ health, safety and security measures meet the standards required by law

■ members of staff with whom they have contact have been trained in health, safety and security procedures

■ they will be told about any aspect of the facility which may present a risk to their health, safety and security.

Criteria

The national tourist boards for England, Scotland and Wales operate a national ACCESSIBLE scheme to identify and acknowledge those places to stay that meet the needs of wheelchair users. There are three Categories of accessibility:

Category 1
Accessible to an independent wheelchair user.
Category 2
Accessible to wheelchair user with assistance.
Category 3
Accessible to wheelchair user able to walk a few paces and up at least three steps.

The minimum requirements for each of the three Categories are shown in this leaflet. It is emphasised that these are the minimum requirements. If an Access inspection reveals that there are other aspects, not dealt with in the criteria, that prohibit access or present serious obstacles, the awarding of an Accessible Category may be withheld until such time as it is confirmed that the situation has been remedied.

Please note:
The measurements included in these criteria are those acceptable to meet the requirements of the three Categories of accessibility. They are not, necessarily, recommended or Ideal measurements. Details of recommended measurements are given in the 'Providing Accessible Accommodation' guide published by the Holiday Care Service, Imperial Buildings (2nd floor), Victoria Road, Horley RH6 7PZ or from your regional tourist board.

Notes
1 Ramps, where present, should not have a gradient at any point of more than 1:12. Removable ramps, unless permanently in situ, are not acceptable for Category 1.
2 Single steps: For Category 2 there can be a succession of single steps, provided there is sufficient space after each step for a wheelchair to sit comfortably and safely, with all four wheels on the ground.
3 Steps to be used by a disabled guest should have risers no more than 19cm, treads no less than 25cm deep and 75cm wide.
4 For Category 1, thresholds to rooms to which the wheelchair user requires access must be no higher than 2 cm.

Extract from 'the 'National Accessible Scheme' published by the English Tourist Board

All leisure and recreation organisations want their customers to use their facilities, products and services safely. It's part of their legal responsibility and part of their ethical responsibility. The manager of a fitness centre explains why they see health, safety and security as a duty they owe their customers:

❝ *Our customers come to us because they see us as fitness experts – both in the instruction we give and the facilities we provide. They trust us to provide a healthy, safe and secure environment. If we fail to live up to that trust, we're failing to do our jobs properly and we shouldn't be in business.* **❞**

DISCUSSION POINT

What would you do as a customer if you felt you were at risk because of an organisation's bad health, safety or security practices?

The environment

Some leisure and recreation activities are a possible threat to the environment. Health, safety and security measures play an important role in avoiding or limiting environmental damage.

The manager of an outdoor swimming pool at a seaside resort describes how they are aware of environmental hazards:

❝ *We thought about setting up another business hiring out motor boats and jet-skis. Local conservationists were worried about the effect the extra noise and activity would have on the wildlife. We also thought about other damage to the environment – for example, the fuel tank of a boat might leak. So we didn't go ahead with the expansion. We built a second swimming pool instead.* ❞

It's not just leisure and recreation facilities that create an impact on the environment – their visitors do too.

ACTIVITY

Design a leaflet which could be given to customers at a leisure and recreation facility you know about to help raise their awareness of the impact they may have on the local environment. Give them some guidelines on positive actions they can take and standards they can keep.

2.1.3 **Public relations**

Public relations is a system of establishing and maintaining good relationships and effective communication channels between an organisation and the general public.

Organisations use public relations to present their image to the outside world. For leisure and recreation organisations, demonstrating to the public that they take the health, safety and security of their staff, customers and the local environment seriously is an important part of their public relations activities.

When something goes wrong, like an accident, an organisation uses its public relations activities to:
- explain its side
- acknowledge any responsibility it has
- reassure the public it is taking preventative measures to stop a similar accident happening in the future.

Public relations activities include:
- dealing with the media
- organising public awareness events
- issuing press releases and statements
- coordinating publicity events
- organising and controlling the way information about the organisation is passed to the media and the general public.

A public relations officer for a theme park describes how important it is for organisations to take into account the power of public opinion:

66 *A failure in health, safety or security measures in one organisation puts the whole industry sector under public scrutiny. It makes the public think: 'If it happened at that facility, it could happen at others.' So we don't just have responsibility for the image of our own organisation: we also have responsibility for the industry sector as a whole. This means that our public relations department has to be geared up to respond to the wider picture, not just our own part of it.* 99

Key questions

1 What would the effect be on an organisation that had a reputation for bad health, safety or security practices?

2 What have customers the right to expect of an organisation in terms of health, safety and security?

3 What is public relations?

4 What is the function of an organisation's public relations department?

5 In terms of health and safety, what are the responsibilities of employees of a leisure and recreation facility?

6 In terms of health and safety, what should employees expect of their employer?

SECTION **2.2**

Health and safety legislation and regulations

Organisations ensure health, safety and security through a range of measures which are either obligatory (which means you have to follow them) or voluntary (which means you can choose whether to follow them or not). In this section you will develop your understanding of the laws and regulations and of the agencies who enforce them. You will also learn how to find out information on the very large amount of legislation which exists on health and safety.

66 We had our regular visit from the environmental health inspector this year. Although there are regulations which everyone preparing food has to observe, we don't have to have big stainless-steel surfaces everywhere because we are not a restaurant and are considered to have a domestic kitchen. 99

owner of a guest-house

66 The main national legislation which affects us is the Children's Act. This requires that we maintain a ratio of staff to children of one to eight. It means that staff don't have unrealistic demands made on them, and the children benefit from better safety standards and more attention. 99

community play officer in a city council

2.2.1 **Health and safety measures**

Obligatory measures

All organisations offering goods and services must meet minimum standards of health, safety and security. These standards are set at local, national or international level. They are described in various documents.

- **Laws** – Rules made by parliament which all individuals and organisations have to follow. Laws are enforced by the courts and local authorities.
- **By-laws** – Regulations made by local authorities which residents and businesses within the area covered by the local authority have to follow.
- **Regulations** – Official rules or orders, usually made by a government department, and authorised by law. They are different from laws in that they do not always apply to everyone.
- **EU Directives** – Regulations which apply to all member states of the European Union. The way they are put into practice, e.g. by law or regulation, is left to the individual state.

Organisations which do not meet the standards may be prosecuted in court. Many of the laws, regulations and directives affecting the leisure and recreation industry are described in section 2.2.4.

Voluntary measures

Laws, regulations and directives set minimum standards of health, safety and security which organisations have to meet. Some sectors of the industry have voluntary measures as well, such as:

- industry codes of practice – voluntary procedures laid down by organisations which represent an area of the industry
- organisational codes and procedures – procedures adopted by individual organisations.

These voluntary codes may:

- describe how laws and regulations – the obligatory standards – should be put into practice
- set standards that are higher than the legal minimum
- lay down additional health, safety and security measures relevant to a particular area of the industry – for example, a company offering diving lessons may have a code of practice relating to procedures which all divers must follow and for using diving equipment safely.

HSC
Health & Safety
Commission

Organisations can send copies of their voluntary codes of practice to the Health and Safety Commission (HSC) for approval.

In 1994 the Activity Centre Advisory Committee (ACAC) drew up a voluntary code of practice for outdoor activity centres. The committee took this action largely in response to an incident at Lyme Bay where four teenagers on a school trip died during a canoeing activity.

The code covers:

■ general conditions (such as statutory obligations and insurance)
■ safety, welfare and care of people using and working in activity centres
■ staffing
■ facilities
■ management of activities
■ environmental considerations.

Centres which follow the code are eligible for accreditation by the Committee if they:

■ can demonstrate that they are implementing the code's guidelines
■ are open to independent inspections
■ have an effective customer complaints procedure.

The Government has incorporated much of the code in a new law on the operation of outdoor centres called the Activity Centres (Young Persons' Safety) Act 1995.

When organisations introduce their own procedures, they generally base them on laws, regulations and industry codes of practice.

Many professional bodies and trade associations produce their own codes of practice on customer care. These often include health, safety and security procedures. Local authorities and government departments may produce statements relating to health, safety and security in their Citizens' Charters.

ACTIVITY

Ask to see the health and safety policy statement of a facility you know. Make a copy of this checklist and tick off each item you find in the policy statement.

■ a general statement of policy
■ a list of responsibilities, including named people who are responsible for some area of safety
■ accident arrangements, including details of first aid
■ general fire safety
■ the address of the local Health and Safety Executive (HSE)
■ special training arrangements
■ the organisation's rules for outside contractors and other visitors
■ notes of hazards
■ housekeeping arrangements, including waste disposal
■ rules for electrical safety
■ dangerous equipment and necessary precautions
■ dangerous substances and relevant precautions, for those covered by COSHH regulations and flammable substances
■ other important hazards such as on-site vehicles.

2.2.2 **Implementing measures**

Setting standards is one thing. Making sure that they are kept to is much harder. It's up to everyone to make sure that the measures described here are put into practice.

- ■ **Individual employees** must be aware of and follow relevant guidelines – whether obligatory or voluntary.
- ■ **Departmental managers** are responsible for making sure that the procedures are used.
- ■ Where security of information is concerned, organisations may have an **information technology (IT) manager** responsible for laying down procedures.
- ■ Large organisations may employ a **health and safety officer** to oversee and coordinate health and safety regulations and procedures.
- ■ In situations where health, safety and security are subject to laws and regulations, **enforcement officers** may visit premises to check that measures are being followed. If they're not being followed, the officers can take action against the owner or directors.

Customers are also important pieces in the health and safety jigsaw. They should be made aware of any health, safety or security procedures which they should observe when using a facility. Customers ignoring the rules in force may put into danger the health, safety or security of themselves and others, and should be asked either to follow the rules or to leave.

DISCUSSION POINT

In what ways might an organisation ensure that health, safety and security procedures are understood and followed by staff and customers?

79

2.2.3 Laws and regulations

Laws are rules that allow governments to set down standards of conduct and behaviour which everyone has to follow — including individuals and organisations. Laws also aim to protect people against the negligence and wrongdoing of others. **Legislation** is the process of establishing law.

Here is a legal adviser's summary of the purpose of health, safety and security laws and regulations:

66 *Laws and regulations provide a framework which organisations and individuals can use to make sure that they work in a way that promotes health, safety and security. As well as setting standards, they also describe actions that may be taken against organisations that don't follow the rules laid down.* 99

DISCUSSION POINT

Following health, safety and security laws and regulations means taking responsibility for yourself and for others. As an employee in the leisure and recreation industry, who would you count as 'others'?

The main purposes of laws and regulations

- To raise individuals' awareness of their responsibility in keeping health, safety and security standards.
- To raise individuals' awareness of their responsibility to other people.
- To reduce risks and dangers – to themselves and other people.
- To set standards which organisations and individuals can follow.
- To make sure that advice is available to organisations and individuals.

Most laws relating to health, safety and security aim to provide a better work and leisure environment. They apply equally to employers and employees.

Enforcement officers are employed to make sure that laws and regulations are followed and to look into cases where the regulations have been broken. They also have a duty to assist organisations to comply with the regulations, by giving information and advice.

The Health and Safety Officer of a local authority makes regular checks on all the public entertainment venues in the area. She describes some of the checks she makes:

ACTIVITY

Pick one of the groups listed below and design a poster to get across to them the message that health, safety security laws and regulations are there for a purpose.

- employers
- employees
- customers.

66 *I go round the venues making sure that all the fire exits can be used. Sometimes I've found chairs in front of them, or that the aisle leading up to them has been narrowed. I also look at the number of people the venue can safely hold, and quite often I've had to reduce it as I didn't feel it was safe. That doesn't go down well with the management as they want to sell more tickets not fewer – but it has to be done.* 99

2.2.4 **Key legislation**

The information in this section applies particularly to England and Wales. Most Acts of Parliament apply throughout the whole of the United Kingdom, but there are often separate provisions dealing with Scotland – the same laws apply, but the way in which they are put into practice may vary. This is because the structure of the legal system in Scotland is different from that of the rest of the UK. Although closely linked, the laws of Northern Ireland also vary; where there are any significant differences the relevant legislation which applies is mentioned.

> If they are not available in your local library, copies of Acts of Parliament may be obtained from:
>
> Her Majesty's Stationery Office
>
> Holborn Viaduct
>
> London WC1V 6HB
>
> It's not much fun reading the whole of an Act. You may find it better to read a summary. Relevant directories often contain summaries – ask in your library where you can find them. The summaries given here are a start.

Health and Safety at Work, etc., Act (1974) and Health and Safety at Work (NI) Order 1978

The Health and Safety at Work Act is commonly referred to as HASAWA or HASWA. It applies to England and Wales. In Northern Ireland, the corresponding legislation is the Health and Safety at Work (NI) Order 1978.

The purpose of HASAWA is to increase the protection of people at work. It applies to everybody at work – employers, employees or the self-employed. It also protects people who are affected by work activities – neighbours, passers-by and customers. It applies to people rather than premises.

The main points to note in the Act are Sections 2, 3, 4, 7 and 33 (see 2.2.6 on pages 89–90 below).

Six-Pack

Six sets of regulations became known collectively as the Six-Pack because they gave effect to six European Directives on workplace health and safety.

1 The **Health and Safety (Display Screen Equipment) Regulations 1992** came into force on 1 January 1993 and lay down minimum health and safety requirements for work with display screen equipment.

2 The **Manual Handling Operations Regulations 1992** came into force on 1 January 1993 to prevent injury from manual handling operations. These regulations replaced all previous legislation concerned with the lifting and carrying of heavy weights.

3 The **Personal Protective Equipment at Work Regulations 1992** came into force on 1 January 1993 and introduced minimum health and safety requirements for the use by workers of personal protective equipment at the workplace.

4 The **Management of Health and Safety at Work Regulations 1992** were introduced to implement measures to encourage improvement in the approach of management towards the health and safety of people at work.

5 The **Workplace (Health, Safety and Welfare) Regulations 1992** consolidate many existing pieces of legislation relating to workplaces and welfare facilities. The Regulations apply to a broad range of workplaces including factories, offices, shops, schools, hospitals, and hotels, and the term workplace incorporates common parts of shared premises such as lifts and stairways and private roads and paths on industrial estates.

6 The **Provision and Use of Work Equipment Regulations 1992** cover the safety requirements of machinery and equipment in the workplace. The Regulations apply to all work equipment, including second-hand, hired or leased equipment.

Working Time Regulations 1998

These cover all aspects of the rights of workers in relation to time in the workplace, including:

- maximum weekly working time
- length of night work
- weekly rest period
- rest breaks
- entitlement to annual leave
- payment in respect of periods of leave.

The regulations also indicate which areas of work are not covered by these provisions, including the police service, the armed forces, domestic service, agricultural work. These areas of employment are covered by other regulations.

The Health and Safety (First Aid) Regulations 1981

These set down the legal requirements for employers. They are supported by an Approved Code of Practice which recommends one first-aider per 50 members of staff during working hours.

ACTIVITY

Find out who amongst the staff at your college or school has responsibilities for first aid. Talk to them about what their responsibilities involve and any training they have to do.

Workplaces should also provide first-aid boxes and kits. Each first-aid box should contain standard items including adhesive and other dressings, a triangular bandage, at least one sterile eye pad and a guidance card or leaflet giving first-aid advice.

Many leisure and recreation facilities have large numbers of people visiting them, and the arrangements for first aid should take account of this. One first-aid box is not enough on a large site or in a large building where there are going to be a lot of customers on busy days.

Disability Discrimination Act 1994

If you are disabled, or have a disability, the Act makes it unlawful for an employer (who employs 20 or more people) to discriminate against you when you are applying for a job. It is also unlawful for people to discriminate against you in the provision of goods, facilities and services, or in the selling or letting of land and property. These are not universal rights – only certain degrees of disability qualify and certain types of organisation are exempt.

Children Act 1989

The Act covers:
■ the welfare of children
■ local authority services for children in need
■ children's homes, community homes, voluntary homes and voluntary organisations
■ fostering, childminding and day care for young children, and adoption.

Data Protection Act 1984

One important aspect of security is security of information. With the increasing use of computers, it has become much easier to store and move information about individuals. The Data Protection Act is designed to protect individuals' rights in relation to computer-held personal data.

The Data Protection Act 1984:
■ forbids organisations or individuals from holding personal data unless they are registered with the Data Protection Registrar
■ gives individuals the right to know whether a data user is holding personal data and the right to look at that personal data
■ gives individuals a right to compensation where personal data held is inaccurate
■ gives the right to have inaccurate data corrected or removed.

Food Safety Act 1990

The Act relates to food preparation and services. There are stringent hygiene procedures to be abided by hotels, restaurants, pub, clubs, take-aways and other tourism venues. Local authority environmental health officers enforce the regulations.

Fire Safety and Safety of Places of Sport Act 1987

An amendment of the Fire Protection Act 1971, this was introduced after the Bradford City Football Club fire where 56 people died. Sporting venues must obtain fire certificates to show that they keep exits clear of obstructions, have regular fire drills, set maximum numbers, provide staff training and keep records on fire safety.

Fire Precaution (Workplace) Regulation 1998 (amended December 1999)

Similar in requirements to the Fire Safety and Safety of Places of Sport Act, the regulation covers virtually all places of work, including sports grounds. Exemptions are mostly private dwelling and self employed people's workplaces.

Voluntary codes of practice

Organisations in the leisure and recreation industry often adopt voluntary codes of practice in order to improve health and safety standards. These codes have no force in law, but they can greatly improve the competence of employees and reassure customers who know that the code is being observed. For example, the Royal Life Saving Society (RLSS) has a Water Safety Code which could be adopted by swimming pools, yacht clubs, or any facility using water in its attractions. The RLSS also provides water safety education and training in resuscitation and publishes the *Beginner's Guide to Water Safety*.

2.2.5 Duties of employers and employees

Employers

Here are the duties of employers under sections 2, 3 and 4 of the Health and Safety at Work Act.

Section 2

- Provide and maintain equipment and appliances and systems of work which are safe and without risk to health.
- Arrange the safe handling, use, storage and transport of articles and substances.
- Provide information, instruction, training and supervision to ensure the health and safety of employees.
- Keep places of work in a safe condition without risk to health.
- Provide safe access to and exit from working premises.
- Provide and maintain a working environment that is as safe as possible and free of risks to health and safety, and in which the facilities and arrangements are adequate for the wellbeing of employees at work.
- Provide a written statement of the general health and safety policy and bring it to the attention of all employees (this does not apply to organisations where there are fewer than five employees).
- Consult the safety representatives of recognised trade unions about making and maintaining health and safety and to set up a safety committee, if two or more safety representatives request it.

Section 3

- Make sure, as far as possible, that people other than employees (clients, visitors, etc.) are not exposed to risks to their health and safety.

Section 4

- Make sure that premises, equipment and machinery may be used without risks to health and safety.

Employees

Here are the duties of employees under sections 7 and 8 of the Health and Safety at Work Act.

Section 7

- Take reasonable care for the health and safety of themselves and persons who may be affected by what they do or don't do at work.
- Cooperate with their employers about any duty placed on them relating to health and safety.

Section 8

- Not to interfere intentionally or recklessly with or misuse anything provided for health, safety or welfare (e.g. fire extinguishers).

Section 33

Section 33 describes what constitutes an offence under the Act. Offences include:

- failing to carry out duties laid down by the Act or by other health and safety regulations
- obstructing inspectors in their work or interfering with the inspection process – for example, by preventing employees appearing before an inspector
- failing to comply with improvement orders, prohibition notices and other court orders
- posing as a Health and Safety Inspector.

DISCUSSION POINT

A waiter employed in a country house hotel was carrying a tray from one of the guest rooms down the service staircase to the kitchens. To save himself two journeys, he had loaded a lot of things on the one tray, but it was still light enough to be carried. The staircase was poorly lit and some of the carpet was badly frayed. The waiter missed his footing and fell down to the bottom. He broke his ankle and received several bad cuts from the broken glass.

- Which sections of the HASAWA are relevant to this incident?
- What did the owners of the hotel do wrong?
- What did the waiter do wrong?

2.2.6 Enforcing the HASAWA

HSE
**Health & Safety
Executive**

HSC
**Health & Safety
Commission**

There are two government-funded bodies whose job it is to make sure that the HASAWA is understood, followed and used:

■ The Health and Safety Commission (HSC) consists of a full-time chairman, representatives from industry and local authorities. Its duty is to promote the objectives of the Act and to develop health and safety policies, provide guidance, codes of practice and proposals for regulations.

■ The Health and Safety Executive (HSE) has a duty to carry out the day-to-day work of the HSC and to put into force the legal requirements of the Act.

The HSE appoints inspectors who have the power to enter any premises, at any time, if they believe that there is a dangerous situation. They have the power to interview anyone who may have information relevant to their examination or investigation.

If an inspector finds any breaches in health and safety laws and regulations, he or she is entitled to:

■ issue a *prohibition notice* which bans the activity which is causing the risk until action is taken to put the problem right – particularly if there's a risk of a serious personal injury

■ issue an *improvement notice* which gives the organisation a specified time for putting the fault right

■ prosecute so that the matter is dealt with by the law courts – if the circumstances demand it, this may be in addition to, or instead of, issuing a prohibition notice

■ arrange to have the source of the danger made harmless or removed – particularly if it threatens to result in serious personal injury or damage to property.

Under HASAWA, people guilty of an offence may be fined up to £20,000. Anyone failing to comply with a notice or court order faces a similar fine, or six months in jail, or both.

Workplace regulations

New laws made under HASAWA – the Workplace (Health, Safety and Welfare) Regulations 1992 came into force for all premises on 1 January 1996. They were published by the HSC together with an approved code of practice (ACOP) which gives more precise guidelines on some topics.

These regulations set out the minimum working conditions for all workers in fixed permanent workplaces – including all offices, shops and similar premises. They also cover hospitals and schools.

ACTIVITY

What does eleven cubic metres look like? If you were working in a room three metres high with several desks in it, how much space would have to be left between the people sitting at each desk? Calculate how much floor space each person can expect as a minimum. Do you think this is a reasonable minimum?

Cleanliness

Premises, furnishings and fittings must be kept in a clean state. Dirt and rubbish must not be allowed to collect. Floors and stairs must be cleaned at least once a week.

Overcrowding

No room in the premises should be so overcrowded as to cause risk of injury to the health of persons working in them. The Workplace Regulations say that there should be enough floor area, height and unoccupied space to ensure health, safety and welfare. The ACOP states that this means at least eleven cubic metres per person (any space above three metres from the floor should not be included in the calculation).

Temperature

A reasonable temperature must be kept in every room in which people are employed to work. The minimum temperature should normally be 16 °C. Equipment used in workplaces, such as photocopiers and computers, must not cause discomfort or danger through fumes – temperatures of up to 32 °C have been found in rooms containing several pieces of electronic equipment.

Ventilation

A constant flow of clean, fresh, draught-free air should be provided.

Lighting

Lighting should be of the right quality and brightness, and, wherever possible, should be natural light. There should be no glare and black shadows.

Sanitation and water

Toilets should be provided for employees. There should be separate toilets for both sexes. Clean running hot and cold water, soap and towels (or suitable alternatives) should be provided. These facilities should be kept clean, properly looked after, properly lit and ventilated. There should be drinking water which employees can easily get to.

Seating

Where employees have to sit down to carry out their duties, suitable seating must be provided. Seating must be safe, and of suitable design, construction and size.

Floors, passages and stairs

Floors, passages and stairs must be of sound construction, properly looked after and free from obstruction. Handrails should be provided on the open side of staircases.

Dangerous machinery

Dangerous machinery must be securely fenced and adequately guarded against all possible injuries.

Sections 1, 7, 8, and 14 of an earlier Act, the Shops, Offices and Railway Premises Act 1963 cover similar areas to the Workplace Regulations. Section 3 of the Act excludes workplaces used for less than 21 hours a week by one staff member or a total of 21 hours between two or more staff members. Section 15 requires organisations to provide a suitable eating place for staff who have to eat on the premises.

The Control of Substances Hazardous to Health (COSHH) Regulations

The COSHH regulations have two main purposes:

- to increase awareness of the hazards posed by chemicals and other substances
- to promote their safe handling and storage.

All employers and self-employed people must follow the COSHH regulations.

All substances are potentially hazardous – even water can burn when it's hot – but the regulations are designed to cover:

- substances which are labelled as dangerous – toxic, harmful, irritant or corrosive
- agricultural pesticides and other chemicals used on farms
- a range of other substances for which exposure levels have been set.

The regulations also cover harmful microorganisms, substantial quantities of dust and any other material, mixture or compound which can harm people's health as a result of breathing it in, swallowing or skin contact.

No work which could expose anyone to hazardous substances may lawfully be carried on unless an assessment has been made and necessary precautions have been taken.

EXTREMELY/HIGHLY
FLAMMABLE

ENVIRONMENTAL
HAZARD

CORROSIVE

OXIDISING

VERY TOXIC/TOXIC

EXPLOSIVE

HARMFUL/IRRITANT

COSHH precautions

- control exposure to exclude or minimise risk
- check that the measures taken work
- ensure that the substances are properly looked after
- monitor substances to maintain proper limits
- keep records of monitoring
- train and instruct employees about the risk and precautions

COSHH has important implications for some areas of the leisure industry – for example, water in swimming pools is treated with chlorine. A farmer describes what he did to observe COSHH when he rented out cottages on his farm to visitors:

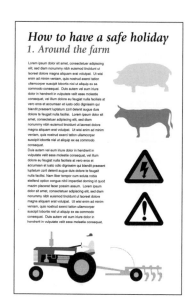

How to have a safe holiday
1. Around the farm

Lorem ipsum dolor sit amet, consectetuer adipiscing elit, sed diam nonummy nibh euismod tincidunt ut laoreet dolore magna aliquam erat volutpat. Ut wisi enim ad minim veniam, quis nostrud exerci tation ullamcorper suscipit lobortis nisl ut aliquip ex ea commodo consequat. Duis autem vel eum iriure dolor in hendrerit in vulputate velit esse molestie consequat, vel illum dolore eu feugiat nulla facilisis at vero eros et accumsan et iusto odio dignissim qui blandit praesent luptatum zzril delenit augue duis dolore te feugait nulla facilisi. Lorem ipsum dolor sit amet, consectetuer adipiscing elit, sed diam nonummy nibh euismod tincidunt ut laoreet dolore magna aliquam erat volutpat. Ut wisi enim ad minim veniam, quis nostrud exerci tation ullamcorper suscipit lobortis nisl ut aliquip ex ea commodo consequat.

Duis autem vel eum iriure dolor in hendrerit in vulputate velit esse molestie consequat, vel illum dolore eu feugiat nulla facilisis at vero eros et accumsan et iusto odio dignissim qui blandit praesent luptatum zzril delenit augue duis dolore te feugait nulla facilisi. Nam liber tempor cum soluta nobis eleifend option congue nihil imperdiet doming id quod mazim placerat facer possim assum. Lorem ipsum dolor sit amet, consectetuer adipiscing elit, sed diam nonummy nibh euismod tincidunt ut laoreet dolore magna aliquam erat volutpat. Ut wisi enim ad minim veniam, quis nostrud exerci tation ullamcorper suscipit lobortis nisl ut aliquip ex ea commodo consequat. Duis autem vel eum iriure dolor in hendrerit in vulputate velit esse molestie consequat,

❝ *I converted an old barn into some cottages, so families could see what it was like living on a working farm. I consulted my professional body, the National Farmers Union, and the local tourist board. I was particularly worried about some of the equipment and chemical fertilisers on the farm that could be very dangerous. I already had strict guidelines for my farm workers about storing and handling these substances. These were tightened to make sure that all these substances were well out of the way of the visitors. I also produced a leaflet for all the visitors on health and safety – a friend who was an artist added illustrations to make it easier for children to understand.* **❞**

Notification of Accidents and Dangerous Occurrences Regulations 1985

Dangerous incidents, including all those where the injured person is in hospital as a result of an accident or incident in the workplace, should be reported to the Health and Safety Executive. Whenever a report is received, the HSE Inspectorate will decide whether further investigations are needed. In Northern Ireland this is covered by the Reporting of Injuries, Diseases and Dangerous Occurrences Regulations (NI) 1986.

Fire Precautions Act 1971

This act details the regulations concerning lighting, heating, means of escape, and precautions to take in case of fire. Regulations are checked up on by inspectors working together with the local authority.

Occupiers Liability Act 1957

'Occupiers' have a duty to protect the lawful visitor who comes on to the premises. The Act applies to the occupier of land and buildings and to those who have furniture and fittings – shelves, cupboards, carpeting, floors and so on – under their control.

Consumer protection

Several laws offer protection to the consumer. The ones which apply to leisure and recreation organisations offering goods or services are:

- The Consumer Protection Act 1987
- The Fair Trading Act 1973
- The Trade Descriptions Act 1987
- The Sale of Goods Act 1979.

These Acts are controlled and regulated by the Office of Fair Trading (OFT) and are administered locally by trading standards officers. The main aim is to look after the rights of customers when they buy goods or services:

- Goods or services must be of a suitable quality.
- Goods or services must be what they claim to be – in other words, they should. match the description given to customers.
- Customers have a right to return goods which are faulty, damaged or don't match the description.

2.2.7 **Relevance of laws and regulations**

Many of the laws and regulations are relevant to particular types of leisure and recreation facilities. For example, COSHH is more important for swimming pools, which use substances such as chlorine, than for museums where the most hazardous materials are likely to be cleaning fluids.

SWIMMING POOL

Following a regular Saturday morning swimming session at the local swimming pool, Jamie Carter slipped on a pool of water in the changing area and fell, cracking his head on the floor. The lifeguard gave him first aid and called an ambulance. Jamie was taken to hospital. A gash on his head needed several stitches and he was kept in overnight with mild concussion.

OUTDOOR CONCERT

The town orchestra was staging its annual open air concert. This was the orchestra's silver jubilee and it decided to stage something really special. Tchaikovsky's '1812 Overture' was performed with cannon fire, smoke and a fireworks display.

MAILING LIST

A sports club bought a computer and transferred their membership list on to a database. The club registered with the Data Protection Registrar even though they were only using the database as a membership record and as an address list for newsletters.

Following an inquiry by the Data Protection Registrar it was discovered that a rival sports club had got hold of a copy of the membership list. The membership secretary had a good idea who had handed the list over.

DISCUSSION POINT

Read through the three case studies again.

■ What laws and regulations are relevant in each situation – either because they have been broken or because they need to be considered to protect customers and employees?

■ What do you think should be the next steps in each situation?

What actually happened

SWIMMING POOL

The lifeguard had to make a full report to the Health and Safety Executive. The health and safety inspector visited shortly afterwards and issued an Improvement Notice requiring non-slip matting to be provided in the changing rooms within 14 days.

OUTDOOR CONCERT

The local fire officer provided the orchestra with advice on fire safety during the performance and also arranged for a fire-fighter to be on duty during the performance. Special arrangements were made for storing the smoke canisters and the stage manager was given special instructions on their use. The fireworks were provided by a specialist firm with an excellent safety record. The company was a member of the Association of Firework Manufacturers who produced a code of conduct which met both health and safety and fire regulations.

MAILING LIST

In this situation the Data Protection Act was clearly broken, but after discussions between the club chairman and the local crime prevention officer, it was decided that a police investigation would create too much bad publicity and would be unlikely to prove who had broken the regulations. The crime prevention officer suggested a number of security measures which could be taken. While on his visit he carried out a security inspection of the premises and made several recommendations about the security of the cash, locks and protection against vandalism.

THORPE PARK

Thorpe Park in Surrey is a leisure park offering a range of indoor and outdoor family entertainments and activities including:

- lakes
- rides
- a shop and a craft centre
- food outlets
- a working farm
- nature and conservation areas
- a collection of scale models of world-famous buildings
- special events such as jousting competitions, water-ski championships, airship displays and open-air drama productions.

It employs around 1,000 people and has up to 18,000 visitors a day. Safety is a top priority and their safety policy aims to ensure:

- safe working conditions for employees
- a safe environment for visitors.

All staff are made aware of their responsibilities for safety. They're given guidance from their supervisors and also written information in the *Terms and Conditions Handbook.*

Staff are expected to:

- take care over the use and maintenance of equipment
- keep their own working areas clean, tidy and hazard-free.

All staff are aware of the procedures for emergencies such as fire or bomb alerts.

Security staff can be contacted by radio from many points throughout the site.

Security responsibilities for all staff include:

- always carrying their security passes
- knowing where to report incidents such as theft or damage
- making sure lost property is passed on to the Information Point.

Key questions

1 Why are good health, safety and security procedures important to:
   – organisations?
   – staff?
   – customers?

2 What is the difference between obligatory measures and voluntary measures? Give an example of each type.

3 Where can you obtain copies of Acts of Parliament?

4 Summarise the responsibilities which the Health and Safety at Work Act 1974 gives to:
   – employers
   – employees.

5 Who appoints health and safety inspectors? What actions can inspectors take against an organisation which fails to meet legal requirements for health, safety and security?

6 How many first-aiders do the Health and Safety (First Aid) Regulations 1981 recommend per 50 members of staff during working hours?

7 Why is COSHH important? What incidents might occur if a swimming pool ignored its recommendations?

8 A small fitness centre has put all its customer details onto a computer database. Which Act will it have to comply with, and what will this entail for them?

SECTION **2.3**

Hazards and risk assessments

Because health and safety law in the UK and the EU is now based on the principle of risk assessment, the onus is on employers to assess health and safety hazards and risks and take appropriate measures to eliminate or control them. In this section you will develop your understanding of risks and hazards and the correct procedures for carrying out a risk assessment.

> 66 *Where employers are involved in putting on events, they have a legal duty under the Health and Safety at Work Act 1974 to look after the safety of their employees and anybody else affected by their work practices. Since 1993, employers' legal responsibilities include the duty to carry out risk assessments. This was laid down in the Management of Health and Safety at Work Regulations 1992.* 99
>
> *safety officer*

> 66 *I have to be especially aware of health and safety issues when we run an event like a gymkhana. Our outside electricity supply has to be checked and we have to have a certificate for it. Any substance or chemical used by anyone on the premises that might be hazardous or dangerous in some way has to be covered by the health and safety legislation. With so much equipment, we also have to make sure things aren't left lying around which people could fall over.* 99
>
> *owner of a riding school*

How to have a safe holiday
1. Around the farm

Lorem ipsum dolor sit amet, consectetuer adipiscing elit, sed diam nonummy nibh euismod tincidunt ut laoreet dolore magna aliquam erat volutpat. Ut wisi enim ad minim veniam, quis nostrud exerci tation ullamcorper suscipit lobortis nisl ut aliquip ex ea commodo consequat. Duis autem vel eum iriure dolor in hendrerit in vulputate velit esse molestie consequat, vel illum dolore eu feugiat nulla facilisis at vero eros et accumsan et iusto odio dignissim qui blandit praesent luptatum zzril delenit augue duis dolore te feugait nulla facilisi. Lorem ipsum dolor sit amet, consectetuer adipiscing elit, sed diam nonummy nibh euismod tincidunt ut laoreet dolore magna aliquam erat volutpat. Ut wisi enim ad minim veniam, quis nostrud exerci tation ullamcorper suscipit lobortis nisl ut aliquip ex ea commodo consequat.
Duis autem vel eum iriure dolor in hendrerit in vulputate velit esse molestie consequat, vel illum dolore eu feugiat nulla facilisis at vero eros et accumsan et iusto odio dignissim qui blandit praesent luptatum zzril delenit augue duis dolore te feugait nulla facilisi. Nam liber tempor cum soluta nobis eleifend option congue nihil imperdiet doming id quod mazim placerat facer possim assum. Lorem ipsum dolor sit amet, consectetuer adipiscing elit, sed diam nonummy nibh euismod tincidunt ut laoreet dolore magna aliquam erat volutpat. Ut wisi enim ad minim veniam, quis nostrud exerci tation ullamcorper suscipit lobortis nisl ut aliquip ex ea commodo consequat. Duis autem vel eum iriure dolor in hendrerit in vulputate velit esse molestie consequat,

2.3.1 **Identifying hazards**

Health and safety law in the UK and the EU is now based on the principle of risk assessment. The onus is on employers to assess health and safety hazards and risks, and then take appropriate measures to eliminate or control them.

> A **hazard** is something that can potentially cause harm.
>
> **Risk** is the chance or level of probability that someone will be harmed by the hazard.
>
> **Risk assessment** is the process of making reasoned judgements about the risks and extent of these risks to people's health and safety, which leads to decisions on how these risks should be managed.

Risk assessment

Evaluating health and safety hazards is about spotting potential dangers then taking steps to prevent damage or injury. This is desirable in any situation. In many situations, it is a strict legal requirement.

> **A risk assessment should:**
> - identify the significant risks that might possibly arise because of the work activity
> - enable the employer to identify and prioritise measures needed to follow the legislation
> - be appropriate to the nature of the work and remain valid for a reasonable period of time.

Health and safety hazards can take many forms – for example:
- a large piece of advertising hoarding swinging loose over a pavement
- a post supporting the hoarding that has rotted inside and is about to give way.

The first of these is a current hazard – it could cause injury to anyone passing by at any time. The second is a potential hazard – it will become a risk when the supporting post gives way and makes the hoarding unstable and likely to fall on someone.

Responsibility for health and safety at an event is usually given to one person as health and safety officer or coordinator. The same person may be responsible for security as well. It is the task of the health and safety coordinator at an event to look out for all sorts of hazards – actual or potential – so that steps can be taken to deal with them.

Hazards may be related to:
- materials
- substances
- activities
- equipment
- the environment.

95

SUMMER EXTRAVAGANZA

Every year a community organisation runs a charity event. All profits made from the event go to local charities. This year the organisers have decided to run a Summer Extravaganza. The event will be held in the grounds of a local hall.

The day will includes stalls, activities for children, displays, catering (food and drink) and an all-day disco in a marquee. Based on the experience of previous years, people will come from a wide area. The event is run by volunteers, and local charities are invited to set up stalls. The disco, drinks tent and refreshments are provided by outside companies.

At their first planning meeting, the team putting on the event draws up a site plan.

Notes

- The site is generally secure with high fencing between the area and the main road. A public footpath runs East to West from the lake to the main road, where there is a stile.
- There are two vehicle entrances from the A1234 suitable for use by emergency vehicles.
- The lake has a maximum depth of 1.5 metres.
- There is public car parking for 160 cars on the south-west edge of the site.

ACTIVITY

Identify hazards for the event. Look at all aspects of the event, then list the hazards under these five headings:

- materials
- substances
- activities
- equipment
- the environment.

96

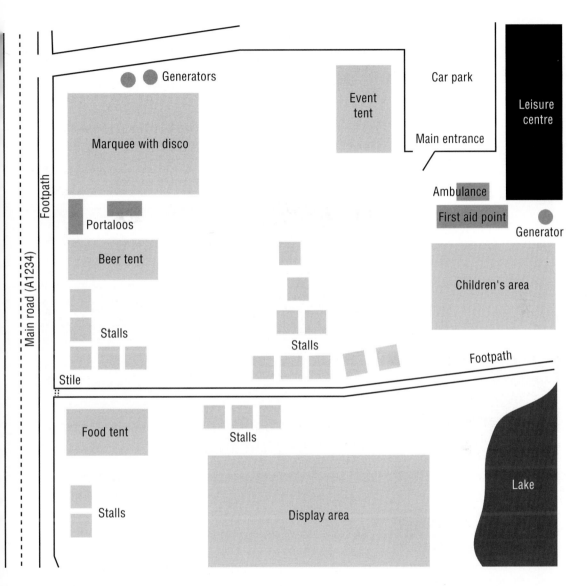

Generators

Event
tent

Car park

Leisure
centre

Marquee with disco

Main entrance

Footpath

Ambulance

First aid point

Generator

Main road (A1234)

Portaloos

Beer tent

Children's area

Stalls

Stalls

Footpath

Stile

Food tent

Stalls

Lake

Stalls

Display area

97

2.3.2 **Evaluating health and safety hazards**

Some health and safety hazards are relatively minor. Others can be highly dangerous. In severe cases, they can result in death – or even many deaths such as a transport incident or fire. Even less serious situations can result in unpleasant problems: injury, pain, financial loss, prosecution by the police and bankruptcy.

When event organisers have drawn up a list of actual or potential health and safety hazards, the next step is to think about:

■ how likely they are to occur

■ how serious their effects would be if they do occur.

DISCUSSION POINT

The team planning the Summer Extravaganza listed these potential hazards and evaluated their probability and severity

	probability	severity
■ people tripping over cables	high	medium
■ a child falling in the lake	medium	high
■ the marquee collapsing on top of dancers	low	high
■ an explosion in one of the generators setting fire to one of the tents	low	high
■ someone being bitten by one of the exotic pets	low	medium
■ someone cutting themselves on a broken glass in the drinks tent	high	low

Do you agree with their assessment of the risk?

ACTIVITY

Look back at the list of hazards you drew up in section 2.3.1 for the Summer Extravaganza. Think about at each one in terms of probability and severity. Decide if they are low, medium or high. Which hazards would you need to pay most attention to?

Produce a summary of your findings, noting:

■ which of the hazards present the greatest risk and will need particular attention

■ why you think they are the highest priorities.

A safety officer gives her view:

❝ *Some hazards are very likely to occur and to cause problems – electrical cables for instance present a real danger to people. These are the hazards that should be given a lot of attention. On the other hand, the marquee is unlikely to collapse because it will be put up by professionals and there are large numbers of supporting ropes. There isn't much that the organisers can do – unless it becomes obvious that the marquee is starting to look unstable, for example if a car accidentally dug up several of the guy ropes. The most careful attention should be given to hazards that are both likely to occur and could cause serious harm. The lake falls into this category, because it's a particular hazard to children and there will be a lot of them about at an event like this.* ❞

Key questions

1 On what principle is health and safety law in the UK and the EU now based?

2 What are hazards and risks? Write a short definition of each of them.

3 What three things should be accomplished by a risk assessment?

4 What kinds of hazards deserve the most careful attention?

SECTION **2.4**

Ensuring a safe and secure working environment

The managers and owners of all leisure and recreation facilities have a duty to provide a safe and secure environment for their staff and visitors. In this section you will investigate the procedures that must be adopted to make this happen. You will learn that ensuring health and safety in the leisure and recreation workplace is a continuous process, needing the support and commitment of all those working for the organisation.

66 *The main safety problems when we put on an outside show in summer are to do with the power supply for the stage lights and the seating. We get professional companies to set them both up for us and they ensure that all the regulations are being met. We also brief our stewards beforehand on what to do if there's an emergency and make sure that there is always someone with a first-aid certificate on the site throughout the performance.* 99

manager of a theatre group

2.4.1 **Risk reduction**

When the planning team has evaluated the potential and actual hazards, the
next job for them is to plan measures that can help reduce or get rid of the
risks.

How can risks be reduced? Read the list of health and safety measures
drawn up by the planning team for the Summer Extravaganza to meet the
hazards they identified and evaluated earlier.

SUMMER EXTRAVAGANZA

- Fence off stallholders' parking area behind the stalls and place restrictions on
  when cars can be driven in and out of the area - no driving allowed during the
  hours of the event.
- Keep electric cabling for the PA system, disco tent and other areas covered or
  hidden and kept off public walkways.
- Site the generators away from areas where the public will be walking and fence them
  off.
- Put up notices saying the lake is strictly out of bounds and erect some sort of
  temporary fencing around it.
- Make trolleys available for lifting and transporting heavy equipment - trestle
  tables, chairs, crates, kegs etc.
- Arrange adequate waste disposal facilities.
- Insist that the company supplying toilet facilities should inspect and clean them
  regularly during the day.
- Arrange for the site to be cleared safely, with supervision.
- Serve drinks in plastic glasses only, and provide additional litter bins in the bar
  tent area.
- Set acceptable noise levels in the disco before the event takes place.

Emergency actions
As well as putting a lot of thought into reducing or eliminating risks, a
planning team also has to think about how they will respond to emergencies
if they do arise.

Examples of emergency actions:
- drawing up evacuation procedures
- calling the emergency services
- having first-aid staff and equipment
- ensuring access for emergency service vehicles
- having fire extinguishers

Realistic measures

All the measures suggested by the planning team were realistic in terms of:
- the people available to carry them out
- finance
- time
- materials.

As one of the team commented:

66 *It seems like a lot to do, but that's what happens when you choose a site like this for an event. We've got people on the planning team who can deal with most things. One's a skilled electrician, so he'll be in charge of setting up the equipment. Another works for the council parks department, so she'll supervise erecting temporary fencing around the lake. Because it's a charity event, the council has agreed to let us have fencing for nothing, and they'll also provide notice-boards. A friend of mine is a solicitor and she has agreed to check the wording of our contracts with the marquee people to make sure that we're fully covered. It takes a lot of time, yes, but it will be worth it in the end.* 99

One of the problems of staging a large-scale event is the number of people involved, including:
- outside companies, such as people running the disco or the bar
- people delivering equipment
- helpers who will only be there on the day.

These people will not be involved in planning of the event. They may not be aware of the potential health and safety hazards, or know about any measures you want to implement.

Outside companies (or contractors) should be consulted about their activities. Only reputable contractors should be used and could be asked to provide evidence of a good health and safety record. Other useful evidence of their competence would be:
- a health and safety policy statement
- membership of a recognised professional body or trade association
- references from other organisations who have used them in the past.

Most health and safety measures depend on people to put them into action. Staffing has to be planned at an early stage. This means asking people to take on particular roles. It also means thinking about training and briefing them about all relevant aspects of health and safety.

Staff tasks
- stewarding and giving information
- controlling the numbers of people
- evacuation procedures – in case of fire, overcrowding or other emergencies
- first aid
- identifying hazardous chemicals and substances
- lifting heavy materials or equipment
- safe waste disposal
- security procedures.

Key questions

1   You are responsible for the erection of temporary seating for a pop concert. What evidence would you want to receive from an outside contractor in order to feel confident from a health and safety point of view that they were the right people for the job?

2   Can you list five things or procedures that you would put in place in order to deal with any emergencies that might occur in a leisure and recreation facility?

3   What would you take into account when deciding whether your proposed safety measures for a sports day were realistic?

4   Six people have volunteered to be stewards at a disco evening which you are organising. In which aspects of health and safety would you train them?

SECTION **2.5**

Security in leisure and recreation

All leisure and recreation organisations must have measures in place to identify security hazards and take steps to minimise security risks. In this section you will gain an understanding both of these risks, present in all facilities and events, and of the main methods used to ensure the security of people, property, money and information in leisure and recreation organisations.

❝ I get advice from the police about security aspects of our events. There's never been any violence, thank heavens, but there's always a risk of stealing when there are so many people around. The biggest risk is theft from cars so now we hire a security firm to patrol the car enclosure throughout the day. It's not something I want any of our volunteers to do – the presence of a uniformed security guard is a good deterrent. ❞

owner of a riding school

❝ The main security risk is leaving expensive equipment on site overnight. Fortunately most of it is heavy and bulky and it would be difficult for anyone to take it away without being observed. Smaller items of equipment, such as the lighting control system, are dismantled and stored in a locked room. One year a small amount of damage was done to the stage fittings but it hasn't happened again. But short of putting on an overnight guard, there's not a lot we can do to stop people getting on the stage. ❞

manager of a theatre group

2.5.1 Identifying security hazards

When people visit a leisure facility, they expect it to be free from danger or risk, either from health and safety hazards or from breaches in security. They assume that managers will have taken steps to make sure that the event is safe and secure.

All leisure and recreation organisations must establish measures to identify security hazards and take steps to minimise security risks. These risks include:

- violence to staff and customers
- theft of property or money
- fraud
- sabotage
- accidental damage
- theft of information.

The degree to which an organisation is exposed to any of these risks will depend on a range of factors such as its scale of operation, location and the sector in which it operates.

As with health and safety, security poses hazards of many different kinds.

Violence

Some locations or types of event may run a relatively high risk of violence. Many violent incidents in public places are connected with abuse of alcohol. Managers of a facility which is licensed to sell alcoholic drinks will need to look into the risk of trouble from people getting drunk.

Many violent incidents are wholly unpredictable – e.g. an intruder at a recreation facility. The organisers could not predict that, but they can plan measures to deal with it, by making sure that there is someone in charge of emergencies.

Theft

Anything that has value can be stolen. This includes:

- obvious items such as cash, cheque books and credit cards
- valuable stock, equipment and property
- information – if a computer containing the only copy of a customer database is stolen, that can have a big effect on how the organisation will be able to communicate with its customers in the future (of course, no organisation should have only one copy of a valuable database).

Fraud

Fraud is a kind of theft committed by people working for an organisation. Fraud can be disguised by passing the theft off as a legal transaction or by altering the records. It's sometimes difficult to detect because it is committed by people who have certain powers and are trusted by other members of the organisation to use those powers properly.

aud Office
to kill off
Leeson suit

Number is up for
lottery fraudster

**Fight promoter
on Lloyd's
fraud charge**

©The Daily Telegraph plc, London, 1995

Sabotage

There are various reasons why someone might practise sabotage:

- a competitor may want to harm a rival's success
- former employees may hold a grudge against the organisation which sacked them
- an individual may have a personal reason for wanting to spoil an event, such as hatred of someone involved in organising it
- a political group may want to stage a protest – for example, animal rights activists may try to sabotage a fashion show that includes products made from animal fur.

Sabotage can be committed in various ways:

- intruders destroy vital pieces of equipment or wreck the premises
- animal rights protesters set up a loudspeaker playing the screams of dying animals outside the hall where the fashion show is about to take place
- a competitor tries to disrupt an event by placing advertisements in the paper saying it has been cancelled.

Damage

Damage to equipment or premises can be a major problem. It may be accidental, such as a car running over marquee guy ropes, or it may be deliberate. Managers have to protect against both. Where damage is serious and deliberate, it can lead to prosecution for criminal damage.

ACTIVITY

Look back at the plans for the Summer Extravaganza described in section 2.3.1. What are the possible security hazards for the event? Remember that security hazards may occur before, during or after an event. Think about which aspects of the event have security implications, including:

- the event itself
- different activities at the event
- customers
- staff
- cash
- equipment and other valuables.

Make a list of security hazards you can foresee.

2.5.2 Evaluating security hazards

Many security problems are relatively minor, but serious security incidents – for example if vandals destroy essential equipment or damage carefully prepared premises – have far-reaching effects.

In planning what measures to take, managers need to look into:
- the likelihood of a security hazard occuring
- what form any resulting loss or damage may take
- how serious the loss or damage might be.

Some security hazards are more likely than others. Vandalism and theft – including pick-pocketing – are more common than sabotage or serious violence. Some people will try to avoid paying the entrance fee to a club, a theatre and so on. If entrances are left open and unattended, people will feel free to walk in.

Managers should pay most attention to hazards that are likely both to occur and to cause a high level of serious damage.

DISCUSSION POINT

At the Summer Extravaganza site, the team make a list of some of the security hazards and evaluate their probability and severity:

	Probability	Form of loss or damage	Severity of loss or damage
• vandals breaking in before the event and damaging stalls, equipment	medium	physical damage	possibly high
• people trying to sneak into the event without paying the entrance fee	high	financial	medium
• theft of items during the event	medium	loss of property	medium
• proceeds being stolen by armed raiders as the event finishes	low	financial loss	high
• fight breaking out in the beer tent	medium	damage to property, customers and reputation	low

Do you agree with their evaluation?

ACTIVITY

Carry out an evaluation of the security hazards you identified in the last activity. Decide whether they have a low, medium or high probability and whether the severity of the damage is low, medium or high. Then note down what form the loss or damage is likely to take.

Produce a summary of your findings, noting which of the security hazards present the greatest risk and will need particular attention.

UNIT

2

SECTION **2.5**

107

2.5.3 **Measures to ensure security**

When managers have identified and evaluated security hazards, they should plan how to cope with them. Many of the measures will aim to reduce the risk from security hazards.

Risk reduction

Read how the planning team for the Summer Extravaganza decided to counter the security risks they identified.

- engage security staff overnight to protect equipment set up the day before
- give passes to participants who need to come on to the site the day before to prepare it
- check security fences in the display and children's activity areas, and around the lake
- controlled spectator access via the car park only – put 'No entrance' signs along the perimeter wall
- make sure that enough stewards are on duty along the footpath leading from the car park
- advise all stallholders that they can store cash in the event office
- make sure that all helpers know the procedures for lost children

ACTIVITY

Take another look at the list of hazards you drew up for the event. What measures would you take to improve security? Note down your ideas.

Emergency actions

Planning also needs to focus on dealing with emergencies. It is impossible to predict when an emergency will happen and what form it will take. But it is possible to be prepared for situations such as:

- fire
- a major accident
- bomb threats
- outbreak of violence
- health emergency such as fainting, heart attacks, sprained or broken limbs.

Any facility needs to have someone responsible for planning and carrying out emergency procedures. Plans will need to be drawn up for evacuation of the site or premises in the event of a major emergency.

Keeping information secure

■ Make sure that at least one back-up copy of information exists.

■ Make sure that the back-up copy is stored in a completely different place from the original.

■ Store copies of important data in fireproof safes.

■ Store sensitive information on computers that can only be accessed through passwords.

■ Don't leave offices or filing cabinets containing important information unlocked.

■ Remember that the storage of computer-based information is governed by legal contraints.

Security and staffing

Many different people are likely to have security roles. For some people it will be their major role – stewards, bouncers or staff employed to patrol the premises. These services can be bought in from professional security firms and may be essential for activities such as guarding premises overnight. Managers have to judge whether it is worth paying for this benefit. For some premises it is essential, especially where large amounts of money or valuable items are involved.

For other staff, security will be just one part of a wider role – e.g. staff serving in a bar who need to ensure the security of both stock and takings.

Both categories of staff will need careful training and briefing. All staff need to be clear about what they themselves would do if faced with a security problem. For example:

■ How would bar staff tackle fighting amongst customers?

■ What should staff members do if they see a customer stealing something?

■ What should stewards do if they see someone coming into a facility illegally?

It is the duty of managers and employers to make sure that staff and helpers are not put at risk – and don't put themselves at risk by entering into an explosive situation. Staff need to know specific procedures for dealing with such situations. They also need to know what the limits are to their roles.

Securing information

The success of many businesses depends on good information – financial, marketing or planning. A database storing details of customers is a good example, as a marketing manager at a facility explains:

66 *We depend on our database to keep customers informed about events and activities. If it got lost or damaged, we wouldn't be able to continue with our normal business. We'd lose touch with customers and lose their confidence. Our database has taken years to develop. It would be a source of highly useful information to competitors. We take strict precautions to keep it safe and secure.* 99

Organisations that store information on computers must comply with the Data Protection Act 1984 (see section 2.2.4) This places a duty on them to take particular care with information they hold about individuals. This includes not allowing it to be passed on to other organisations.

Realistic measures

Security measures, like health and safety measures, have to be realistic. Factors to consider include:

- people – find out whether staff and helpers have the necessary skills and whether enough people will be available
- finance – balance the cost of security measures against the level of security needed
- time – assess how much time can be devoted to planning and putting security measures into practice, given the demands of planning other aspects of the event and the event schedule
- materials – work out what materials are needed, are available and can be hired or bought, such as fence posts and rope, to create fences, or stationery for distributing information.

Achieving the ideal situation is not always possible. Compromises may be needed to ensure that organisers concentrate on what is essential.

DISCUSSION POINT

Look back at the security measures you suggested for the Summer Extravaganza. Are they realistic in terms of people, finance, time and materials?

Key questions

1 What is sabotage?

2 What would be the consequences for an organisation if its database was lost or damaged?

3 What potential security problems should an organisation plan for? Pick a leisure or recreation facility and note down:
   - the likeliest security problems
   - steps that can be taken in advance to minimise the effects of these problems should they occur.

4 What are the factors to be considered when deciding what security measures to take?

Assignment

Part of your evidence for this unit is to present the results of an investigation into the health, safety and security measures provided by two leisure and recreation organisations of your choice.

Make a list of possible organisations you could use. For each suggestion, how easy will it be to get information about the organisation? If it is a local organisation, will you be able to visit it? You may need to do some research to start with, e.g. telephoning or visiting the organisation to find out how helpful they would be.

When you have considered the list of possibilities, choose two of these organisations to investigate as case studies which will illustrate what the health, safety and security laws and regulations mean in practice.

Present your conclusions in an induction booklet for each of the two leisure and recreation facilities. The booklets should be aimed at new members of staff and should be designed to acquaint them with relevant health and safety information.

Begin your investigation by assessing the importance of health and safety in your two chosen organisations. Your booklets should outline the benefits of health and safety to:
- the organisation, facility or event
- staff
- customers
- the environment.

Each booklet should include sections on the following:
- Legislation and regulations
  How do the organisations meet the relevant legislation and regulations to ensure a safe environment for customers and staff? Describe any obligatory measures and voluntary measures taken by the organisations.
- Risk assessment
  How do the organisations carry out risk assessment? Describe any measures taken by the organisations to evaluate health and safety hazards.
- Working environment
  How do the organisations ensure a safe working environment for both staff and customers? Describe any measures taken by the organisations to reduce or eliminate risks and to prepare for emergencies.
- Security
  How do the organisations ensure security for staff and customers? Describe the main methods used by the organisations to protect people, property and information.

KEY POINTS:

- Each booklet should clearly describe health, safety and security policies, and procedures within the organisation.
- Bear in mind that the booklet is aimed at new members of staff who will be unaware of the people, systems, resources and layout of the organisation.
- Use plain language and avoid jargon – if you have to include jargon words, explain them.
- Don't describe procedures in a lot of detail – it's more important to describe who to contact and how, and where to find out more information

KEY SKILLS

You can use the work you are doing for this part of your GNVQ to collect and develop evidence for the following key skills at level 3:

when you	you can collect evidence for
	communication
gather evidence and examples as part of your investigation of health, safety and security	key skill C3.2 read and synthesise information from two extended documents about a complex subject; one of these documents should include a least one image
	working with others
gather evidence in a group and then discuss this research as part of your investigation of health, safety and security; conduct risk assessments	key skill WO3.1 agree realistic objectives and the action and resources needed to achieve them; provide information, based on appropriate evidence, to help agree responsibilities; agree suitable working arrangements with those involved
gather evidence in a group and then discuss this research as part of your investigation of health, safety and security and then present this as part of a group; conduct risk assessments	key skill WO3.2 organise and carry out tasks in ways that help you to be effective and efficient in meeting your responsibilities; seek to establish and maintain cooperative working relationships, agreeing ways to overcome any difficulties; exchange accurate information on the extent to which work is meeting expected time-scales and quality, agreeing changes where necessary to achieve objectives
evaluate your research and presentation into safe working practices; conduct risk assessments	key skill WO3.3 agree the extent to which the objectives have been met; identify factors that have influenced the outcome; agree ways the activity could have been done differently to enhance work with others
	improving own learning and performance
undertake and plan research into safe working practices	key skill LP3.1 seek information on ways to achieve what you want to do, and identify factors that might affect your plans; use this information to agree realistic targets with appropriate others; plan how you will manage your time to meet targets, including alternative action for overcoming possible problems and use of support from others
undertake, plan and evaluate research into safe working practices	key skill LP3.2 prioritise and manage your time effectively to complete tasks, making revisions to your plan as necessary; seek and actively use feedback and support from relevant sources to help you meet your targets; use different approaches to learning, drawing on learning from other tasks and adapting methods to meet new demands
	key skill LP3.3 provide information on quality of your learning and performance, identifying factors that have affected the outcome; identify targets you have met, seeking information from relevant sources to establish evidence of your achievements; exchange views with appropriate others to agree action for improving your performance

when you	you can collect evidence for
	problem-solving
conduct a risk assessment and decide how to minimise this risk	key skill PS3.1 recognise that a problem exists with no immediate solution; select and use appropriate methods for exploring the problem and describe its main features; agree the standards which have to be met to show the problem has been solved successfully
	key skill PS3.2 select and use appropriate methods for generating different options for tackling the problem; compare the main features of each option, including resource needs, timescales and risk factors; select the option which has the most realistic chance of success, and justify your choice
	key skill PS3.3 plan how to carry out chosen option and obtain agreement to go ahead from appropriate person; implement your plan, effectively using support and feedback from others to assist this process; review progress towards solving the problem and revise your approach as necessary
	key skill PS3.4 agree with an appropriate person methods to check whether the standards have been met for solving the problem; apply these methods accurately and fully describe the results; review your approach to problem-solving, including whether alternative methods and options might have proved more effective

UNIT **3**

The sports industry

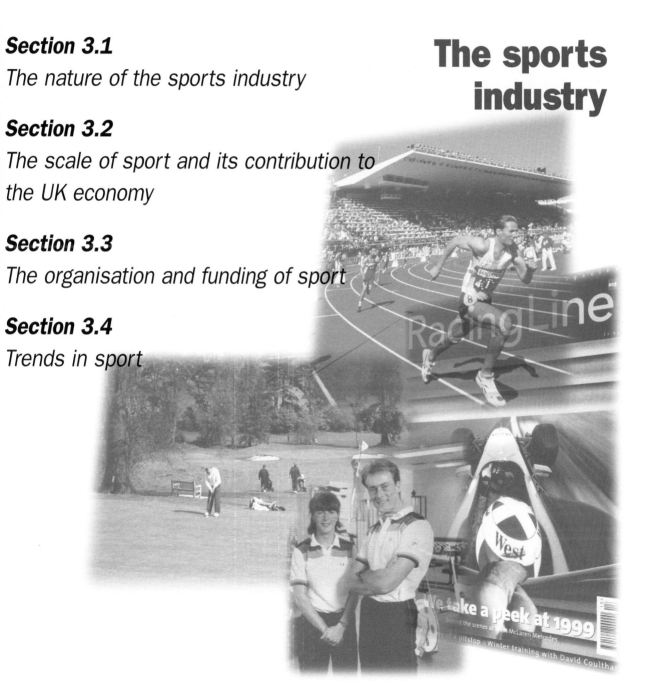

About this unit

Sport is big business. The industry has a complex structure, a large turnover, and an impact on many people's lives through the media as well as participation. In this unit you will investigate the structure, economic impact, organisation and funding of the sports industry as well as current trends in sport and the relationship between sport and the mass media.

SECTION **3.1**

The nature of the sports industry

To understand fully the nature of the sports industry you need to understand its various components and have a broad overview of what these components consist of. Thousands of people work in the sports industry, from professional athletes to assistants in sports goods shops, doctors practising sports medicine to ski instructors, sports development officers to people working in betting shops, and many, many others. In this section you will develop your understanding of the diversity of the industry.

> **❝** Sport means all forms of physical activity which, through casual or organised participation, aims at improving physical fitness and mental well-being, forming social relationships, or obtaining results in competition at all levels. **❞**
>
> *Council of Europe, European Sports Charter*

> **❝** Sport development is never ending. We can always find more people to work with, more initiatives to implement, more projects to support. It is important to be organised, disciplined, and to plan well. If you can manage to do that, it makes the job more manageable and enjoyable. **❞**
>
> *Greater London Regional Hockey Development Officer.*

Sporting goods

A visit to any high street sports shop is enough to convince us of the vast range of goods available. These include racquets for badminton, squash and tennis, footwear for all sports, swimming goggles and trunks, cricket bats and balls.

There is the kind of equipment that may be bought by individuals but is also likely to be bought by leisure centres, health clubs, or sports clubs. This equipment includes:

- rowing machines
- stationary bikes
- treadmills
- free weights
- weight resistance machines.

It is clear that there is a huge industry involved. The Sports Industries Federation (SIF), which represents the interests of manufacturers, distributors, suppliers and retailers, calculates that the industry is worth over £5 billion and employs 75,000 people. The members of the SIF include autonomous trade associations, including the Golf Facilities Association, the Racquet Sports Association and the British Association of Seating Equipment Suppliers. Many of the companies which make sports goods have themselves become internationally famous: Adidas, Nike, Slazenger, Reebok.

> Slazenger is one of the most famous names in sports goods manufacturing. They produce goods for a wide range of sports. The company is associated in the minds of a lot of people with tennis in particular because of their long association with the Wimbledon tennis championships. Slazenger have supplied the balls for the championship since 1902 and currently supply 36,000 balls for the fortnight at Wimbledon. Of course, tennis is one of the six sports that Slazenger feature on their web site (cricket, squash, golf, hockey and badminton are the others). On-line coaching from David Felgate, Tim Henman's coach, is offered on the web site, as is a link to the official Wimbledon site.

High street shops are not the only places where sporting goods can be bought. For example, the professional at a local golf club is likely to have a shop on the course in which members can buy golf clubs, balls, shoes, waterproof clothing and so on. Some people will prefer to buy their equipment there because the professional is able to offer expert advice.

Some sports goods are suitable for use only by one person, but many others can be hired as the occasion demands. Many people wait until they reach their resort and then hire skis; items like squash racquets can be hired in most leisure centres. Leisure centres also sell goods, either as an in-house operation or by granting a franchise to an outside contractor.

ACTIVITY

Visit your local sports goods shop and look at the range of equipment that is on offer. Which manufacturers appear most often? What techniques do they seem to use to persuade you to select their goods? Which sports seem to be best catered for?

Alternatively, visit the SIF web site (*http://www.sportslife.og.uk*). It has links to web sites for Slazenger, Adidas, Nike and Reebok. Compare what you find on the various sites.

DISCUSSION POINT

What are the main factors behind the growth in the sporting goods industry?

3.1.2 Sports coaching

Participants at all levels of sport can benefit from good coaching. The governing bodies of most sports run courses to enable people to gain a coaching certificate.

Coaching can be a voluntary occupation, often carried out by an enthusiast with few qualifications, or a well-paid professional occupation. All professional football teams have at least one coach, and most top tennis players, golfers and boxers have their own coach.

Coaches must have knowledge of:

- the techniques and tactics of the sport
- psychology
- fitness, nutrition, and physiology
- safety
- individual abilities.

Technological developments have had a significant input to coaching. Scientific research has produced greater understanding of how the body responds to exercise. Coaches (sometimes called 'trainers') are able to use computer simulations to show the results of different types of training. Computers can also analyse the movements of a sportsperson in minute detail. The coach is then able to suggest improvements to the performer's technique. The performer and the coach can also watch instant video replays of training sessions as a further aid to improving performance. Modern watches can check pulse rates and blood pressure during the training session.

The National Coaching Foundation (NCF)

The National Coaching Foundation (NCF) is based in Leeds, with regional offices within Sport England's ten Regional Training Units for Sport, and the Coaching Units of Northern Ireland, Scotland and Wales.

The NCF works with many other organisations to improve coaching. The NCF had an annual turnover of £3.4 million in 1998/9. Its main sources of funding are:

- 72.7% grant aid from Sport UK and Sport England
- 22.2% earned income
- 5.1% other grant aid and donations.

The NCF provides a wide range of services to coaches of all levels and from all sports:

- BSc (Hons) in Applied Sports Coaching for experienced coaches
- specialist seminars and workshops for high-performance coaches
- recognition of coaching success with annual awards
- membership and subscription services
- access to up-to-date coaching information through the subscription service inFORM and the NCF web site

- books, videos and cassettes on coaching, sports science and sports medicine topics.

The NCF works with national governing bodies (NGBs) of sport to enhance performance by developing highly competent coaches at all levels. They do this by:

- offering customised, sport-specific NCF resources and courses to key partners
- supporting NGBs in developing coaches who work within national and regional development programmes
- developing new resources with NGBs
- providing training for tutors and assessors of coaches
- helping NGBs to implement national standards for coaching, teaching and instruction
- supporting coaches working, or hoping to work, in the high-performance environment
- helping to advise NGBs on performance planning and lottery revenue funding.

ACTIVITY

Visit the NCF web site at *http://www.ncf.org.uk/infoserv/aboutncf.htm*. Look at the national standards for coaches and make a note of the skills needed for each of the five levels.

DISCUSSION POINT

What are the main reasons why sports agencies promote sports education and training?

3.1.3 **Facility provision**

Sports facilities are provided by:

- the public sector
- the private sector
- the voluntary/not for profit sector.

Before looking at these three sectors, it will be useful to look at one of the biggest projects ever contemplated by the sports industry in the UK – the replacement of Wembley Stadium by a new English National Stadium which would strengthen England's bid to host the Football World Cup in 2006.

Wembley National Stadium

The creation of a major sports centre has an enormous impact on the area in which it is built. There will be jobs not only in the centre itself, but in pubs, restaurants and shops in the area. The influx of money will be considerable, but development on a large scale, whether it is a sports centre, a motorway, a supermarket, the Millennium Dome, or a housing estate, also generates opposition from people who fear negative effects on the environment or who dislike the fact that the nature of the area will change.

It is necessary to obtain planning permission before embarking upon a building project. Objectors are allowed to state their case and permission is granted only if the plans conform to the appropriate laws and regulations.

The Town and Country Planning Act of 1990 (as amended in 1991) sets out the primary legislation for the operation of much of the town planning system in England. Within the act there are numerous sections, dealing with various reports of the planning system, and at section 106 (S.106) reference is made to planning obligations. It enables anyone with an interest in land – usually someone applying to develop a piece of land – to enter into a planning obligation.

So far as the new Wembley is concerned, the two main points that had to be addressed were:

■ the ability of the road and rail network to cope with the expected number of spectators

■ the negative impact of additional numbers of spectators on local residents.

You do not have to approve or disapprove of the proposed Wembley National Stadium project, but a consideration of the scale of what is involved should convince you that the sports industry can make an enormous impact on local and national economies.

The new Wembley will be a 90,000 all-seater stadium. It will be developed as an all-year-round business and will include a hotel, themed restaurants and a visitors attraction.

Wembley National Stadium Ltd is a wholly owned subsidiary of the Football Association. It acquired the existing stadium from Wembley plc in March 1999 for £103 million and will spend a further £200 to £355 million on building the new stadium. The project has received £120 million from the National Lottery. The remainder will be raised by the company.

The Stadium will generate £229 million of spending in the UK economy each year, £26 million of which will be in the local economy, and directly create 2,100 permanent jobs. Including indirect job creation, 7,520 permanent job opportunities (4,920 full-time equivalent jobs) will be created.

The National Stadium complex will pay £4 million in business rates every year. Wembley Stadium currently pays £1 million.

ACTIVITY

The information given above is available on the National Stadium web site. There is much more information on the site. Look at *http://212.158.20.37/new/ section106.htm* and write a report on how the owners of Wembley answer concerns about the adequacy of the transport system and the impact of the development on local residents.

The National Stadium is to be located in the London Borough of Brent, an area which has under-performed in the UK economy throughout the 1990s. Based on the DETR Index of Local Deprivation, Brent is the twentieth most deprived of the 354 English local authorities.

The area suffers from high unemployment, over-reliance on manufacturing and distribution activities and declining local employment opportunities.

The Wembley area is currently attracting little new retail, industrial or business development. There are some speculative hotel and leisure proposals which are awaiting the development of the National Stadium. Wembley is also the focus of some regeneration initiatives to improve transport infrastructure, the general environment and the work skills of local people.

The Wembley area has a declining employer base and needs a major stimulus to halt its decline. A project with the scale of development of the National Stadium is likely to stimulate further investment and regeneration initiatives which may succeed in turning the area around. It may be that the area's future role will be as a comprehensive leisure and sports related quarter of London.

ACTIVITY

Carry out a small survey in your area and find out the range of sports facilities provided by the local authority and the annual spend on these facilities.

The public sector

The government provides national sports centres (through the sports councils), sports facilities for the armed forces, and national parks (through the Countryside Commission).

Local authorities are the main providers of basic sport and recreation facilities for the local community. In England they manage over 1,500 indoor sports centres. Other facilities include parks, lakes, playing fields, playgrounds, tennis courts, artificial pitches, golf courses and swimming/leisure pools. Local authorities, which spend more than £1 billion on sport every year, have a legal obligation to provide sports facilities for education.

National sports centres

The national sports centres and their specialist facilities are:

England
- Crystal Palace (athletics, swimming, diving)
- Bisham Abbey (tennis)
- Lilleshall Hall (football, gymnastics)
- Holme Pierrepont (water sports)
- Plas y Brenin (outdoor activities)
- Manchester (cycling)

Scotland
- Cumbrae (water sports)
- Inverclyde (all purpose)
- Glenmore Lodge (outdoor activities)

Wales
- Cardiff (all purpose)
- Plas Menai (outdoor activities)

Northern Ireland
- Tollymore (outdoor activities)

These twelve sports centres are managed by the four sports councils.

National parks

The seven national parks of England are:
- Dartmoor
- Exmoor
- the Lake District
- North Yorkshire Moors
- Northumberland
- the Peak district
- the Yorkshire Dales.

The Norfolk and Suffolk Broads and the New Forest have similar status.

The private sector

Most facilities provided by the private sector represent commercial ventures which must be run at a profit. They fall into two categories:

- facilities for the public to use at a price – these include, tennis courts, ice rinks, golf driving ranges, tenpin bowling halls, health and fitness centres
- facilities for professional sports people (and animals) to perform in – football and cricket grounds, race tracks for dogs and horses, stadiums for athletics and gymnastics.

The Local Government Act of 1988 introduced Compulsory Competitive Tendering (CCT). It required many local council-operated facilities and services to be offered out to competitive bids. By the end of 1993, all sports and leisure facilities in England and Wales had to put their management contracts out to CCT.

This is not the same as privatisation. The council retains ownership of the facility, but the day-to-day running and operations can be carried out by a contractor from the private sector working to a specification drawn up by the council.

The intention was to introduce competition into the running of leisure centres which, it was believed, would ensure better facilities and service for customers. Many leisure centres have now had their management taken over by contractors.

The Labour Government which came into office in 1997 developed Best Value (BV) as a key element in its programme for modernising local government. The intention of Best Value is to put the customers first and provide them with quality services at affordable costs. Sports provision is one of many services to be affected by this new programme.

BV imposes a duty on local authorities to:

- secure continuous improvement with regard to economy, efficiency and effectiveness
- consult with taxpayers, local businesses, service users and other interested parties
- conduct Best Value reviews of all their functions
- prepare a performance plan for each financial year.

The duty of Best Value applies to a wider range of services than those covered by CCT and will apply to all services delivered directly or indirectly by local authorities, including all elements of the sport and recreation services. This does not necessarily mean that services must be privatised, but nor is there any reason why services should be delivered directly by a local authority if other, more efficient means are available.

ACTIVITY

Extend your area survey, researching into the range of sports facilities provided by the private sector and the annual spend on these facilities.

ACTIVITY

Research the facilities and annual budgets for sports provided by the voluntary sector. Prepare a table comparing the facilities and annual budgets for the public, private and voluntary sectors.

Are there other providers of sports facilities who do not easily fall into these categories, such as university facilities which are also available to the public?

The new duty of Best Value came into effect for all local authorities in England and Wales from 1 April 2000. Once the BV regime is in place, there will be no compulsion for councils to put their services out to tender. Under BV, sport will continue to compete with numerous other services for a share of public resources.

The voluntary sector

In every town and many larger villages there are sports clubs which often concentrate on one sport and are run by enthusiasts. Clubs that have been established for a long time (for example golf, bowls, tennis or cricket clubs) may own their own facilities.

Newer clubs, or ones that do not have a lot of money, will be able to hire facilities, perhaps at the local sports centre, school, playing field or church hall.

Over 150,000 voluntary sports clubs are affiliated to the national governing bodies of sport. Some local clubs cater for indoor recreation, but more common are those which provide sports grounds, particularly for cricket, football, rugby, hockey, tennis and golf.

In addition to sports clubs, there are community associations in villages or towns who hire the village green for cricket in the summer and hockey in the winter. Village and church halls can be hired for indoor sports such as badminton and table tennis.

Some of the national governing bodies own their own facilities – for example, the Rugby Football Union owns Twickenham. Athletics and swimming do not have their own national facilities, and neither do many other major sports.

For many years the Football Association (FA) used, but did not own, Wembley Stadium, which was owned by a company in the private sector.

3.1.4 Sports development

Sports development is essentially about encouraging people to participate in sport, making it easier for them to do so, and helping to ensure that there are good facilities available.

The agencies involved in sports development include:
- the sports councils
- local authorities
- governing bodies of sport
- voluntary sector sports clubs
- schools/education sector

A local authority development manager for a London borough says:

66 *To me, sports development is about providing people with choices about what activities they want to take part in. The sporting diet given to many of our young people at school is very limited. The average inner-city primary school may only offer football, rounders and netball as the main team games. Occasionally cricket and a bit of short tennis creep in if there is a half-decent member of staff, and swimming will usually only exist as an activity because 'it has to be done for the National Curriculum'.*

At secondary level the options are a bit better with hockey, rugby, basketball and athletics being the most common additions at Key Stage 3. Swimming will usually have disappeared unless the school has its own pool. We often have to wait until Key Stage 4 before we see the introduction of taught badminton, volleyball, trampolining and tennis, and even then it's usually only through the GCSE PE groups or a Year 11 option system. Activities like canoeing, sailing, aerobics or orienteering are the treasured domain of the post-16 option group and are left to last like a reward for staying the course.

Therefore, I feel my job is to give young people as many opportunities as possible.

My team of ten full-time development officers is divided into three teams. One team deals with all issues relating to schools, both curricular and extra-curricular activities. The second team works in the community by supporting clubs, associations and governing bodies. This team can be a vital link for those young people who have been encouraged by the education team. If there are no clubs for a particular sport, this team will set up its own club and encourage parents, coaches and governing bodies to take on areas of responsibility.

The last team is the events section. They have the responsibility of ensuring that young people living in the borough have the opportunity of taking part in competitions for their chosen sports. These range from inter-school tournaments and borough championships to the London Youth Games and the Special Olympics.

Everything we do is encapsulated in our mission statement. This states that we set out to provide opportunities for all people living in the borough to take part in the sport of their choice and to perform to the best of their ability. **99**

Many of these organisations will employ sports development officers (SDOs) who perform a number of different functions. These fall into three categories:

- **community sports development**, seeking to promote mass participation in sport, 'Sport for All', especially among target groups – young people, women, over 50s, disabled people, ethnic minorities
- **sports specific development**, promoting specific sports to improve levels of participation, performance and excellence
- **facility development**, promoting and extending the use of existing facilities and contributing to the planning process for new provision.

There are areas of work common to all three approaches and most SDOs will try to establish links between participation and performance, coach and leader training, and in the programming of facilities.

Here is what a hockey development officer says about her work:

66 *I came into sports development following a brief career as a physical education teacher. My love has always been hockey and to be offered a post that allowed me to give all my energies to it was a dream come true.*

The first main task was to make sure that all the communication channels were open between the various partners involved in the sport. One of the main barriers to sports development is people not sharing ideas. Time is wasted by people reinventing the wheel or working in small pockets of development rather than combining resources.

The next task was to give people access to opportunities and support them. In a large area it is important that you develop clubs, schools, local authorities to a point where you can walk away and the work still carries on.

There are many things I enjoy about my work – helping clubs, working with young people – but there are also drawbacks. To be a sports development officer, one really needs to learn how to say 'no'. There is no real end to the work that you can do. There is never a time when you can stand back and say: 'Right, that's me finished.' Whatever you achieve, whoever you help, there is always more that you can do. There are always more people that you can help.

Sports development is a very enjoyable job, but one has to have a number of skills and personal attributes to survive. Good time management, self-motivation, enthusiasm, bags of energy, good communications skills and a very big sense of humour. Get those and you're most of the way there! **99**

Effective sports development requires behavioural change on the part of providers and participants. SDOs need to balance their objectives with the interests of numerous stakeholders, including:

- sports councils, national and local
- politicians, national and local
- current and potential clients
- national governing bodies of sport
- voluntary sector sports clubs
- schools/education sector.

The National Association for Sports Development (NASD) works in association with The Institute of Sport & Recreation Management (ISRM) to provide support, advocacy and professional development for those involved in the development of sport.

The objectives of the NASD are:

- to raise the profile of sports development and sports development officers
- to identify and disseminate examples of good practice in sports development
- to provide a professional development programme for those in sports development
- to represent the views of those involved in sports development to appropriate external agencies (e.g. national sports organisations, government departments)
- when appropriate, and when invited, to work closely with regional and local sports development networks to encourage and support their creation and development.

ACTIVITY

Find out which sports development initiatives are running now. Try to contact a sports development officer and ask if he or she will come to your college to talk to you and your colleagues.

131

3.1.5 Sports recreation

Sports recreation occurs when people visit an area to watch, or to take part in, sports events. Some areas or cities are identified with particular sports, either at one time in the year (e.g. tennis at Wimbledon or TT races on the Isle of Man), or on a permanent basis (e.g. golf at St Andrews).

Countries or cities also bid for one-off sporting events like the football World Cup, or the Olympic or Commonwealth Games.

Hosting an event such as the Commonwealth Games is attractive because:
- revenue is generated for the area as visitors spend their money in hotels, restaurants, shops, pubs and so on
- facilities built for the event (e.g. cycling tracks or swimming pools) remain after the event for use by the local population.

Manchester is hosting the Commonwealth Games of 2002. The focal point for the Games is Sportcity which includes the new City of Manchester Stadium. This 38,000-seater stadium will become the home of Manchester City Football Club in 2003/4.

A new swimming pool has been built on the campus of Manchester University.

Salford Quays in Manchester is a good example of brownfield site regeneration. The triathlon at the Commonwealth Games will be held there, the Lowry Centre houses the works of the painter L. S. Lowry, and the Imperial War Museum is also there. There are also watersports facilities.

You can find out more about Manchester's Commonwealth Games by visiting *http://www.commonwealthgames2002.org.uk/2002.*

ACTIVITY

Develop a proposal which sets out a case for your town or area to host a major sports event. As well as listing the advantages, try to think of some possible pitfalls.

A **brownfield site** refers to an area which has been built on before and where the buildings have decayed or are no longer wanted. A greenfield site is an area which has not been built on before. It is usually considered more environmentally friendly to regenerate a brownfield site than to build on a greenfield site.

3.1.6 Professional sport

Professional sport is a very big business in the UK and its stars earn huge sums of money. This is particularly true of boxing, tennis, golf, and football. This is a recent development and is the result of:

■ commercialisation, including sponsorship
■ the media
■ social changes which have increased leisure time and given the majority of people more time to watch sport.

UK Sponsorship Market (by sector), 1997

	£ million	%
Sports	322	56
Broadcast	111	19
Arts	96	17
Other	45	8
Total	574	100

Source: Mintel, Sponsorship

Professional sport attracts sponsorship because companies see an opportunity to advertise their products. Formula one racing cars are covered with the logos of companies that sponsor the team that is running the car; professional footballers have logos on their shirts; the Wimbledon tennis tournament and the Olympic Games each has a host of official sponsors.

It costs between $80 million and $100 million a year to run a top formula one motor racing team. Much, and perhaps all, of this expenditure can be recouped through sponsorship.

The main sponsor of a team pays $35m–$40m with a secondary sponsor contributing as much as $20m. A further two or three backers each pay $5m–$10m. A range of lesser deals are each worth $1m – 3m. $1m is the minimum a sponsor would have to pay to gain exposure on the car.

The sponsors' reward comes in the 'package', which is the essential part of any deal. The package includes:

■ branding on team gear using the association in the sponsor's advertising and endorsements
■ corporate hospitality at the races and during testing.

In 1999, Jordan entertained 2000 VIPs at test sessions. The guests have greater access to the drivers and the team during testing than they would on race days.

Source: Observer 5 March 2000

It is the televising of sport that makes sponsorship such an attractive proposition for companies. A company's name and logo are seen by millions of people around the world. If you watch any international sports event on television you are almost bound to see the logos of Coca-Cola, McDonald's, and many other multinational companies.

The extent to which commercialisation and sponsorship is involved in football can be understood by looking at the activities of Manchester United, and the scale of Manchester United's operations is indicated by the fact that their official web site registers 75 million hits a month.

Manchester United runs its own TV station, MUTV, on which subscribers can see live coverage of Manchester United reserve matches, and a range of news and information programmes centred on the team and its stars.

The club runs restaurants and shops, including a megastore, at its Old Trafford headquarters.

The famous companies which have sponsorship deals with Manchester United include Sharpe, Umbro, Carling, Lotus, Sun Microsystems, Western Union, Pepsi, and Woolmark.

On 11 February 2000, Manchester United announced that they had signed an agreement under which Vodaphone became the principal sponsor and telecommunications and equipment services partner to the club. Vodaphone will provide mobile phone and wireless Internet services to Manchester United's worldwide supporter base. The agreement, worth £30 million over a four-year period, started on 1 June 2000.

In return for its investment, Vodaphone gained:

■ the right to display its logo on the team's playing kit

■ the right to use Manchester United's mark in promotions and advertising

■ hospitality access and perimeter signage at all Manchester United's home games (excluding the European Champion's League)

Peter Bamford, Chief Executive of Vodaphone UK Limited, commented:

66 *Manchester United is one of the best sporting brands in the world and supported by millions of fans of all ages. This ground-breaking agreement goes beyond a pure shirt sponsorship and will bring a new range of mobile information services to a loyal massive supporter base. There is additional business potential in the bringing together of the world's largest telecommunications company and the world's best known football club.* 99

3.1.7 **Sport-related gambling**

Gambling has flourished in Britain for hundreds of years. Between the late Sixteenth and early Nineteenth centuries, successive governments organised state lotteries which helped to fund, among other things, the wars against Napoleon and the building of the British Museum. Gambling on sports events was also popular, although some of the events would not be considered as sports today. It was possible to bet on foot-racing, prizefighting or wrestling, horse-racing, cock-fighting, dogfighting and bull-baiting. There were even bets laid on races between men with wooden legs.

From the earliest times it was recognised that gambling encouraged cheating and criminal involvement in sport. Prizefighting, cricket and horse-racing all introduced rules to try to ensure that both the competition and the gambling were fair.

Gambling is now legal, strictly controlled, and taxed by the government, although from time to time evidence is found that someone has tried, sometimes successfully, to influence the outcome of a boxing match, horse race, football match or some other event.

The gambling industry in the UK is a large and growing business. In 1999, expenditure on gambling was £6,700 million, an increase since 1989 of 124% at current prices. £1,125 million was spent on bingo, an increase since 1989 of 31%. (Source: the 16th annual British lifestyle survey published by the market researchers Mintel.)

Most betting in the UK continues to be on horse-racing and greyhound-racing, although betting on other sporting events, notably football, is becoming more popular. Bets may be placed with on-course bookmakers at racecourses and greyhound tracks, or off-course through over 8,000 licensed betting offices.

A form of pool betting – totalisator betting – is organised on racecourses by the Horserace Totalisator Board (the Tote), which also has a credit betting operation and a chain of off-course betting offices. A proportion of horserace betting turnover by bookmakers and the Tote is returned to the racing industry though an annual levy. The levy is based on a scheme agreed each year between the Bookmakers' Committee and the Horserace Betting Levy Board. If agreement cannot be reached, it is determined by the Home Secretary. The Levy Board distributes the levy to promote the improvement of horse breeds, and for the advancement of veterinary science and the improvement of horse-racing. In May 1999, the Government announced its intention to introduce legislation to sell the Tote.

It is possible to bet on almost any sports event (just as it is possible to bet on the outcome of a general election or whether there will be a white Christmas). Bets can be placed in a betting shop or, very often, at the venue where the event is occurring. It is also quite common to have an account with a bookmaker which allows you to phone in your bets.

On-line sports betting, in which customers can use the Internet to place bets and watch races, is almost certain to be an increasingly important element in the sports gambling industry.

It used to be the case that bets were almost always on the outcome of the event, which person or animal would win. There is now a wide range of possibilities. For example, you can bet on which player will score the first goal in a football match, which cricketer will score the most runs or take the most wickets.

> In February 2000, Sports Internet, the sports content, statistics and betting company, joined forces with Freeserve, the Internet service provider, to provide Freeserve's customers with an on-line betting service. Freeserve's customers were enabled to bet on line through Sport Internet's Surrey International bookmaking subsidiary.
>
> In the same month, Arena Leisure, which owns or operates six UK racecourses, launched an Internet betting service in a joint enterprise with Autotote, the US betting system operator. Arena's role in the project was to broadcast live races over the Internet while Autotote, which controls more than 60% of the world tote market, supplied the betting operation. The new service allowed horseracing fans worldwide to place bets, watch races and collect their winnings through mobile telephones and digital television as well as the Internet.
>
> *Source: Financial Times 10 February 2000*

DISCUSSION POINT

Try to find out the latest figures for the money that the Government takes from sport in tax, and the amount of money that the government gives to sport. Do you think that the discrepancy is fair?

There are certain events which inspire people who do not consider themselves to be gamblers to have a bet. The Derby and the Grand National are horse races which come into this category.

New opportunities for the betting and gaming industry, and the consumer, have arisen through a relaxation of membership conditions and advertising of casinos (of which there are over 100 in Britain) and on broadcast advertising of commercial bingo.

3.1.8 Sports medicine

Sports medicine is particularly concerned with the treatment and prevention of injuries, as well as dietary advice and analysis.

The majority of general practitioners (GPs) have no training in sports medicine, although some will have a little experience of treating sports injuries. The National Health Service (NHS) has a number of sports injury clinics whose facilities are normally accessed by referral letter from a patient's GP. Unfortunately, immediate treatment is not always available and delay can be detrimental to an elite or developing athlete.

Sports medicine in the private sector is a growth area. Clinics provide their service at a cost, with fees varying from clinic to clinic. A number of insurance companies offer policies which can help to offset the cost of treatment at a private clinic.

The National Sports Medicine Institute (NSMI) is situated at the Medical College of St Bartholomew's Hospital in London. Its facilities include a physiology laboratory, library and information centre.

The NSMI provides accommodation for the British Association of Sport and Medicine (BASM). BASM organises in-service education programmes and maintains a register of sports injury and physiotherapy clinics, which is published in the form of a directory.

In Scotland, a network of 26 accredited sports medicine centres provides specialist help with sports injuries. Wales has eleven sports medicine centres accredited by the NSMI. The Northern Ireland Sports Medicine Centre is a partnership between the Sports Council for Northern Ireland and a local healthcare trust.

The following web sites contain up-to-date information about sports medicine:
- National Sports Medicine Institute (*http://www.nsmi.org.uk*)
- British Journal of Sports Medicine (*http://www.bmjpg.com*)
- International Federation of Sports Medicine (*http://www.fims.org*).

3.1.9 **Health and fitness**

Since the 1980s there has been a boom in health and fitness clubs in the UK, and no one who takes even a brief glance at some statistics could doubt that there is room for improvement in the health and fitness of the nation.

Figures published by the World Health Organization (WHO) in the 1980s revealed that Scotland and Northern Ireland recorded an annual death rate from coronary heart disease among 55- to 64-year-olds of over 1,000 persons per 100,000 of the population. The corresponding figure in Japan was 100 persons. These figures indicate a major health problem brought on by too much smoking and drinking, unhealthy diet, and lack of exercise.

In 1998, the UK population spent £2.25 billion on participating in sports and keeping fit. The balance of spending is shifting away from sports and games and towards fitness. This demand for 'pure fitness' activity has seen councils investing in gyms and health suites in the late 1990s.

There are around 1,600 leisure centres in the UK, developed by local authorities to provide for a wide range of activities, centred on:

- swimming
- sports hall games
- racquet sports.

These centres are subsidised from local taxation but may be privately managed or run by council staff.

Private health clubs, which offer sophisticated equipment and an exclusive environment, are increasingly favoured by affluent professionals. There are over 3,500 health clubs in the UK and although the numbers are still growing there are indications that the market is shifting towards the larger clubs owned by specialists such as Cannons or Fitness First.

The leading groups are:
- Whitbread (David Lloyd, Curzons, Marriott clubs) 200,000 members
- Cannons 80 sites and 125,000 members
- Fitness First 45 sites 100,000 members.

In 1999, 6.4 million adults (nearly 14% of the population) either used a gym regularly or had joined a health club. (Source of figures: Executive summary of Key Note Ltd report on Health Clubs and Leisure Centres.) Health clubs provide opportunities for exercise, advice on diet and lifestyle. Those who can afford it take the further step of acquiring a personal fitness trainer.

Community-based organisations also provide classes and facilities aimed at groups in their community and also target these at special interests (e.g. gentle keep fit for the unfit, stretching for the elderly). The public leisure centre infrastructure is less dynamic than that of the private sector but National Lottery funds are contributing to upgrades.

David Lloyd Leisure, which is owned by Whitbread, operates 47 private Racquet Health and Fitness clubs in the UK. The clubs focus on racquet sports, but also contain gyms, aerobic studios, swimming pools and tenpin bowling.

There is a children's fitness programme and swimming lessons for both children and adults. All instructors are fully qualified. There is wheelchair access to all of the clubs.

Other famous brand names owned by Whitbread include Beefeater, Boddingtons, Murphys, Pizza Hut, Thresher Wine Shop and Travel Inn.

DISCUSSION POINT

Can you think of ways that people on low incomes could be helped to recognise the importance of a healthy diet and regular exercise?

Health and fitness is also a home-based industry. People do not necessarily need to go to a gym to use exercise machines or to keep fit.

One problem is that people on low incomes, who are likely to be on unhealthy diets, will be unable to afford visits to health clubs, and certainly cannot afford personal fitness trainers.

ACTIVITY

Carry out an investigation into the health and fitness facilities in your area. Write a short report on the range and the providers of those facilities. What conclusions can you draw from this research?

GP referral schemes

In the early 1990s, pilot projects for GP referral schemes were begun. Doctors worked with leisure centres to provide an alternative form of treatment for many illnesses and medical conditions.

Doctors and health workers register with the project by signing a copy of the project manual. Doctors can then refer patients to the liaison officer for the project via a prescription which states:

- the name of the patient's doctor
- the name of the doctor referring the patient (if different)
- the nature of the exercise recommended by the doctor
- any further information (e.g. medical/physiological limitations).

The liaison officer monitors the patient's activity during the programme. On completion of the programme, patients return to the doctor for evaluation.

In its basic form, the project is designed to improve the fitness levels of the referred clients. However, since the scheme attracts large numbers of people who would not normally use a leisure centre there are important secondary benefits.

3.1.10 **Outdoor and adventure activities**

There is a wide range of activities in this category, including:

- gliding
- canoeing
- mountaineering
- rambling/orienteering
- mountain biking
- sailing
- scuba diving.

The National Mountain Centre at Plas y Brenin is in the heart of the Snowdonia National Park. It offers facilities for mountaineering, climbing and canoeing.

On-site facilities include:

- a climbing wall (up to 13 metres)
- a training wall
- an indoor canoe training pool
- a 60-metre ski slope
- a fitness room.

The centre's programme includes governing body award courses, multi-activity holidays and specialist courses like Alpine climbing. There are also accredited safety and leadership courses.

The National Mountain Centre is operated by Mountain Training Trust Ltd, a non-profit-making company comprising expertise from the British Mountaineering Council, the United Kingdom Mountain Training Board and, on behalf of Sport England, the Mountain Leader Training Board.

Many of these activities have traditionally taken place in some of the more remote and inaccessible parts of the country. Access is now easier because of

- increasing levels of participation
- improved transport networks
- the rise of private car ownership.

Many of the activities are also free but they may require equipment or specialist clothing and footwear. They are a major contributor to the sports industry.

The popularity of outdoor activities has also inspired a growth in activities taking place in an urban environment:

- indoor climbing walls
- skiing at the Crystal Dome, Milton Keynes
- skiing at the SnowDome in Tamworth
- skiing at World of Snow in Telford.

In recent times, sailing has enjoyed the most spectacular increase in popularity of any outdoor activity.

It is possible to pursue winter sports in England on a year-round basis. The SnowDome at Tamworth opened its ski slope in 1994. The slope is 150 metres long, 30 metres wide and has a 90-degree bend. The temperature is 4 °C and the snow is groomed four times a day. Uplift is provided by two travelator lifts. The Dome also has shops, a bar and a restaurant.

The World of Snow opened on an industrial site on the outskirts of Telford in 1992. There is tobogganing as well as skiing, and discos and junior and adult group events are also organised. Gloves must be worn and users must be able to complete a basic snow-plough (wedge) turn or take lessons.

Key questions

1 What is Compulsory Competitive Tendering?

2 Why is sponsoring sport an attractive proposition for companies?

3 What does the GP referral scheme aim to achieve?

4 What are the benefits to a city or area in hosting a major sporting event? Are there any disadvantages?

5 Into which three categories can the work of sports development officers be divided?

6 What factors have contributed to easier access to some outdoor activities such as canoeing, gliding and scuba diving?

7 What is Best Value and what effect do you think it will have on the provision of sport in your area?

8 Which sectors are involved in the provision of sports facilities?

SECTION **3.2**

The scale of sport and its contribution to the UK economy

The sports industry has grown hugely in the UK since the 1970s. In this section you will develop your understanding of the scale of the sports industry and the contribution it makes to the economy. You will also examine the participation rates in sport.

❝ Sport and related activity provide more jobs than the motor manufacturing, chemical, gas, coal or agricultural industries. ❞

Sports Council, Sport in Society factsheet

❝ The business is great but we now see new opportunities for advertising on the Web. We hope to attract US customers to come and learn competitive sailing in Wales. ❞

manager, sailing sports centre

❝ The modern football club doesn't just sell kit anymore. There's a whole lifestyle around the club and its players and it's generated all kinds of merchandising – mugs, even dolls and teddy bears. And our web site gets more and more important. ❞

web developer at a football club

3.2.1 People employed in sport

The large sports industry in the UK is relatively new. It stems largely from the jogging boom of the 1970s, the health and fitness boom since the 1980s and the range of new facilities that have opened up. Sport is now a significant employer. In the UK industry as a whole, there are around 1.5 million employees and about 180,000 self-employed. Sport provides over 400,000 paid jobs and the voluntary sector the equivalent of 108,000 full-time jobs.

Numbers employed in the sports industry

1985	1995	1998
324,470	425,056	437,460

from a report for the UK Sports Council

3.2.2 People who participate in sport

It is estimated that 25 million English people take part in some sport or active recreation at least once a month.

Participation in the most popular sports, games and physical activities: by gender and age, 1996–7

United Kingdom — Percentages

	16–19	20–24	25–34	35–44	45–54	55–64	65 and over	All aged 16 and over
Males								
Walking	57	57	50	53	51	50	37	49
Snooker/pool/billiards	54	45	29	19	13	9	5	19
Cycling	36	24	19	18	12	8	5	15
Swimming	18	17	17	20	10	7	5	13
Soccer	47	28	17	10	2	1	-	10
Females								
Walking	45	43	44	45	49	43	25	41
Keep fit/yoga	29	28	24	20	14	12	6	17
Swimming	23	21	26	22	14	12	5	16
Cycling	14	11	10	12	7	4	2	8
Snooker/pool/billiards	24	17	6	3	1	-	-	4

Source: General Household Survey, Office for National Statistics; Continuous Household Survey, Northern Ireland Statistics and Research Agency

'Social Trends 30', Office for National Statistics © Crown Copyright 2000

A survey for the Sports Industries Federation showed that:

- adults participating in at least one sporting activity (excluding walking) rose from 62% in 1987 to 67% in 1990, 68% in 1993 and to 70% in 1999.
- regular participation in sport has fallen from 46% in 1996 to 43% in 1999
- there has been a decline in team and racquet sports, particularly squash
- activities which have shown some growth include health and fitness activities, particularly aerobics for women and weight training for men
- football and cue sports have seen some growth, particularly among 18- to 24-year-olds
- participation by women has increased, with 51% actively involved in sport compared to 49% of men
- there is an emphasis on activities that are done for fitness, particularly use of home gym equipment, rather than competition
- swimming remains the most popular sport, but numbers are falling
- participation levels in golf have remained virtually static since 1993.

It is estimated that there are 150,000 sports clubs in the country covering a wide range of sporting and recreational activities. The top ten sports in terms of club membership are:

	Members	Number of clubs
Football	1,650,000	46,150
Billiards/snooker	1,500,000	4,500
Golf	1,217,000	6,650
Squash	465,000	1,600
Bowls	435,000	11,000
Sailing	450,000	1,650
Angling	392,000	1,750
Rugby union	284,000	3,250
Lawn tennis	275,000	2,800
Swimming	288,000	1,950

ACTIVITY

A *Directory of Sport* may be obtained from the appropriate regional office of Sport England. (Maybe you can find a copy in your local or college library.) Use the directory to find out about sports facilities in your region. Are there gaps in provision? What do you think can be done about this, and who should do it?

3.2.3 Consumer spending on sport

UNIT

3

SECTION **3.2**

Value added is a term used by economists to measure the value of the output of an economy or a particular part of it.

Consumer spending on sport in the UK was £10.4 billion in 1995 (£8.5 billion in England), representing 2.24% of total consumer expenditure. The fastest growth in consumer expenditure on sport was in the categories 'subscription charges and fees for participant sports', 'sports clothing', and 'sports footwear'.

Value added to the UK economy in 1995 by sport-related economic activity was £9.8 billion, double the figure of 1985. Local government contributed 9.32% to this value added, compared to the contribution of 0.35% from central government.

For every £1 of central and local government support received, sport gives back £5 to the taxpayer, not counting invisible gains to the economy through sport tourism, reduced use of the National Health Service and greater fitness in the workplace.

Key questions

1 What is 'consumer spending'?

2 Can you think of any reasons why team sports have shown a decrease in popularity while health and fitness activities have become more popular?

3 What factors have contributed to the huge growth in the sports industry?

SECTION **3.3**

We are no longer thinking about what society can do for sport, but what sport can do for society. That people are thinking of sport as a vehicle for regenerating and improving communities is, I believe, a real step forward.

Chris Smith MP, Secretary of State for Culture, Media and Sport

The organisation and funding of sport

The organisation and funding of sport at local, national and international levels involves a complex network of institutions and many thousands of people. In this section you will learn about many of the organisations involved in the promotion and running of sport for those who participate for fun, as well as for those top performers for whom sport provides a very good living.

3.3.1 **The organisation of sport**

The provision of sport can be at local, regional, national or international levels. Many sports would not survive without managerial and administrative support, nor would they survive without financial support from central or local government, participants, sponsors or other benefactors.

The Department for Culture, Media and Sport is the central UK government department responsible for government policy on the arts, sport and recreation, the National Lottery, libraries, museums and galleries, export licensing of cultural goods, broadcasting, film, press freedom and regulation, the built heritage, the royal estate, and tourism.

A 'Sports Cabinet' was established in 1998 to identify strategic priorities for sport. It is headed by the Secretary of State for Culture, Media and Sport and includes the ministers responsible for sport in England, Scotland, Wales and Northern Ireland.

Sports councils

Government responsibilities in sport and recreation are largely channelled through five sports councils:

- the United Kingdom Sports Council, operating as UK Sport
- the English Sports Council, operating as Sport England
- the Sports Council for Wales
- the Scottish Sports Council, operating as sportscotland (sic)
- the Sports Council for Northern Ireland.

UK Sport takes the lead in all aspects of sport and physical recreation which require strategic planning, administration, coordination or representation for the UK as a whole. It works alongside the Sports Cabinet in undertaking its main functions, which include:

- coordinating support to sports in which the UK competes internationally (as opposed to the four countries separately)
- tackling drug misuse
- coordinating policy for bringing major sports events to the UK
- representing British sporting interests overseas and increasing influence at international level.

National governing bodies (NGBs)

Individual sports are run by over 400 governing bodies. Some have a UK or Great Britain structure while others are constituted on a home country basis (i.e. England, Scotland, Northern Ireland, Wales).

The functions of the NGBs include:

- drawing up rules
- holding events
- regulating membership
- selecting and training national teams.

Some of the NGBs are:

- **Basketball** – Basketball Association of Wales, British & Irish Basketball Federation, English Basketball Association, Irish Basketball Association, Scottish Basketball Association
- **Cycling** – British Cycling Federation
- **Netball** – International Federation of Netball Associations, All England Netball Association, Scottish Netball Association, Welsh Netball Association
- **Nordic Skiing** – English Ski Council Nordic Committee.

The British Amateur Gymnastics Association (BAGA) is the NGB for gymnastics in the UK. In 1996, it evolved into British Gymnastics for all operational purposes, but the company name has remained unchanged.

Gymnastics includes the following individual disciplines and activities:

- men's artistic gymnastics
- women's artistic gymnastics
- rhythmic gymnastics
- sports acrobatics
- sports aerobics
- general gymnastics
- disability gymnastics.

The BAGA is divided into three Home Nations (Wales, Scotland, Northern Ireland) and ten English Regions (North of England, North West, Yorkshire, West Midlands, East Midlands, East England, South West, South, South East, London). See their web site (*http://www.baga.co.uk*) for more details.

The Association is a member of the World Governing Body for Gymnastics (FIG) and the European Governing Body for Gymnastics (EUG). It is also a member of the British Olympic Association (BOA) and the Central Council of Physical Recreation (CCPR).

Governing bodies receive funds from the sports councils and they are required to produce development plans from the grass roots to the highest competitive levels. In order to have access to money from the National Lottery for their top athletes they need to prepare 'world-class performance' plans with specific performance targets.

Most sports clubs in the UK belong to, or are affiliated to, an appropriate NGB.

Sport for disabled people

The NGBs are increasingly taking on responsibility for sport for people with disabilities. As well as those concerned with individual disabilities and single sports, the key organisations are:

- Disability Sport England, which organises regional and national championships in many sports and also runs training courses. Scottish Disability Sport, the Federation of sports Associations for the Disabled (Wales) and Disability Sports NI have similar coordinating roles. In England, Sport England and disability organisations have cooperated in the formation in April 1999 of the English Federation of Disability Sport, which aims to integrate disability sport into mainstream sporting activities as much as possible.

- The United Kingdom Sports Association for People with Learning Disability (UKSAPLD), a coordinating body with a membership of over 20 national organisations, promotes and develops opportunities in sport and recreation for people with learning disability.
- The British Paralympic Association (BPA) which organises participation by British athletes in the summer and winter Paralympics.

All distributing bodies of National Lottery funding are required to ensure that applicants incorporate access and availability for people with disabilities. Sport England has provided nearly £20 million for 200 projects which specifically target disabled people. The Government also wishes to see better facilities for disabled spectators. New facilities at football grounds will include a minimum number of wheelchair spaces offering an unobstructed view of the pitch, and funding from the Football Trust will only be given on the condition that football clubs consult disabled people before work begins.

The Women's Sports Foundation (WSF)

The WSF is a registered charity with five key aims:
- to increase awareness about the issues surrounding women and girls involvement in sport
- to support women and girls to become involved in sport at all levels and in all capacities
- to encourage organisations to improve access to sporting opportunities for women and girls
- to challenge instances of inequality in sport and seek to bring about change
- to raise the visibility of all British sportswomen.

In addition, the WSF has cooperated with the Institute of Sport and Recreation Management, Sport England, and the Equal Opportunities Commission (EOC) to promote single-sex sport and leisure provision.

The creation of women-only sessions has been seen as particularly successful in promoting a range of sport or recreation activities among women who for reasons such as religion, culture or lack of confidence, had previously not been keen to participate.

Single-sex provision can be challenged under the requirements for equal treatment of men and women in the Sex Discrimination Act 1975 (SDA) or the Sex Discrimination (Northern Ireland) Order 1976. However, in passing the SDA, Parliament decided that there should be exceptions to the general rule of equal treatment in certain special circumstances. Of these exceptions, the most important for sport and leisure facilities is in section 35 (1) (c). This section allows facilities to be restricted to one sex if it can be demonstrated that:
- the facilities or services are such that users of one sex are likely to suffer serious embarrassment at the presence of the opposite sex

OR
- the facilities or services are such that a user is likely to be in a state of undress and might reasonably object to the presence of a user of the opposite sex.

The SDA also permits single-sex provision if physical contact is likely between users of the opposite sex and there might be reasonable objection to this. In addition, the Act permits voluntary groups of various kinds to cater for one sex only. Such organisations may restrict membership, benefits and facilities to one sex and may provide public services to one sex only. Where sport and leisure services are provided by a single-sex voluntary group committed to that purpose therefore, they would not normally be in breach of the general requirement of equality between the sexes.

The Institute of Sport and Recreation Management (ISRM)

The ISRM is the national professional body for sport and recreation facility managers. Its aim is to improve the management and operation of recreation centres, sports facilities and swimming pools through the provision of training, information and consultancy services. In particular, the Institute places great emphasis on the management of the technological aspects of sport and recreation facilities, especially swimming pools.

The Institute of Leisure and Amenity Management (ILAM)

The Institute is a registered charity with the aim of representing every aspect of leisure, cultural and recreational management. Its objectives are:
- the improvement of management standards in the leisure industry
- promotion of the benefits of leisure and healthy lifestyles
- the enhancement of the quality of experience of those participating in leisure activities
- the representation, development and advocacy of professional standards
- the provision of a continuing professional development (CPD) programme
- the provision of a professional qualification scheme
- dissemination of information.

Central Council of Physical Recreation (CCPR)

The CCPR speaks and acts to support the work of its membership of over 300 national governing and representative bodies of sport, 150,000 voluntary sports clubs, and everyone who regularly participates in sport and recreation in the UK.

The CCPR is increasingly called upon to advise the government on matters such as the National Lottery, VAT on sport, child protection in sport, and access to the open countryside.

SPRITO

SPRITO is the trading name of the national training organisation (NTO) for the sport and recreation industry. It was founded by the key employer and trade associations, professional bodies, and sector networks in the industry. The NTO is responsible for setting and implementing training standards. These standards are not only the basis for establishing Scottish and National Vocational Qualifications, but will be the basis of establishing a framework of education and training and other national awards. The participating organisations of the NTO (including the British Olympic Association, the National Coaching Federation and the Central Council of Physical Recreation) represent all the key trade (employer) associations, professional bodies and representative networks across the breadth of the industry.

3.3.2 **Major sources of funding**

ACTIVITY

Find out how your local authority spends money on sport. How much does it spend, and how is it decided which sports should receive money?

For most sports, the major sources of funding are:

- grants – e.g. money given by central government (via a sports council) or local authority
- sponsorship – e.g. money given to a sport, or to a particular event, by a private company
- charges for activities – e.g. the money that you pay to hire a squash court
- membership fees – e.g. an annual subscription to a golf club
- fees for media coverage – e.g. the money that television pays to broadcast Premier League football matches
- National Lottery – e.g. money distributed by Sport England for the development of sport in England.

Sponsorship

Sponsorship may take the form of financing specific events or championships, such as horse races or cricket leagues, or grants to sports organisations or individual performers. A joint Department of Trade and Industry/Sports Industries Federation competitiveness analysis estimated that the sports sponsorship market was worth £353 million in 1998. Sponsorship is encouraged by a number of bodies, including:

- the Institute of Sports Sponsorship (ISS), which comprises some 100 UK companies involved in sponsoring sport
- the Sports Sponsorship Advisory Service, administered jointly by the CCPR and the ISS and funded by Sport England and similar advisory services of the Scottish Sports Council and the Sports Council for Wales.

Under the European Union's Tobacco Advertising Directive, the Government intends to ban tobacco sponsorship of sport from 2003 in most cases and from 2006 for certain exceptional global events. It has set up a task force of business and sponsorship experts to help the sports affected. Seven sports have sought assistance to make the transition: rugby league, clay pigeon shooting, billiards and snooker, pool, darts, ice hockey, and angling.

Recent examples of sponsorship:

- The 1999 Cricket World Cup had four official sponsors – Emirates Airlines, National Westminster Bank, Pepsi, and Vodaphone.
- The Nationwide Building Society sponsors the England football team to the tune of £15 million over four years.
- The airport operator BAA is the lead sponsor of the Millennium Youth Games – a series of events over three years in which more than 300,000 people will take part, with a Grand Final in Southampton just before the Sydney Olympics.

We should not only think of sports sponsorship in terms of the huge sums that companies spend in promoting professional sports events, clubs, or star players. Many companies have found it advantageous to sponsor grass-roots sports.

Sportsmatch was started in 1992 by the UK government on similar lines to a scheme that had been used to fund the arts. Now every year around £3 million is available to match every pound of sponsors' money with a pound from the Department of Culture, Media and Sport, channelled through Sport England.

Sportsmatch is administered in England by the Institute of Sports Sponsorship which in just over six years has made 2,500 awards to sport. Together with sponsors' money this has generated £40 million of sponsorship for grass-roots development programmes. Similar schemes are funded separately in Scotland and Wales.

Any grass-roots amateur sport can apply for an award. The applicant must come up with a project for sponsorship that fits the Sportsmatch criteria and find a company that is interested in supporting it. Sportsmatch money is available to match the sponsor's money, either to make up the project cost to the full amount, or to double the money to increase the size of the event or project and the number of people participating.

Priority for awards is given to:
- disabled people
- young people
- school sports
- community projects.

Big names like Coca-Cola, Umbro, TSB, Nike, Pizza Hut have contributed, but so have a host of small companies.

National Lottery money

Sport is one of the main recipients of funds raised by the National Lottery. By June 1999, awards totalling over £1 billion had been made to 3,000 projects in the UK.

Some of the funds from the Millennium Commission were also for sporting and recreational developments. Major schemes include £46 million for the Millennium Stadium in Cardiff and £42.5 million for a new national cycle network.

The Sports Council, which distributes National Lottery money, welcomes applications from:
- voluntary sports clubs, charitable trusts, playing fields associations, youth clubs, community associations
- area sports associations, provided they are made up of local sports clubs

- national governing bodies of sports recognised by the Sports Council
- local authorities and other public bodies.

Commercial bodies can apply only if the project:
- is not primarily oriented towards individual personal gain or shareholders' dividends
- resolves a real shortage of facilities
- delivers significant community benefit with significant guaranteed public access through a Community Use Agreement (this applies to professional sports clubs too).

Schools, universities and colleges can apply only if they have a shortage of facilities and will guarantee public access through a Community Use Agreement. Only independent and grant-maintained schools can apply to the Sports Council; others must go through their local education authority (LEA).

The range of projects which can qualify for lottery money is very wide, but they must be capital projects. That is:
- construction (building pitches, swimming pools, bowling greens, jetties and slipways, etc.)
- buying land
- upgrading facilities.

Revenue costs – salaries, maintenance, insurance, etc. – are not normally eligible for Lottery grants.

Funding of around £20.5 million a year from the National Lottery Sports Fund is being earmarked for two main schemes designed to promote sporting excellence:
- The World Class Performance Programme provides support to the UK's most talented athletes to enable them to improve their performance and win medals in major international competitions. Since April 1997 grants totalling nearly £65 million have been committed to more than 30 sports in the programme, and 2,100 athletes have received support.
- The World Class Events Programme aims to ensure that major international events can be staged successfully in the UK. About £3 million a year is available to support funding of up to 35% of the cost of bidding for and staging events. By mid-1999, £4.6 million had been awarded to assist with the bidding for and staging of 13 international events, the largest award being £3 million to assist with England's bid to host the football World Cup in 2006.

A trend to reduce direct government spending on sport started in the 1990s. Sports council grants were reduced each year from 1993/4 and the councils were expected to raise money from other sources and to reduce their running costs.

ACTIVITY

Try to find out if any club or organisation in your area has been successful in obtaining some Lottery money. What did they do with the money, and could they have carried out their plans without it?

3.3.3 Organisation and funding of sport at international level

International sport is controlled by the international sports federations (ISFs) and the International Olympic Committee (IOC).

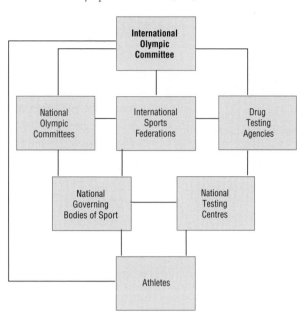

The ISFs are independent organisations consisting of members representative of the governing bodies in countries where the sport is played. Their role is to:

■ encourage the worldwide development of their sport
■ make sure that their rules agree with the rules of the IOC
■ control all international fixtures and competitions
■ change and enforce the rules of the sport.

The ISFs are funded by national governments, the private sector through sponsorship of events, and by the fees for televising international fixtures.

The IOC (founded in 1894) is an independent club of non-elected members. Its headquarters are in Lausanne, Switzerland. The membership of about 90 is responsible for electing new members.

The IOC is in complete control of the Olympic Games. It works through national Olympic Committees and its aims are:

■ to promote the physical and moral aspects of sport
■ to encourage international understanding and friendship
■ to spread the Olympic principles throughout the world
■ to bring sportspeople together every four years at the Olympic Games.

The members of the IOC are responsible for selecting the host cities of the Olympic Games, both summer and winter. The IOC is financed by selling the television rights to broadcast the Olympics and by companies who pay for the right to be official sponsors of the Olympic Games.

The British Olympic Association (BOA) is an independent voluntary organisation, founded in 1905, and is the National Olympic Committee of the UK. The BOA represents a constituency of 35 National Governing Bodies of Sport who are members of the National Olympic Committee, and the athletes from these sports.

It is totally independent of government, which was highlighted in 1980 when the Government asked the BOA to boycott the Olympic Games in Moscow following the invasion of Afghanistan by the Soviet Union. Nevertheless, the British team participated in the Olympics and won medals, notably Alan Wells, Sebastian Coe and Steve Ovett. The team from the USA did boycott the Moscow Olympics. The Soviet Union and other countries then boycotted the 1984 Olympics in Los Angeles.

The BOA:
- seeks to foster interest in the Olympics throughout the UK
- runs the British Olympic Medical Centre
- helps the governing bodies of Olympic sports to prepare their teams
- organises the British team for each Olympic Games (summer and winter).

The BOA has established a warm weather training camp in Florida. It is run by the Orlando Regional Health System and uses the Disney Wide World of Sport facilities. Athletes chosen by the various NGBs are able to have year-round training with comprehensive medical and administrative support.

The BOA is financed by the public (through the British Olympic Appeal), by sponsorship from companies, and by companies who pay to be official BOA sponsors.

3.3.4 Organisation and funding of sport at national level

Funding

SportsAid

SportsAid is an independent charity which has three main objectives:

- to further the education of young people through the medium of sport
- to encourage those with social or physical disadvantages to improve their lives through sport
- to enable those living in poverty to take advantage of the opportunities offered by sport.

SportsAid also awards grants both nationally and regionally to promising young sportspeople. A typical national grant is £500 a year, and a regional one is £150–£250 a year.

To qualify for a national SportsAid grant, an athlete must be:

- aged between 12 and 18 (special cases may be made for under-12s and for 19-, 20- and 21-year-olds)
- in genuine financial need and therefore not in receipt of a National Lottery World Class Performance grant
- a member of a national squad.

SportsAid regions raise funds to assist local competitors who are not receiving National Lottery funding or a national SportsAid grant. To be considered for a regional grant, an applicant must have top-six national standing and/or be in a national squad.

A representative from a national governing body must support all SportsAid grant applications.

Public Sector

Council tax is levied on individuals living in its area by the local authority. **Uniform business rate** is paid by local businesses for the services which they receive from the council.

The **European Social Fund** is a European Union fund which is allocated to bids for special projects. A local authority could bid for some of this money for a sports project in its area.

Local authorities can use their discretionary powers to channel money towards sport. This money comes from:

- central government
- council tax and uniform business rate
- European Social Fund
- charges for services (swimming pools, leisure centres, etc.)
- the National Lottery

Local authorities also have a legal obligation to provide sports facilities for education.

Private sector

The private sector in sport does not receive guaranteed income from central government or local taxes. Private sector companies rely on income received directly from customers. This can come from direct admission charges (paying to enter a stadium) or from membership fees (an annual subscription to a gym).

Private companies can bid for grants from funding agencies, including:
- sports councils
- the National Lottery
- the Department of Trade and Industry (enterprise schemes)
- the Football Trust
- the Foundation for Sport and Arts

These bids are more likely to be successful if they include an element of partnership with the public or voluntary sectors.

Voluntary sector

This sector is vital to the provision of sport in the UK, but its diverse nature makes it hard to define. Its main objectives are the provision of a service for a group sharing mutual interests (e.g. people interested in hockey, tennis, or football) and the wish to help other people with similar interests and to contribute to the mutual funding of activities.

Voluntary sector clubs and organisations have no guaranteed source of income and need to fund their operations in a variety of ways:
- **Membership fees**. Anyone joining a sports club will probably have to pay an annual membership fee. The amount will depend on the number of members, the extent of the activities, and the upkeep of any premises owned by the club.
- **Match fees**. Sports club members usually pay a fee every time they play. This may help to cover the cost of refreshments, transport, referee's fees, washing kit, etc.
- **Grants**. A voluntary-sector sports club may apply for a grant to any of the grant-awarding bodies mentioned above. Some governing bodies are large enough, rich enough, or willing to grant aid to clubs, and this can be an essential source of club income.
- **Loans**. A club may take out a bank or other loan to fund its operations, perhaps for ground or clubhouse improvements. The ground or clubhouse may be used as collateral to guarantee the loan.
- **Sponsorship**. Any club can seek out commercial sponsorship. Of course, the largest deals are found in the world of professional sport where companies sponsor teams, prize money or whole events, but smaller sums can be important to clubs in the voluntary sector. A local company might provide the team's kit or make a contribution to transport costs.

ACTIVITY

Pick a local voluntary sports club and find out how it funds its operations. If it receives any commercial sponsorship, list the benefits and drawbacks of this as a source of funding.

Key questions

1 Usually, only capital projects can qualify for National Lottery money. What are capital projects?

2 What could a private company do to increase its chances of receiving a grant from a funding agency such as the Foundation for Sport and Arts?

3 How is the British Olympic Association financed?

4 What is the function of the Sports Cabinet?

5 Can you name the five sports councils operating in the UK?

6 Which government department is responsible for government policy on sport?

7 When would it be legal to restrict sports facilities to one sex?

8 What is SPRITO?

9 On what basis does Sportsmatch distribute money?

10 What is the role of the ISFs?

SECTION **3.4**

Trends in sport

The sports industry is continually changing and developing. You need to understand the many trends involved in the industry in order to work within it and react to these trends effectively. This section will help you to understand the importance of sport to the mass media, and the equal importance of the mass media to sport. You will also develop your understanding of various factors, including participation rates, changing expectations and markets, technological developments and the way in which fashion can influence the sports industry.

66 *The vast majority of people who use our sports hall are young, mainly in their teens and early twenties. It's evident that as people get older they do less active sport; the few that do probably join clubs. They are looking for something different.* 99

supervisor, city sports hall

66 *The Premier League will hope the option of showing matches on club channels and Internet sites within 48 hours will keep the big clubs happy.* 99

Daily Telegraph, 4 April 2000

3.4.1 **Involvement of the mass media**

The relationship between sport and the mass media is a close and interactive one. Most people experience sport through the mass media rather than through active participation or by watching events live, and it is likely that this trend will become more marked in years to come. The mass media includes:

- television (terrestrial, cable, satellite, video)
- radio
- print (newspapers, magazines, books)
- the Internet.

Television

The 1998 World Cup football match between England and Argentina was watched on television by 23.7 million people, the highest ever ratings figure in the UK for a sports event.

The amount of sport on television has increased greatly in recent years. At one time, the governing bodies of sports were worried that the relatively small payments for television rights would not compensate for the reduced numbers of spectators who would pay money to see events live. Several factors contributed to a change in the position:

- colour television and other technological developments improved the coverage of sports events
- the banning of cigarette advertising on television led to tobacco companies sponsoring sports as a way of getting round the ban; money for sponsorship and television rights greatly increased
- satellite television allows us to watch sports events from around the world and gives us the choice of a large number of channels

> DISCUSSION POINT
>
> Should a sport accept sponsorship from a tobacco company?

Satellite television has meant that many minor sports are seen regularly on television. However, many people are worried that more and more of the major sports events are available only on satellite television, thus denying those who cannot afford to pay the subscription for satellite television the chance to see those events. The Government decided that a number of events are too important to the nation to be sold to only one company. These events include:

- the FA Cup Final
- the Scottish Cup Final
- cricket Test Matches in England
- the Derby
- Wimbledon
- the Olympic Games
- the Grand National
- the FIFA World Cup Final.

Interactive digital television has introduced new opportunities. People can select the angle they wish to view a match from and replay moments of their choice. These facilities are expected to increase the audience size for sport.

Television exerts a powerful influence on the organisation of sport. For example, professional football used to be played only on Saturday afternoon. This was the only time that most spectators could go to a match (they worked during the week and often on Saturday mornings as well). Now, because of the demands of television, Premier League matches are played on Saturday and Sunday afternoons and Monday evenings.

Matches in the rugby Five Nations Championship (Six Nations since the inclusion of Italy from 2000) used to kick off at the same time. Now, again because of television, kick off times are arranged so that all of the games can be broadcast live on various channels.

Radio

The BBC and some commercial radio companies provide a wide coverage of sport. The BBC, having lost the television coverage of many events to commercial and satellite companies, uses Radio Five Live to broadcast live football commentaries, and coverage of boxing, athletics, tennis, golf and other sports. The BBC has suffered some setbacks even in its radio coverage. For example, Talk Radio won the rights to broadcast commentary on England's overseas cricket Test Matches.

Print

Sports books tend to fall into three major categories:

- biographies or autobiographies of famous players, managers, etc.
- histories of sport in general, or of one particular sport
- instructional books designed to help people to improve their skills.

Sports magazines are usually dedicated to one sport (with names like *The Cricketer*) and usually carry news items, articles about points of controversy in the sport, articles on famous players or teams, reports on the latest match or tournament. Magazines are usually published monthly, so they cannot compete with television, radio or newspapers in bringing the latest news to their readers, but they can aim for greater depth and a wider coverage of the sport than is provided by other media.

Newspapers, whether tabloid or quality, provide extensive sports coverage, although not all sports receive a lot of attention. Several newspapers have separate sports sections on certain days of the week. Some newspapers like to deal in controversial issues, urging the sacking of managers, enquiring into the private lives of star performers and so on.

> ### DISCUSSION POINT
>
> Should, or could, the BBC have done more to retain a big share of the televised sports market?

> ### ACTIVITY
>
> Look at the sports coverage in copies of six different newspapers. Which sports receive the most coverage? Compare the coverage on, say, football and hockey. Do women receive as much coverage as men do? Whatever you decide the position is, try to explain why it is so.

The Internet

In February 2000, the *Financial Times* reported that NTL and BskyB, rivals in a race to negotiate a new broadcasting deal with football's Premier league, were competing against each other to form an alliance with Sports Internet, the sports web site and on-line betting company. BskyB had recently taken a 5% stake in Sportal, another sports web site operator.

BskyB held the rights to televise most top-flight British football until the end of 2000. NTL and other media groups were anxious to compete for these rights.

Both groups owned stakes in football clubs. BskyB had shares in Aston Villa and Newcastle United; ntl in Manchester United, Leeds United, Sunderland, and Manchester City.

Sports Internet ran the official web sites of more than 20 clubs through its Planet Football subsidiary.

An alliance between ntl and Sports Internet could pave the way for live and recorded video broadcasts of Aston Villa and Newcastle United games to be shown on the clubs' web sites.

Sports Internet was also attractive to media groups because of its on-line betting service. Broadcasters were increasingly keen to offer subscribers the ability to bet while they watched.

DISCUSSION POINT

What are the commercial opportunities for sport via the Internet. What are the commercial imperatives behind Mick Jagger's cricket web site?

The Internet has a major impact on information about and access to sport. Major cricket and football events are now accessible via the Internet.

Premiership football clubs have their own web sites. On these sites, it is possible to buy goods from the club's shop (books, football shirts, souvenirs of all kinds). The official Manchester United site has 75 million hits per month so the commercial opportunities for the club to make money are evidently enormous.

ACTIVITY

Use the Internet to investigate the range of sporting sites. Visit *http://www.sportszine.co.uk.*

From here you can find the best sites for a very wide range of sports. Report on the main sites and what they are trying to achieve.

DISCUSSION POINT

How important do you think the Internet will become as a provider of sport over the next five years?

3.4.2 Participation

Participation is increasing in some sporting activities and decreasing in others. This is an important point for the makers of sports clothes and equipment, the providers of facilities, existing or potential sponsors, television executives, sports councils and so on. Many organisations will spend a lot of time in trying to find out if an increase (or decrease) is a quickly passing phase or represents a definite trend that will continue for a long time.

DISCUSSION POINT

What have been the main factors in the increasing popularity of:

- home-based activities?
- specialist sports clubs (e.g. rugby)?
- golf?

ACTIVITY

Find out what sports are on offer at your school or college – whether as classes or as extracurricular activities. If possible, find out which of these has the highest enrolment or participation.

66 *Adults participating in at least one sporting activity (excluding walking) rose from 62% in 1987 to 67% in 1990, 68% in 1993 and has now risen slightly to 70% in 1999. However, regular participation in sport has fallen from 46% in 1996 to 43% in 1999.* 99

The Sports Industries Federation

3.4.3 Expectations

Many people, both participants and spectators, have changing expectations of the industry.

- At one time footballers were tied to the club they played for, could be denied a transfer and were restricted to a maximum wage of £20 a week. Nowadays they can leave the club when their contract runs out, and many Premiership players earn £30,000 a week; a few earn £50,000 a week.

- Spectators used to stand in the open air in dreadful weather to watch an event in old-fashioned stadiums which had inadequate toilet and catering facilities. Today, people are much more likely to demand a seat and decent facilities. They have many more options than spectators used to have, and if they are not treated well they are likely to go elsewhere.

Professional footballers in England, who were restricted to a maximum wage of £20 a week during the football season and £17 a week in the summer, threatened to strike in 1961. The Football League gave in only 48 hours before the strike was due to begin. The first player to benefit from the abolition of the restrictions was Johnny Haynes of Fulham, who immediately became England's first £100-a-week footballer.

In 1990, Jean-Marc Bosman's contract with RCF Liege expired and the Belgian club offered him a new deal, but with a 60% wage cut. Bosman said that he would rather move to Dunkerque. Liege demanded a transfer fee of more than £250,000, twice what the French club were prepared to pay. This left Bosman unable to play professional football so he took legal action citing restraint of trade. The case was fought all the way to the European Court of Justice who found (in 1995) for Bosman and also announced that the current transfer system was a breach of the free movement of labour between countries. The court also declared that the limit on the number of European Union players a team could field was unlawful. The verdict meant that once a player's contract had expired he was able to move to any club in the EU without a transfer fee.

The improvements in professional football stadiums were forced on the clubs by the Government following the publication of the Taylor Report into the tragedy which occurred at Hillsborough in Sheffield. In 1989, 96 fans were crushed to death during an FA Cup semi-final. Taylor recommended that:

- Football League grounds should become all-seater
- fencing should be safer
- improvements be made to policing and medical facilities.

Safety considerations have greatly reduced the maximum number of people who are allowed in football grounds. For example, Wembley Stadium used to hold crowds of 100,000, but the capacity was reduced to 80,000.

Some people believe that we will reach the stage of stadiums with no spectators – that the event will take place in silence while millions watch it on television.

DISCUSSION POINT

What do think of the idea of a stadium with no spectators? List the points in its favour and the points against it.

3.4.4 **Changing markets**

The UK has what is known as an 'ageing population'. This means that more people are living longer, and improved health has resulted in more retired people staying active for longer. This increases the market for goods and services in many sectors of the sports industry, including walking, golf, bowls, sailing and many others.

Other factors which influence markets include the economic health of the nation. If the majority of people enjoy an increase in their standard of living and have more disposable income (i.e. money to spend), they will spend some of that money in the sports industry, either as players or spectators.

The success of a UK sportsperson or team influences the market in that sport. After England won the World Cup in 1966, attendance increased at Football League matches. This made football more attractive to advertisers. If Tim Henman won Wimbledon, we would expect increased sales of tennis racquets, tennis clothes, and rising membership of tennis clubs.

DISCUSSION POINT

How do the media influence the sports market for individuals?

3.4.5 Technological developments

Technological developments have always had a dramatic impact on the sports industry.

Footballs used to be made of leather and had laces. On a wet day they absorbed a lot of water, became heavy, and were unpleasant to head.

Grass, the traditional surface for many sports, is subject to extremes of weather which can cause the fixture to be cancelled or have an adverse effect on the performance. The situation changed for many sports in the 1960s when artificial surfaces were developed. For example, hockey is now almost always played on artificial pitches at international level.

At the level of community sport, artificial pitches mean that a facility can be open at all times, whatever the weather. They are also less expensive to maintain than a grass pitch.

Companies which manufacture sports equipment are constantly in search of improvements in design and in the fabrics and materials used to construct their products. There are many examples:

- formula one racing cars
- graphite tennis rackets
- skis
- golf clubs (the 'woods' are now often made of metal).

At the top level of sport, a very small improvement in equipment can mean the difference between victory and defeat – for example, new running spikes that can take hundredths of a second off someone's time for the hundred metres.

New equipment is unlikely to have such a dramatic effect on the performance of the person who is participating for fun, but people like to use the same equipment as the top performers.

Technological developments can also be used to regulate a sport. In cricket matches, the third umpire is now regularly called upon to view a video playback and adjudicate on an appeal for a run-out. Rugby league was the first contact sport to use video playbacks. The expense of providing the appropriate technology means that those who play their sport on a non-professional basis are unlikely to encounter video playbacks and will have to rely on the human umpire or referee.

3.4.6 Sport and fashion

Sport has had an important impact on fashion in recent years. For example, large numbers of people, especially young people, began wearing trainers and fleece jackets as casual rather than sportswear. One effect of this was to make sports footwear a fashion item and to drive up the price of trainers.

It also became fashionable to wear rugby or soccer shirts, not only at matches but also in social situations.

The proportion of footwear sales attributable to sport rose from 11% in 1985 to 33.5% in 1990. The expenditure on sports clothing, including footwear, in the UK was £2.01 billion in 1990.

DISCUSSION POINT

Consider your own wardrobe. Do you own any items of casual clothing which are sports-related.

ACTIVITY

Visit some of the web sites of sports clothing manufacturers and retailers. (A search engine will find a lot of these if you use "sports clothing" for your keyword search.) To what extent are the goods advertised as being suitable for the sport, and to what extent are they advertised as being fashionable?

Key questions

1 In what ways can technological development influence sports?

2 What were the main recommendations of the Taylor Report?

3 Why would a sports clothing manufacturer be interested in sports participation rates?

4 What are the advantages of artificial pitches for hockey or cricket?

5 What factors have led to increased coverage of sport on television?

6 Why do some newspapers deal as much in the private lives of sports stars as in reporting matches and events?

7 What effect did the banning of cigarette advertising on television have?

Assignment

Conduct an investigation into the sports industry by analysing two sports of your choice. Use your findings to prepare a written report or presentation. If you choose to write a report, use illustrations, graphs and tables to support your evidence. If you prefer to make a presentation, prepare handouts which highlight your main points.

Your report or presentation should include the following information:

- The scale and economic importance of each sport
  How many people are employed in each sport in the UK? How many people participate in the sport as a leisure activity? How much is spent on the sport by consumers?
- The organisation and funding of each sport
  How is each sport organised and funded at the international level? At the national level? At the regional and local levels?
- The importance of each sport for the mass media
  What role does mass media play within the context of each sport? In what ways has the interest of mass media influenced each sport?
- Major trends in each sport
  What major trends have influenced the development of each sport in the last several decades? What trends are currently shaping the direction that each sport takes within the industry?

KEY SKILLS

You can use the work you are doing for this part of your GNVQ to collect and develop evidence for the following key skills at level 3.

when you	you can collect evidence for
	application of number
obtain relevant information from different sources to support your research with appropriate statistics	key skill N3.1 plan, and interpret information from two different types of source, including a large data set
	communication
gather evidence and examples as part of your investigation	key skill C3.2 read and synthesise information from two extended documents about a complex subject; one of these documents should include at least one image
produce the results of your investigation	key skill C3.1b make a presentation about a complex subject, using at least one image to illustrate complex points (if the results are produced in the form of a presentation)
	key skill C3.3 write two different types of documents about complex subjects; one piece of writing should be an extended document and include at least one image (if the results are produced in the form of a written/wordprocessed report)
	information technology
gather evidence and examples as part of your investigation	key skill 3.1 plan, and use different sources to search for, and select, information required for two different purposes
produce the results of your investigation	key skill 3.3 present information from different sources for two different purposes and audiences; your work must include at least one example of images and one example of numbers
	working with others
investigate two sports	key skill WO3.1 agree realistic objectives and the action and resources needed to achieve them; provide information, based on appropriate evidence, to help agree responsibilities; agree suitable working arrangements with those involved
	key skill WO3.2 organise and carry out tasks in ways that help you to be effective and efficient in meeting your responsibilities; seek to establish and maintain cooperative working relationships, agreeing ways to overcome any difficulties; exchange accurate information on the extent to which work is meeting expected time scales and quality, agreeing changes where necessary to achieve objectives
	key skill WO3.3 agree the extent to which the objectives have been met; identify factors that have influenced the outcome; agree ways the activity could have been done differently to enhance work with others

when you	you can collect evidence for
	improving own learning and performance
plan your research and carry out your investigations	key skill LP3.1 agree targets and plan how these will be met, using support from appropriate others
	key skill LP3.2 use the plan, seeking and using feedback and support from relevant sources to help meet the targets, and use different ways of learning to meet new demands
	key skill LP3.3 review progress in meeting targets, establishing evidence of achievements, and agree action for improving performance using support from appropriate others

UNIT **4**

Marketing leisure and recreation

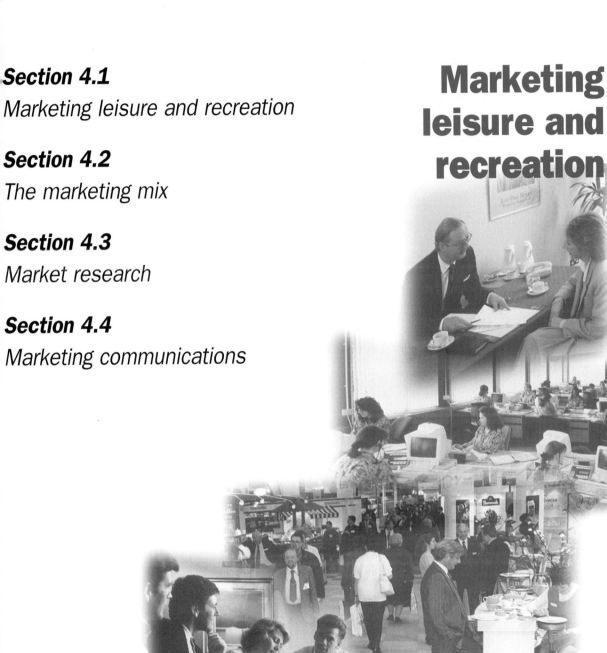

About this unit

In this unit you will investigate the marketing process and the way in which it can help leisure and recreation organisations to achieve their objectives. Marketing is a continuous process that involves anticipating and identifying customers' needs, and supplying products and services to meet them. You will investigate the part that market research plays in identifying customer needs and consider the main marketing communications used by organisations to make customers aware of their products and services.

SECTION **4.1**

Marketing leisure and recreation

You can see the results of organisations' marketing activities all around you: advertisements on TV and in magazines on billboards and so on. Organisations often spend large amounts of money to make sure their products or services are well known and easily available to people who want to buy them. In this section you'll be looking at the way organisations set about marketing and how the results of marketing activity affects the way they change their products. You will learn that marketing is a continuous process that embraces everything that an organisation does to identify, anticipate and satisfy customer needs and expectations.

66 *Marketing is always a very difficult thing – you can spend a fortune and get little or no return. I have advertised my classes in newspapers in the past, but now I find it more effective to advertise every month in the specialist riding magazines.* 99

owner of a riding school which also provides holidays

66 *We have a full marketing team working at our head office. They analyse the economy and other aspects of the industry, such as competitor activity. We receive a report every quarter explaining the company's marketing objectives and plans.* 99

regional manager of a large chain of sporting goods stores

66 *Marketing is a process that starts with research and ends with new products. We collect statistics on how many customers we've had and what films are the most popular. We promote the store by placing advertising in local press and by offering special deals to our regular customers.* 99

owner of a video rental shop

4.1.1 Marketing principles

Marketing activities for all industries are based on five key principles:
- identifying customers' needs and wants
- satisfying customers' needs and wants
- finding new markets for the organisation's products or services
- influencing customers' buying attitudes
- getting the products and services into the right markets.

All marketing activities aim to provide:
- the right product or service to customers
- at the right price
- in the right place
- using the right method of promotion.

Marketing is the life-blood of the leisure and recreation industry because of its highly competitive nature and its volatility due to changing expectations and fashions.

Marketing activities are a continuous process in leisure and recreation. They happen at every stage of the buying process – from encouraging people to buy a product or service, through to providing after-sales service and customer care.

DISCUSSION POINT

The Institute of Marketing defines marketing as '*the management process responsible for identifying, anticipating and satisfying customer requirements profitably*'. Look at the list of marketing principles and the aims of marketing activities and think about the Institute of Marketing's definition. Is marketing just the responsibility of the marketing department, or would other areas of the organisation be involved?

4.1.2   Setting marketing objectives

Mission statements

Organisations often summarise their objectives officially in a mission statement. A mission statement often embraces the organisation's philosophy about its products or services. It is used to publicise the organisation's goals and to motivate its staff.

Blackpool Pleasure Beach's mission statement is: '*to make adults feel like children again'*.

An organisation needs to state its marketing objectives clearly in its marketing plan. It can then look back at the plan after carrying out activities, and evaluate whether the objectives have been achieved, and whether they need to be changed.

Key marketing objectives of leisure and recreation organisations:

- to analyse the needs of the market
- to satisfy customer requirements
- to manage the effects of change
- to manage the effects of competition
- to coordinate activities (relating to market information, customer requirements, competition, change)
- to maximise income
- to make a profit
- to improve people's lives
- to improve people's opinions of a product or service

The key marketing objectives of a profit-making organisation will characteristically focus on growth and increasing profit.

The key marketing objectives of not-for-profit organisations will characteristically focus on promotion, continuation and expansion of the public or charitable service it offers.

Analysing market needs

To make sure that it is producing the right products and services, at the right price and in the right place, an organisation has to know as much as possible about what the market is demanding. The information gathered from market analysis provides an organisation with criteria for assessing:

- how well it is meeting market needs
- new opportunities the market may offer.

Satisfying customer requirements

The marketing function isn't just about identifying needs. It's also about checking continuously that the products and services that the organisation provides meet the customers' requirements and expectations. The marketing officer of a small cinema describes how they thought they'd provided what the customers wanted – but the customers thought otherwise:

66 *Our research showed that customers wanted the cinema to be seen as more than just a place to watch films. They wanted it to be more of a meeting place and a social venue. So we developed our snack bar into a licensed bar and offered a range of hot and cold meals. We thought we'd done well and we conducted customer surveys expecting they'd confirm what we thought. They didn't. Although the bar attracted new customers and the meals were popular, our cinema customers complained that the noise from the bar and the smell of the food was spoiling their enjoyment of the films. Additional soundproofing and more effective extractor fans solved the problem. But if we'd just assumed our*

DISCUSSION POINT

Think of a leisure and recreation organisation you know about. What sort of changes can you foresee in its markets? How might the organisation be affected and how might they respond positively to the changes?

perception of the level of customer satisfaction was right without checking it, we'd have lost a few of our cinema customers. 99

Managing the effects of change

All markets are subject to change. A key objective of marketing is to keep in close touch with their existing and potential markets. External factors like political, economic, social and technological changes also must be closely monitored. Keeping a continuous watch on all factors likely to result in change enables an organisation to respond to and anticipate changes. It puts them in a stronger position for dealing with the effects of change and gives them a head start in developing their products and services to keep pace with the changes in customer demands.

Managing the effects of competition

All organisations need to keep a close eye on what their competitors are doing and evaluate the effects of their competitors' activities on the market. The fiercer the competition, the more effort an organisation has to put in to differentiate itself from its competitors. A key marketing strategy for differentiation is known as the unique selling proposition (USP). The organisation defines what is unique about its products and services that makes them more attractive and beneficial than those of its competitors. The managing director of a gym explains how they used their USP to hold on to their customers when a new competitor entered the market:

66 *Six months ago, a new gym opened in the town. Its membership fees were 10% cheaper than ours were and it offered a wider range of exercise facilities. We saw that as a serious threat to our business. We couldn't afford to drop our fees without affecting the quality of the products and services we offered and, besides, we'd spent eight years building up the business to provide quality rather than quantity. That gave us our answer. In comparison with our new, cheaper and more diverse competitor, our USP was experience, quality and specialisation. So we focused on these aspects in our promotion and highlighted the additional benefits customers got from us – like the café and the crèche which our higher prices enabled us to provide. It worked: we gained more customers than we lost.* 99

Coordinating activities

Marketing involves the whole organisation, from the directors who decide on the organisation's objectives to the staff who deliver the products and services to the customer. This means that everything an organisation does must be geared towards achieving its aims in a professional and effective way. Everybody in the organisation needs to have a clear idea of what the organisation is aiming to do and make sure that their work contributes.

Maximising income

Maximising income is the result of carefully targeted spending. Everything an organisation does will cost them money so it needs to ensure that the money will be recouped from the income gained by selling its products and services.

A marketing consultant explains the principle:

66 *It doesn't matter if you're generating a huge income or a modest one – it's being able to use it effectively that matters. It involves ensuring cost-effectiveness, planning and targeting spending and keeping within your budgets.* 99

Making a profit

To make a profit, an organisation needs to make sure that its income is greater than its expenditure. The amount of profit an organisation wants to make will be part of its business plan. All its marketing activities will be directed towards making the plan a reality.

Improving people's lives

In the 1960s, the American marketer Theodore Levitt stated that people don't buy drills, they buy holes. The hole is what they want, the drill is the thing that gives them what they want. So the benefit of buying the drill is that they can use it to make the holes they want. Effective marketing always promotes the benefits the product or service provides. This is particularly true of the leisure and recreation industry. For example, people don't buy skis, they buy the benefits the skis will give them – relaxation, a new experience, fun, adventure and so on.

Improving people's opinion of a product or service

All organisations work hard at presenting a positive image of themselves and their products and services. Marketing is the means of presenting an organisation's image, raising awareness of what it has to offer and encouraging customers to see the benefits they can gain by having the product or using the services.

The marketing plan

The marketing plan is an important document in any organisation. It:

■ summarises what the organisation aims to achieve by selling its products and services

■ identifies and explains the marketing activities that will help achieve those aims.

The first step in developing a marketing plan is to identify the organisation's objectives. What it is trying to achieve in the long term will affect the type of marketing activities it carries out.

Listed below are some typical leisure and recreation facilities. For each one, state the benefits its products or services offer the customer.

- a theatre
- a swimming pool
- a tenpin bowling alley
- a heritage site
- a nature reserve
- a theme park

Leisure and recreation organisations usually have one or more of these three objectives:

- to succeed financially and make a profit
- to help the community by providing facilities and events for local people to use
- to develop their business and grow (this is often linked to making a profit).

DISCUSSION POINT

What do you think would be the objectives (one or more) of these leisure and recreation organisations?

- an old people's club which runs activities in a local hall
- an out-of-town multiplex cinema
- a local authority leisure centre operating under competitive tendering
- a national hotel chain

A marketing consultant explains how objectives affect an organisation's marketing activities:

❝ If the organisation's objective is to increase profits, its marketing activities will focus on increasing sales by selling more to its existing market and finding new markets for its existing products and services. Its promotional activities will be directed at keeping existing customers and attracting new ones.

If an organisation's objective is to provide a community benefit, its marketing activities will focus on raising public awareness, encouraging people to make use of the products and services and encouraging funding bodies to provide financial support. Its promotional activities will be directed at publicising its activities, informing the public of the issues and highlighting the social or cultural benefits that the products or services offer.

If an organisation's objective is growth, its marketing activities will focus on finding new markets for its existing products and services and creating new products and services that will get it into a new or different market. Its promotional activities will be directed at launching the organisation into new markets and launching new products and services.

Whatever the objectives, marketing activities will always include continuous market research to identify and anticipate the needs of the markets the organisation wants to be in. ❞

Talk to the marketing manager of a local leisure and recreation facility about the organisation's objectives. How do they influence the marketing activities which the organisation carries out? Does the organisation's marketing plan include a description of objectives?

UNIT

4

SECTION **4.1**

Writing objectives

Good marketing plans have clear objectives, which state exactly what an organisation hopes to achieve through its marketing activities. The organisation can then use these objectives to evaluate different activities by looking at:

- how far objectives have been achieved
- whether objectives need to be reviewed and amended
- what new objectives may have been created.

Adding 'how' and 'why' to an objective helps organisations decide what marketing activities to carry out, and then makes it easier to evaluate whether they have been successful.

Objective	How	Why
To analyse market needs	Identify customers' needs and wants through primary and secondary research	To change existing or develop new products or services to meet customers' needs
To satisfy customer requirements	Deliver the goods or services which customers need and want	To increase the likelihood of repeat business and maintain or improve current levels of business
To manage the effects of competition	Maintain market share by promoting products and services	To keep market position
To manage the effects of change	Through public relations	To minimise the bad effects that change may have on the market
To coordinate marketing	Provide marketing information to staff involved in the delivery of products and services to customers	To ensure that staff are aware of developments in the market which may affect their ability to deliver a quality service and provide cost-effective marketing
To maximise income and generate profit	Develop and implement pricing and sales strategies	To ensure the continuing survival and profitability of the organisation
To generate community benefit	Provide or sponsor services which offer a direct social or cultural benefit to the community but which are not necessarily profitable	To create goodwill in a competitive and changing environment and to ensure that customers are not deprived of leisure and recreation products or services because of disadvantage, disability or discrimination
To help customers see the product in the best possible way	Run special promotions emphasising quality and value for money	To maintain or improve levels of sales in the long term

Melanie is head of marketing for a large entertainment venue which puts on events ranging from rock concerts to opera, Shakespearean plays to alternative comedians. She is responsible for:

- the box office – where tickets are sold, information is available and publicity material displayed
- front-of-house staff – including stewards who check tickets and sell programmes at events
- promotion and publicity officers – who deal with the press, write promotional material, and so on
- customer service staff – who answer customers' queries, problems and complaints
- a team of distributors – who deliver leaflets, put up posters, and so on.

Melanie tells all her staff that they contribute directly to marketing the venue. They help to promote events, have contact with customers, and provide direct customer care. She also says they are great sources of information about what customers want, think and feel – information which is fed back into the department's research into the market.

Melanie is convinced that she also needs to involve staff from other areas of the organisation in marketing activities. This includes the financial, catering and technical (backstage) staff, as she feels their work has an important effect on whether the venue meets customers' needs.

ACTIVITY

Look through the different objectives given at the start of this section. Choose three that you think would interest Melanie. Why would these interest her so much? How should she try to achieve them? Make notes on your ideas and discuss them with one or two other people.

4.1.3 **Analysing internal influences on the business environment**

DISCUSSION POINT

Think of the sector of the leisure and recreation industry that you'd most like to work in. What sort of opportunities and threats do you think exist for that sector? What sort of strengths do you think are needed by organisations operating in that sector of the industry?

Companies must have a good understanding of the market in which they operate so that they can target their marketing activities well.

Most organisations analyse the marketing environment by carrying out a 'SWOT' analysis of:

■ Strengths – what the organisation is good at, the skills and expertise they have, successful business activities

■ Weaknesses – where necessary skills and expertise are missing, unsuccessful business activities

■ Opportunities – new markets, new needs in existing markets

■ Threats – competitors, shrinking markets.

The results of a SWOT analysis show an organisation:

■ strong areas to build on

■ weak areas to overcome or eliminate

■ opportunities to take advantage of

■ threats to guard against, or convert to an opportunity.

ACTIVITY

A friend already runs one popular gym, and is thinking about opening up another in a nearby town. She has asked you to analyse the marketing environment by carrying out a SWOT analysis. She gives you the following information:

■ Membership of her existing gym has doubled in the past year, and it's clear that fitness training is very popular, with young people in particular.

■ There is already one gym in the town. It is very busy and customers have complained that they have to queue to use equipment. It is located on the outskirts of town. Women have said that the facilities and classes for them are inadequate.

■ There are still a couple of empty sites in a new shopping centre which has opened. One would convert well into a gym.

■ A tennis club in the town is also building a gym complex for its members.

■ Several new retirement homes are being built in the town, and the area is developing a reputation as being for older people.

Use this information to carry out a SWOT analysis, and recommend what your friend should do.

ACTIVITY

A squash and badminton club is preparing its marketing plan for the year. The club is run on a voluntary basis, and its main aim is to provide facilities and events for the local community. However, it also needs to make enough money to cover its costs. The club's committee has carried out a SWOT analysis of the marketing environment, which identified the opening of a new leisure centre as a threat, but showed that the club still has plenty of strengths and opportunities it can make the most of. The committee thinks it should investigate the possibility of offering new products and services to meet customer's needs.

What do you think the club's marketing objectives are? Which should the club include in its marketing plan? Suggest three ways you think the club could work towards achieving these objectives.

A dance studio prepared the following SWOT to analyse their marketing environment and to look for ways to hold on to existing customers and find new ones.

■ **Strengths**

a good team of fully qualified dance instructors

dance classes are consistently popular and well-known forms of exercise

school-age children make up a large and consistent segment of the market

■ **Weaknesses**

dance is perceived as too technical and too demanding for some people

dance is perceived as girls-only activity

■ **Opportunities**

an untapped market amongst older women and males of all ages

■ **Threats**

competition from local fitness centres offering dance aerobics and other forms of dance-based exercise

On the basis of the SWOT, the owners of the studio decided on the following marketing objectives:

■ to raise awareness of the benefits of dance
■ to dispel the myth that dance was only for girls
■ to increase the number of older and male customers.

They decided to run the following promotional activities:

■ adverts in the local press
■ posters in local schools, youth centres, the library
■ dance displays in local schools.

All the promotional activities would present a fun image of dance. The press adverts would be used to send the message that dance can be enjoyed by all age groups and both sexes. The posters in the schools and youth centres would be aimed at young people. The poster in the library would be aimed at all age groups.

4.1.4 **Analysing the external influences on the market**

The products and services a leisure and recreation company offers – and the way it markets them – can be influenced by factors outside the industry. Organisations need to analyse the whole marketing environment in order to market their products and services well. To do this, they consider a range of different factors, or 'environments'.

Environment	Possible influences
Political	Changes in international, national and local governments, policies and legislation
Economic	Effect of factors such as unemployment, rises or falls in taxation, the cost of living, interest rates and so on
Social	Changes in local or national population (e.g. growing numbers of retired people), fashions, lifestyles and cultures
Technological	Effect of new technology on how organisations operate and on people's buying habits

This type of marketing environment analysis is known as a 'PEST' or 'STEP' analysis – an acronym using the first letters of the four factors listed in the box.

ACTIVITY

Think of any leisure and recreation organisation. Do a PEST analysis of the changes outside the organisation that might influence the products or services it offers. What benefits might come from these changes? What problems might they create?

4.1.5 Analysing the needs of customers

Think of a time when you've
been:

- satisfied with an
  organisation's products and
  services
- dissatisfied with an
  organisation's products and
  services.

What was your opinion of the
organisation in each case?

One of the main aims of marketing is to make sure that customers are
satisfied.

The marketing manager of a fitness centre sums up the importance of
satisfying customers:

66 *Good customer care encourages repeat business – if customers are
satisfied, they are likely to buy the product or use the service again. That means
you stay in business. They're also likely to recommend you to their friends. So
that means you could increase your business. If customers aren't satisfied,
they'll look around for an organisation that can satisfy them. That means you'll
lose business – and your loss is your competitor's gain.* 99

Analysing and targeting markets

To meet customer needs and wants, organisations have to:

- know who their customers are
- target marketing activity towards them.

This means analysing the markets carefully. For example, one technique that
is often used is called segmentation. This is simply the process of assessing
customers by such factors as age, social class, income and lifestyle. This
allows an organisation to direct its efforts towards those people who are
most likely to want its goods or services. So, a company would direct its
advertising of a pop concert at young people rather than the elderly. In this
case, young people are the market segment at which the product is aimed.

Market analysis

- By segmentation – classifying potential customers according to what
  segment of the market they fall into. This is done by assessing factors
  such as age, social class, income and lifestyle. By classifying
  customers in this way, products, services and marketing activity can be
  geared towards a particular market segment.

- By looking at the competition – finding out what products and services
  competitors provide, which customers they aim for, what gaps there
  are in the markets.

- By targeting – focusing marketing activity on particular clients or
  groups of clients. This helps ensure that promotional time and money
  is spent attracting the right customers.

- By positioning – the part of the market the organisation aims to occupy
  in relation to the market position of its competitors.

Influencing buyers' decisions

People buy products or services for many different reasons. Marketing identifies:

■ why people want to buy products or services

■ who decides what to buy (for example, in families and organisations).

The behaviour of buyers changes as their lifestyles change. For example, as people get older their needs, wants, income, likes and dislikes change – all of which affect the decisions they make about what they buy. So a teenager and an elderly person are likely to want very different things from a holiday.

Effective marketing makes use of what motivates people to buy products and services.

> What motivates people to buy leisure and recreation products and services?
>
> ■ safety and security – e.g. martial arts classes for young women
>
> ■ health and well-being – e.g. saunas, fitness clubs, sports centres
>
> ■ exclusivity – e.g. membership of a private golf club
>
> ■ peer group status – e.g. designer-label sports clothing
>
> ■ value for money – e.g. family membership of a leisure centre.

Customers usually go through several stages, shown in the chart on the left, when deciding whether to buy a product or service, or choosing which one to buy. Their final decision will be based on which option best meets their needs.

ACTIVITY

Think of a purchase you've made recently. List the steps you went through in making your purchase and the factors which influenced you at each step.

Compare different products or services

Look for more information or advice about them

Ask questions about them

Talk to their family or friends

Decide to buy the product or service they like best.

4.1.6 Evaluating marketing

Evaluation tells you how successful you've been in achieving your objectives. It also gives you an opportunity to analyse what went well and what went less well, so that you know what to do and what not to do next time.

Evaluation techniques

There are two common evaluation techniques:

- comparison
- surveys.

Comparisons are useful when your objective can be measured by quantities, like increasing sales or bringing in new business. The important thing to do when making comparisons is to compare like with like. For example:

- sales figures for the month following the promotion with sales figures for the month preceding the promotion
- proportion of first-time buyers amongst all buyers.

Comparisons rely on the consistency and accuracy of record-keeping methods.

Surveys are useful for collecting quantitative measures, but they can also be used to get qualitative information – that is, information based on feelings, attitudes and perceptions rather than just numbers. A survey would be a good way to evaluate how successful an organisation had been in activities to raise people's awareness, influence people's opinions or promote a cause.

It's often useful to use both strategies – for example, to compare current figures with past figures then use a survey to test the validity of any conclusions the figures suggest.

Evaluation criteria

A **criterion** is a set standard (the plural form of criterion is criteria – one criterion, several criteria)

To evaluate something, you need to have some way of measuring performance. Evaluation criteria provide those measures. The clearer the measures, the easier it is to show how well an activity has been performed. Evaluation criteria always relate to the objective and set the parameters for performance in specific terms of quantity or quality. For example, if your objective is to eat 40 biscuits in half an hour without leaving any mess, the criteria would be:

- the number of biscuits
- the timescale
- the tidiness of the area after you've eaten the biscuits.

The first two are quantitative criteria – they can be assessed by numerical measures. The third is a qualitative criterion – it can be assessed in terms of quality.

ACTIVITY

Why is evaluation important? What does it achieve?

191

ACTIVITY

For each of the following, describe the evaluation criteria you would use. Say whether your measures would be quantitative, qualitative or a combination of both and explain why.

■ a promotion aimed at increasing membership of a health and fitness club

■ an advertising campaign using the national press and television to raise awareness of the benefits of keeping fit

■ a launch of a new product to existing customers

■ a strategy for attracting customers away from your competitors

Common marketing criteria

■ Volume of sales — The number of sales achieved in a given period. Useful for judging if business has increased and for judging the success of promotional activities.

■ Repeat business — The number of customers who buy the product or service again. Useful for judging the hold on market share.

■ New business — The number of first-time buyers for a product or service. Useful for judging an increase in market share and growth.

■ Brand loyalty — The number of customers who choose the organisation's products or services in preference to similar ones produced by competitors. Useful for judging the hold on market share.

■ Customer loyalty — The number of people who buy from the organisation because they trust its reputation. Useful for judging perception of an organisation's image and the quality of products and services.

■ Public awareness — The level of recognition of or familiarity with an organisation's products, services, activities, name and image. Useful for judging market share and effectiveness of promotional activities.

■ Market share — The proportion of the total number of customers in a market who buy from the organisation. Useful for judging competitiveness and growth.

■ Keeping within the budget — Implementing the marketing plan within a set budget. Useful for judging staff performance, cost-effectiveness, marketing methods and processes and the levels of funding being allocated.

Key questions

1   What do all marketing activities aim to provide?

2   Why is marketing important to the leisure and recreation industry?

3   What is the purpose of a marketing plan?

4   What is a SWOT analysis?

5   What is a PEST analysis?

6   What is market segmentation?

7   What is achieved by evaluating marketing? List two evaluation techniques and explain why they are useful.

SECTION **4.2**

The marketing mix

Marketing is the result of hard work and creativity. The term 'marketing mix' is used to describe the key elements that an organisation offers in order to meet its customers needs and expectations. This section will help you to understand how each element of the marketing mix is developed and how they all interact.

66 *My job is to liaise with the press and other media, both nationally and locally. I write and send out press releases and arrange press interviews. I set up photo opportunities, try to encourage press interest in all the acts we have appearing and liaise with promoters. I'm also responsible for arranging posters and photos to be available. Sometimes I arrange competitions to increase interest in our productions. when we were putting on an opera we got in touch with a local restaurant which had the same name as the opera and arranged for children to design a pizza. The winner's idea was then on the menu for the following week.* 99

press and publicity officer at an entertainments venue

4.2.1 Balancing the marketing mix

> The **marketing mix** is the combination of factors used to achieve marketing goals.

The components of the marketing mix are often called the Four Ps.

The Four Ps
- Product – establishing a product range, quality, level, name
- Place – selling products in the right places
- Price – selling the products at the right price
- Promotion – publicising the products in the right way and to the right people

The relationship and interaction between these four factors is critical in understanding an organisation's market aims and position. Applying the Four Ps to product strategy and marketing activities helps an organisation to:
- concentrate its resources in the right areas
- increase the likelihood of selling its products and services
- achieve customer satisfaction.

The marketing officer of a local authority sports hall explains:

66 We match the Four Ps to what we know about our customers – who they are, where they are, what they like. The right products are defined by what our customers want. The right price is what we know our customers are willing to pay. The right place is where we know our customers are and where our customers can make use of our products. The right promotion is the best way to make contact with our customers to let them know about our products. 99

Product
Product describes what an organisation offers to its customers, whether that's merchandise or service. It also includes the brand name and the after-sales service available through manufacturer's or extended warranties.

Leisure and recreation organisations develop new products and redevelop existing products all the time. For example:
- theme parks introduce new rides every year
- restaurants develop new menus
- cinemas run newly released films.

This constant process of developing and redeveloping products is an important part of meeting customer needs and maintaining quality.

Another way of marketing products is branding them to give them a clear identity and to raise customers' expectations. Many leisure and recreation organisations have strong brand identities: Adidas, Nike and many more. Building on these brands can help to ensure the success of products.

Leisure and recreation products include activities or experiences, such as a visit to a theme park or a film, or services, like information or guided tours round a country house.

Place

Place is the term used to describe how a product or service reaches the customer – available in the right place at the right time. It includes:

- the type of outlet or facility used by the organisation
- the location of the facility
- the distribution channels.

Type of outlet

Several aspects must be considered when choosing or designing a site for an organisation:

- The size of the building or space must be appropriate. For example, a successful shop may seek larger premises to accommodate both the increase in the number of customers and the increase in stock.
- The layout must satisfy the purpose it serves. For example a take-away restaurant will have the cash till near its entrance for quick and convenient payment. A gourmet restaurant, however, may place its cash till in a discreet area where it does not disturb the dining area.
- The cost of the premises. For example high street and prime shopping centre spaces cost significantly more to rent or buy than sites in less prominent areas such as ring roads or industrial estates.

Location

Getting the location right is a major step towards establishing a successful business. Many leisure and recreation facilities need to be located:

- in a place with good transport links
- close to where a large number of people (potential customers) live or work

For businesses like cinemas, theatres and restaurants this often means being in, or just outside, towns and cities. People are willing to travel further to reach attractions and accommodation where they spend time. But they still want an easy journey, and sites with good transport connections will have an advantage.

Distribution

Products often pass through two or three distribution channels before they reach the customer. For example, products sold in National Trust shops come from various sources – some from the Trust itself, others from different suppliers. Consumer goods also pass through the hands of wholesalers and retailers before they reach the customer.

Price

Price is the amount of money that a customer pays for the product or service. It includes the selling price as well as any credit terms that are part of the sales arrangement.

ACTIVITY

You are at the cinema on a Saturday night and decide to stop at the concession stand and buy a large box of popcorn. What distribution channels do you think the popcorn travelled through before it was sold to you? Produce a flow chart, using photographs or illustrations, to show how this distribution channel worked.

If customers feel that the product is fairly priced, they are more likely to buy it. So pricing is a key marketing decision and not an accounting responsibility.

ACTIVITY

Look through a magazine specialising in a leisure activity, for instance, a sports, music, or gardening magazine, and consider the advertisements.

How do the prices for similar products and services compare?

Do they offer special discounts, offers, or peak and off-peak rates?

Write a short summary of the pricing policies you observe in the magazine, explaining what they show you about the organisations' aims, the competition, and the demand for their products.

How do the leisure and recreation organisations decide the price of

HOW MUCH DOES IT ACTUALLY COST?
In order to make a profit, the organisation has to charge more for the product than it costs to produce.

WHAT ARE THE AIMS OF THE ORGANISATION?
Does the organisation aim to make a profit? or can it offer reduced prices for the benefit of the community?

WHAT PRICE SHALL WE CHARGE?

HOW MUCH DO COMPETITORS CHARGE?
If a competitor is charging half as much for a similar product, the organisation's product won't sell.

WHAT IS THE DEMAND FOR THE PRODUCT?
The number of people wanting to use facilities and buy products varies throughout the year. Organisations need to change the price of their products in line with this.

Leisure and recreation organisations use a range of pricing methods in different situations:

- peak and off-peak pricing – prices vary depending on the time of day or year, in line with the number of people wanting to use the facilities
- group and special discounts – discounts are reductions for parties of people or particular sections of the community; for example, special discounts or 'concessions' are often offered to pensioners, students and people with disabilities, so that they can afford to use facilities
- special offers – low prices offered on a temporary basis to attract people to use a facility or to encourage them to buy a particular product; for example, a tour operator might offer two-for-one price deals on short-break holidays.

Promotion

Once you have the right product, at the right price and in the right place, you need to promote it – let your customer know that it's there and waiting to be bought.

Leisure and recreation organisations use different promotional techniques, such as:

- advertising
- direct marketing
- public relations
- sales promotion
- sponsorship.

These techniques are examined in more detail in section 4.4.

ACTIVITY

Make a collection of 15 to 20 newspaper advertisements, magazine articles, letters and brochures promoting leisure and recreation products.

What is each item in your collection trying to do?

Is there any relationship between the aims of different promotional activities and the promotional methods used?

Promotion:
- tells or reminds customers of the products and services on offer
- raises the profile of a product – and makes people want to buy it
- influences customers to choose one product rather than its rivals
- provides incentives for customers to buy or use particular products.

4.2.2 **Growth through market share**

The marketing mix will be affected by an organisation's market share. This is the percentage of customers in a market who choose your products and services. There are two ways that an organisation can increase its market share:

■ by attracting customers away from competing organisations
■ by picking up customers from organisations who have moved out of the market.

The marketing director of a council-funded sports centre explains how they increased their share of the local leisure and recreation market:

66 *With the increasing popularity of fitness as a recreational activity, our centre was in danger of losing its customers to two new private sector fitness centres in the area. We identified that we had a market advantage because our public funding meant we could offer low membership and concessionary fees. So we promoted that aspect heavily. As a result, our membership has gone up and our share of the local market has increased from 28% to 35%.* 99

Ansoff's matrix

Ansoff's Matrix was developed by Igor Ansoff. It is a tool for identifying ways an organisation can grow through increasing sales. The options are:

■ sell more existing products or services to existing customers (i.e. getting further into the market – market penetration)

■ sell existing products or services to new customers (i.e. expanding existing markets or getting into new ones – market development)

■ develop new products or services to sell to existing customers (product development)

■ develop new products or services to sell to new customers (developing new products for new markets – diversification).

Organisations can use Ansoff's Matrix to ask:

■ Will existing customers continue to buy existing products?

■ Can the existing products attract new customers?

■ Will new products appeal to existing customers?

■ Will new products have to attract new customers?

■ Can the existing and new products both be marketed to existing customers?

■ Can the existing and new products both be marketed to new customers?

■ Will any of the above strategies increase the market share?

■ Can the existing products or services be sold by targeting a different group of customers?

Ansoff's Matrix

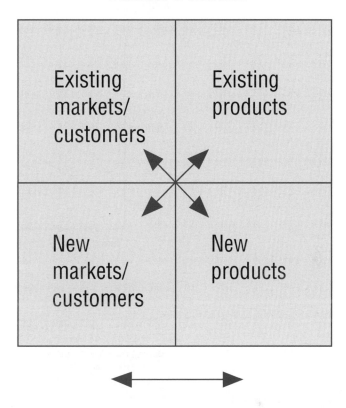

Answers to these questions will help them to decide whether marketing activity should be customer-focused or product-oriented:

- If the market is saturated, i.e. no new business is being generated, they will need to consider new markets.

- If there is no scope for growth in new markets, they will need to focus on new products.

Product life-cycle

Most products and services have a limited lifespan. There are many reasons for this, including changes in fashion and technology that can quickly make a product obsolete.

Products and services often go through a five-stage cycle, as shown in the graph.

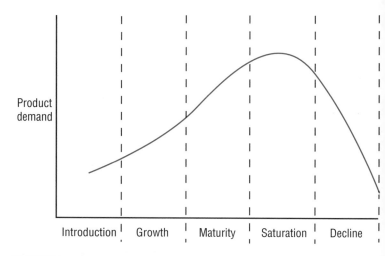

Introduction:	Low initial sales until product or service awareness develops.
Growth:	Steady, sometimes rapid, increase in sales as demand increases.
Maturity:	Sales continue to increase but at a slower rate, as the market for the product is fully targeted.
Saturation:	All customers needs and wants for the product are satisfied.
Decline:	Sales of product decline as the popularity of the product decreases.

The strategies adopted to promote them will vary according to which point in the life-cycle they have reached. A sportswear manufacturer comments:

66 *We put a lot of promotion effort into a product as it is introduced, including things like special offers, promotional events and an advertising campaign.*

As the product matures, our aim is to maintain a high profile in the market and ensure that as many potential customers as possible are being reached, for example through targeted direct mail or selective advertising.

As the product nears the end of its life-cycle, we cut down promotional activity and change focus, perhaps offering reduced prices or special terms to milk the last few sales out of the product. 99

The Boston matrix

The Boston matrix is used to assess where products are within the product life-cycle.

Different types of product or service produce different levels of income for organisations. They are classified according to their position, in terms of relative market share and how quickly the market is growing:

- **star** – high share in a growth market
- **problem child** – a product in a growing market but with a low market share
- **cash cow** – large market share in a mature market
- **dog** – weak in market share, or in a declining market

The Boston Matrix

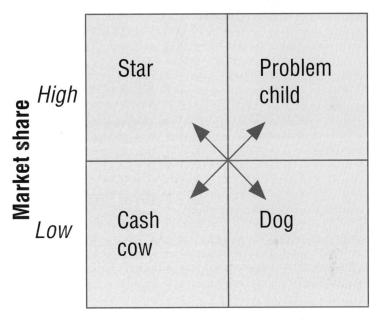

Pricing products and services – deciding what price to sell them for – is an important part of marketing. If an organisation charges too much, people will buy competitors' cheaper products; if it charges too little, it won't make a profit.

Using the case study on the right as a model, select two nationally known leisure and recreation organisations and write a short report on their marketing activities. Your report should identify their marketing activities, objectives and pricing policies, and investigate how they achieved growth.

Virgin is a company owned by Richard Branson. He started as a sole trader, and since then the business has grown into one of the world's leading leisure organisations with interests in entertainment, travel, catering, publishing and broadcasting.

Key features of Virgin's marketing activities.

- Most, although not all, Virgin products are branded.
- The product range of Virgin follows a reasonable, logical sequence of diversification.
- The products are marketed both internally and externally (e.g. Virgin drinks are available on Virgin Airlines and in Virgin pubs).
- Virgin is a high-profile sponsor of national and community events and voluntary causes.
- The organisation has an effective public relations division which succeeds in placing Virgin or Richard Branson in the news.
- Virgin products are widely merchandised through special promotions at point-of-sale (T-shirts and baseball caps).
- The market segmentation of Virgin products is targeted primarily at teenagers and young professionals.
- Pricing is geared towards achieving mass-market penetration by undercutting the prices of Virgin's main competitors.

Key questions

1 What do you think is the most important element in marketing: the customer, the organisation, or the product or service being offered?

2 Which elements make up the marketing mix? Why are they important?

3 In what ways does the status of an organisation (profit-making/not-for-profit) influence or determine the sort of marketing activities it undertakes?

4 How does Ansoff's matrix analyse product development?

5 What are the five stages in a product's life-cycle?

6 How does the Boston matrix assess where products are within their life-cycle?

SECTION **4.3**

Market research

A crucial aspect of any organisation's marketing activity is the understanding of customers' needs and their reaction to products and services. This section will help you to understand the complex processes of market research, which is the gathering of information about customers and its use for management purposes.

> *We carry out market research in schools to find out what children like and want. Provision for children can actually be difficult to get right because what they want tends to change within the space of six months. It is clear that the media influences them – at the moment a lot of basketball is being shown on Sky TV and is very popular with the children.*
>
> community play officer in a local authority

> *Our target market is really everybody in the community. One of the ways we carry out marketing research is to develop a 'ticketing history' which allows us to see what has sold well and who likes coming to what. We have also distributed questionnaires to selected audiences to see what people thought about ticket prices, whether they liked the shows we were offering and what they thought about the venue.*
>
> press and publicity officer in an entertainments venue

4.3.1 **The elements of market research**

Organisations carry out marketing research to find out as much as they can about the customers they want to sell to. Through market research they identify:

- what markets exist
- the characteristics of potential markets
- market trends and changes
- opportunities for market and product development
- promotion opportunities and the effectiveness of promotions
- who their competitors are and what they are doing.

The information they gather helps them to make sure that they're offering:

- the right product or service
- to the right people
- at the right price
- in the right place.

A marketing consultant made this comment on the importance of market research and the cost of not doing it:

66 *Some organisations think that market research is too costly. Their approach is to use their money to develop products or services they think are good ideas and then try and find customers who agree with them. If they can't find enough customers, they're not going to sell enough products or services to be profitable or even to cover their costs. And nothing is as expensive as making a product or providing a service that nobody wants to buy.* 99

Marketing research tries to predict the future from research and analysis of the present and the past. There are three main components to marketing research:

- identifying your potential customers – which involves classifying your customers into key segments (e.g. socio-economic group, age, income levels); this is called segmentation
- primary research (also known as field research) – this involves direct contact with current and potential customers, and it is usually based on questioning or direct observation of customers
- secondary research (also known as desk research) – this involves analysing data about customers from different sources; it is usually used to identify and predict market trends based on statistics.

Segmentation

Organisations make good use of government statistics about social data which help them to classify potential customers according to what segment of the market they fall into. This is done by assessing factors such as age, social class, income and lifestyle. By classifying customers in this way, products, services and marketing activity can be geared towards a particular market segment.

Social Trends has been published annually by the Central Statistical Office since 1970. It draws together statistics from a wide range of government departments.

The main sources are:

- *Social Trends*
- National Statistical Office (*http://www.ons.gov.uk*).

Secondary marketing research

When producing a marketing plan, organisations need to decide whether they are going to use:

- internal secondary data sources – information collected from inside the organisation, such as visitor records
- external secondary data sources – information collected from other organisations, such as national statistics.

The marketing manager of a theatre explains:

> 66 *It's important to decide from the start what marketing research methods you're going to use, otherwise you tend to waste a lot of time. That's why we always state what research methods we're going to use in our marketing plan. Our latest plan concentrates on secondary marketing research using a combination of information provided by our box office on ticket sales, where customers live, our 'friends of the theatre' scheme; and data on national leisure trends published by leisure organisations. External data helps to give us the wider picture, while internal information gives us the current state of play.* 99

DISCUSSION POINT

Why do you think that organisations might waste a lot of time if they didn't plan their marketing research activities carefully?

Primary marketing research

A plan for carrying out primary marketing research might include:

- qualitative research – looking in depth at customers' needs, wants and attitudes; this usually involves asking customers to fill in a questionnaire, or interviewing them
- quantitative research – providing results which can be measured as statistics; this usually involves counting customers and watching the way they behave
- interviews – with individuals or groups
- surveys – face-to-face, over the telephone or in writing; these often involve questionnaires
- observation – counting people and watching the way they behave
- experiment – carrying out experimental trials by asking customers questions about a product or service, its price, packaging, and so on.

The plan should also say how the organisation is going to contact its customers to carry out primary marketing research. This may be:

- by mail – using mailshots to send out questionnaires to a large group of people
- by telephone – ringing up customers and asking them questions
- personal contact – speaking to people face to face.

ACTIVITY

Imagine you are the marketing manager of an entertainments venue. You want to find out more about the needs of customers in the 16 to 21 age range. Write a short section for the venue's marketing plan, explaining what primary marketing research methods you will use and how you will contact customers.

4.3.2 Sources of secondary marketing research

There are two main types of marketing research data collected from secondary sources:

- **internal** data – information collected from inside the organisation, such as visitor records
- **external** data – information collected from other organisations, such as national statistics on the number of foreign visitors coming to the UK.

Internal sources of secondary marketing research data

Most organisations working in leisure and recreation collect information about their customers and service users from:

- sales records
- occupancy/usage figures
- financial information
- the customers themselves.

This information may be collected by one department in an organisation and used by another. For example, the marketing department may use financial data collected by the accounts department. Because of this, people involved in marketing often have to work closely with other departments to collect and interpret information.

To be useful, data must be:

- relevant – to the subject area, to the research objectives, to the time period
- accessible – easy to get hold of, easy to understand, easy to share.

Sales records

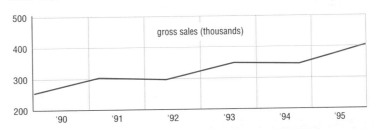

These are usually presented as a graph showing sales over a period of time. Leisure and recreation organisations use sales records as part of marketing research to spot trends and seasonal variations in sales.

Occupancy and usage figures

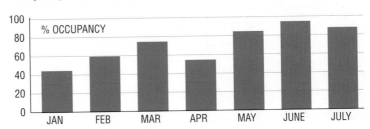

207

Hotels and leisure facilities such as sports centres use occupancy and usage figures as a source of secondary marketing research data. They use these figures to work out when they are likely to be busy and, more importantly, when they have space for more customers. Occupancy and usage figures are measured by time and capacity.

Financial information

Leisure and recreation organisations use financial data in secondary marketing research to find out:

- overall sales
- growth or fall in sales of particular products and services
- the profitability of different products and services.

Customer databases

Customer databases are made up of information collected in many different ways. For example, customers may fill in membership application forms or complete booking forms for events/holidays, or they may supply information in surveys. This information is then stored in a database, which organisations can use to find out marketing research data such as where customers live, their age, sex, income, and preferred activities (what, when, where and how often).

Personal details kept on computer for future quick checking in and mailshot →

Details for help with target marketing in promotions and mailshot →

For safety and security →

Customer history tells us what sort of break and price bracket these guests fall into – which helps with mailshot and future promotions →

A) For customer convenience. Already on file helping with quick and easy payment.
B) For hotel security against bad debtors
Helpful not to make the same mistake twice →

CUSTOMER DETAILS	
NAME:	MR. B. FARREL
ADDRESS:	2 HONEYWOOD RD
	MUNFORD THETFORD
PHONE:	01589 333125
OCCUPATION:	SALES REP
AGE:	33
MARITAL STATUS:	MARRIED
CHILDREN:	3
CAR REG:	M859 22Q

HISTORY:

1. 24.12.98 – 1.1.99 'CHRISTMAS BREAK' £760.00 PER ROOM, ALL INCLUSIVE PACKAGE 2 ADULTS, 2 CHILDREN.
2. 1.4.99 ONE NIGHT £110 FOR ROOM, NOT INCLUSIVE

CREDIT CARD NO: 4039 7920 7991 9134

COMMENTS / COMPLAINTS

If you prefer to pay by cheque, please put your Booking Reference Number on the back to ensure it is correctly attributed to your holiday and ensure it is fully completed before posting.

Data Protection: 'Summerside Holidays' may forward your name and address to other reputable companies whose products and services may be of interest to you. Please tick here if you do not wish to receive information from these companies. ☐

I am over 18 years of age, I have read the Booking Conditions and agree to be bound by them.

Signed _____ Date _____

External sources of secondary marketing research data

To get a clear picture of what is happening in the marketplace as a whole, organisations use data from external sources as well as internal data.

Government publications

The government publishes a wide range of data which can help leisure and recreation organisations decide how to meet their customers' needs and wants. This is collected from many different sources, including:

- population census returns
- household surveys
- industry surveys
- information provided by government departments.

Useful government publications include:
- *Annual Abstract of Statistics*
- *The British Household Survey*
- *The Employment Gazette*
- *Social Trends.*

Professional organisations, trade journals and periodicals

There are a number of leisure and recreation associations – professional organisations – which play an important role in the industry. They provide information, promote training, and speak on behalf of the industry.

 ILAM (Institute of Leisure and Amenity Management) is a professional body which encourages professionalism through the endorsement and development of career paths and qualifications within the sports, leisure and recreation industries. Its particular focus is at management level.

They also produce and contribute to publications – trade journals and periodicals – which are an important source of secondary marketing research data for leisure and recreation organisations. These give information about new products, services, competition, trends, and general developments in the industry.

Useful trade journals and periodicals include:

- *Campaign*
- *Countryside Commission News*
- *Floodlight*
- *Journal of Leisure Research*
- *Leisure Management*
- *Leisure Studies*
- *Marketing Weekly*
- *The Caterer.*

National organisations

Government-funded organisations – such as the Sports Council, English
Heritage and other national heritage bodies – also publish useful data about
leisure and recreation markets.

Commercial data

Some companies specialise in collecting information and passing it on to
organisations to use for marketing research. These include cuttings services,
which collect articles and reports on the industry from national, regional and
local newspapers.

Other external sources

- national, regional and local newspapers
- on-line databases, which provide statistical information using computer
  technology
- annual and financial reports published by organisations
- opinion polls
- reference libraries

4.3.3 Primary marketing research methods

Organisations usually carry out primary marketing research by talking to the
people who buy their products or services – the consumers. Primary
marketing research gives organisations a clearer picture of their customers'
needs, preferences, attitudes and feelings.

Leisure and recreation organisations use a range of different methods to
collect primary marketing research data.

Sampling

Sampling is the process of selecting a small part of any leisure and recreation
market and taking their views as representative of the whole. For example, a
leisure centre manager who wanted to find out what customers thought
about a new reception area used sampling:

❝ *We'd been having complaints about the amount of time it took to book in and long queues were forming at busy times. So we reorganised the whole area, separating out the booking facilities from general services. Customers were certainly going through faster but I wanted to know if they had any other problems. It would have been very time consuming talking to every customer! So we simply decided to interview every twentieth person and hoped that the sample would reflect people's views generally.* ❞

Opinion polls

Opinion polls are a good example of large-scale sampling. The two largest organisations in the country producing opinion polls are Gallup and MORI. Both carry out polls for private companies, and also run opinion polls on public events such as general elections. Gallup and MORI interview thousands of different people and ask them questions about particular products and services.

Qualitative and quantitative research

Primary marketing research is either qualitative or quantitative.

- **Qualitative** marketing research looks in depth at consumers' feelings, desires and views. Organisations usually carry out qualitative research by asking customers to fill in a questionnaire, or by interviewing them. It provides useful information on customers' needs, wants and attitudes.
- **Quantitative** marketing research is more formal and structured than qualitative research, and the results can be measured as statistics. Organisations usually carry out quantitative research by watching and counting the number of customers behaving in a particular way, and then producing statistical data from these numbers. For example, a football club would use quantitative research to find out how many spectators are at a football match.

Interviews

Interviews – with individuals and groups – are one of the most common ways to collect primary data. Marketing research interviewers ask two main types of questions:

- **closed questions** – these can either be answered 'yes' or 'no', or the interviewee can choose an answer from a list of options; interviewers use closed questions to collect quantitative data.
- **open questions** – these allow customers to talk freely and express an opinion in their own words; interviewers use open questions to collect qualitative data.

Surveys

Surveys – often involving questionnaires – are another way that leisure and recreation organisations find out customers' views on their products and services. Surveys may be carried out face-to-face, over the telephone, or in writing.

A marketing researcher who was asked to sample 100 customers at a museum to find out their views on a new exhibition hall explains his approach:

66 *The first question I asked was: 'Do you like the new exhibition hall?' Of the 100 customers, 63 said 'yes' and 37 said 'no'. This gave me the qualitative evidence that most customers liked the hall, but a significant proportion didn't. I then asked two further questions: 'What is it that you particularly like about the exhibition area?' and 'What do you particularly dislike?'*

These questions enabled customers to give a qualitative opinion about the design and layout of the facility. I found out that those who disliked the hall thought the lighting was too bright, and as a result the brightness of the lighting was reduced by 10%. A month later I repeated the survey, and 90% of those interviewed said that they liked the exhibition hall. **99**

Guidelines for writing questionnaires

- Set an overall limit for length. How long do you want your questionnaire to be? Remember that you want to encourage customers to fill it in and not be put off.

- Decide whether you are going to ask open questions, closed questions, or a mixture of the two.

- Think about how to organise and number the questions. A clear numbering system will not only make the questionnaire easy to follow; it may help you organise your questions into topics. You can then present your findings using the same numbered headings.

- Decide on layout. How will you make your questionnaire attractive and easy to use? Your design will be affected by how much space you need to leave for answers, whether you want to use boxes, and so on.

- Think about how you will use the questionnaire. What sampling method will you use to select the people to survey?

- Avoid leading questions – that is, a question which contains a prompt for the expected answer, for example, 'You do like the exhibition hall, don't you?'

Observation

Carrying out marketing research by watching and counting people – observation – is useful if organisations need to collect data quickly, but don't need to know what customers think. For example, a leisure centre might decide the best place to put a brochure rack by watching the way customers walk around the foyer.

ACTIVITY

Have you ever been asked to test a product and answer questions about it? For example, in a supermarket, have you ever tasted a new cheese, or new biscuits? Do you think your answers were useful for the company?

Experiments

Experimental trials – sometimes called market testing – are used to work out how successful new products might be.

In experimental trials, organisations ask customers a range of questions about a product or service, its packaging, price, and how it should be promoted. They then use these findings to work out how to promote the product or service.

4.3.4 **Contact methods**

Marketing researchers make contact with consumers in three main ways:
- by mail
- on the telephone
- face to face (personal contact).

Mail

Leisure and recreation organisations often use mailshots to carry out primary marketing research. This usually involves sending questionnaires either to a large number of households, or to people in a particular socio-economic, geographic or age group. It's a good way to gather quantitative information. The more carefully organisations choose their targets, the more likely they are to get a response and to get relevant information.

The disadvantages of using mail methods are:
- it's a one-way flow of information so if the response isn't clear you can't ask the person what they meant
- there's a lot of it about and people often regard mailshots as junk mail and put it straight in the bin.

To encourage people to fill in and return a mailshot, organisations often offer incentives, such as entering the names of people who reply in a prize draw, or giving them a reduction on products and services.

As well as generating primary research data, mailshots can give organisation useful information about their customers. They can then store this in a database and use it for future mailshots and promotional activities.

Telephone

Telephones are useful for gathering quantitative and qualitative information. They can be used in a number of ways, for example:

- as a first method of contact (also known as cold calling) when marketing researchers pick a number of targeted people and interview them over the phone
- as a follow-up method of contact when marketing researchers ask people who've taken part in a written questionnaire or responded to a mailshot to say if they'd be willing to take part in further research over the telephone
- as a follow-up to a sale or loss of sale to find out why the person has chosen to buy or not buy the product or service.

The advantages of using the phone

- It's direct.
- It's personal contact.
- It can't be thrown in the bin unanswered like a mailshot can.
- It allows an immediate two-way flow of communication.

The disadvantages

- Finding the right people to talk to and the right time to call them can be time-consuming.
- People are sometimes guarded because they suspect you might be trying to sell them something.
- It may use time from the person's working day.
- Callers need training to ensure that they get the relevant information from what people say and to keep the conversation on track.

Personal contact

Although marketing researchers can usually collect very useful information if they speak to customers face to face, this is not always possible. Samples are often too large for everyone to be interviewed individually, and one-to-one surveys are time-consuming and expensive. Many leisure and recreation companies are now replacing personal contact with telephone research, and are exploring electronic methods such as e-mail.

A large sports and leisure shop publishes a magazine which it mails free to all customers on its database. The shop collects the names, addresses and telephone numbers of customers when they buy products under guarantee.

The magazine contains some articles of general leisure interest, and others about new products and services. After it has been sent out to customers, researchers telephone a sample of customers and ask them questions about the magazine. They then look closely at the data they collect and develop future marketing plans.

How marketing research contributes to marketing decisions

DISCUSSION POINT

Why did the leisurewear manufacturer take these decisions? Based on the research findings, what else might you do to sell this range of leisurewear?

Organisations don't carry out marketing research for the sake of it. They use its findings to make decisions about products, prices, place and promotion – the 'Four Ps' of the marketing mix.

A sporting goods manufacturer was planning to introduce a new range of clothing in purple, green and blue, and decided to carry out marketing research to find out customers' views.

Summary of primary marketing research:

The clothing was displayed at 30 leisure centres around the country. Customers at the centres were asked their opinions on the design, range of colours, and logo on the clothing. They were also invited to enter a prize draw to win a family holiday in Florida. More than 30,000 people entered the competition.

Key results:

- 40% of competitors were from the C1/C2 socio-economic grouping (office supervisors/skilled manual workers).

- Most competition entries came from leisure centres in the North.

- Most customers liked the design range; but quite a lot of people disliked the purple colour.

- 10% of people said that even though they were not regular sports players, they would be prepared to wear the clothing as leisurewear.

The range of children's wear was particularly popular.

Summary of secondary marketing research:

- The most popular leisurewear carries a logo.

- The most popular leisurewear manufacturers spend a lot of money on sponsorship of professional sports players.

- Leisurewear stays fashionable for about eight months.

- Similar clothing produced by a competitor was selling in the shops for £60 per outfit (children's range £22).

- The busiest sales time for leisure clothing is in mid-July, just after the Wimbledon Tennis Championships.

As a result of the marketing research findings, the sporting goods company made the following decisions about the marketing mix for its new clothing.

Price

The adults' range of clothing should be priced at £58; the children's at £20.

Everything not sold in the January sales (if not sooner), should be sold off at a very reduced price.

Place

The range of clothes should go on sale in the men's and ladies' leisurewear departments of stores, rather than in sports departments.

Product

As a result of its primary marketing research, the company decided to market the green and blue ranges only – the idea of a purple range was abandoned.

Promotion

The company decided to promote the children's range particularly strongly, and to use children as much as possible in the advertising campaign. It targeted the Manchester area as a particularly good market, and decided to run special promotions there.

4.3.6 Undertaking marketing research

Carrying out marketing research needs careful thought and planning. Organisations work through five main steps to make sure that all goes smoothly.

Steps in research

1 Decide what you hope to achieve and write it down clearly.

2 Decide the best ways to carry out your research, bearing in mind cost and time. Will you use primary or secondary research methods? Make sure that the methods you choose are likely to give you the information you need. Think in advance about problems you might face; for example, how long it will take, the money it will cost, and the number of people you will need.

3 Carry out the research.

4 Collect information.

5 Work out what you have learnt from your research, and use the information to decide your marketing mix.

DISCUSSION POINT

Think of a project you carried out recently which involved research. What were the broad objectives of your research? What were your specific objectives? Do you think it would have helped you achieve your objectives if you had identified them clearly before starting your research?

Setting objectives

Organisations need to set both broad and specific marketing research objectives.

A company which manufactures rollerblades set the following broad and specific objectives.

Broad objective	Specific objective
To identify market trends (e.g. whether the market for rollerblades is growing)	To determine the growth in sales of rollerblades in Wales and north-west England in the last six months
To spot opportunities for products (e.g. rollerblades for the under-5s)	To find out what parents think about their young children wearing rollerblades. What are their top three worries?
To find out what the competition is doing (e.g. special offers on rollerblades in the run-up to Christmas)	To find out what were the top and lowest prices for rollerblades in all city stores in the six weeks before Christmas last year.
To evaluate how effective our promotion is	To find out how many more rollerblades we sold in the three months after a regional TV advertising campaign

Selecting suitable research methods

As you have already seen in this section, there are many different ways to carry out primary and secondary marketing research. Organisations need to ask themselves a range of questions in order to decide which research method to use in a particular situation.

Questions	Examples
How much will it cost to use this research method?	If a company is considering carrying out a detailed telephone survey, it needs to work out whether it will cost too much.
How much time will it take to use this research method?	If a company does decide to carry out a telephone survey, it needs to consider how much time it will need to carry out the interviews. Working with a short multiple-choice questionnaire would be quicker than working with a number of long answers.
How accessible is the method – how easy is it for people to understand?	If a company designs a questionnaire, it needs to assess how easy it is for respondents to fill in.
Will the results be valid (well-grounded and fair)?	If a company wants to carry out a survey of leisure facilities for young people in a town, it would be wrong to go to just one school. For results to be valid, it would need to go to several schools to see what a range of young people think.
Will the response, and the results, be reliable (consistent and accurate)?	If a company hands over a large number of questionnaires to respondents, how can it be sure that it will get any replies back? Or that the replies it gets will be honest?
Is the method fit for its purpose – is it suitable for the customers involved and will it produce the information needed?	If a company is dealing with people with learning difficulties, it can't give them a long written questionnaire. A short questionnaire with simple questions worded in plain English would be fit for the purpose.

Carrying out the research

Once an organisation has determined its marketing research objectives and the research methods to use, it can carry out the research.

Putting research into practice can be an expensive business – primary marketing research is usually more expensive than secondary research, because people have to be paid to collect the information. Secondary research is cheaper and quicker, but may not produce the information an organisation needs. The owner of a small, local agency specialising in marketing research explains:

66 *There's no point advising clients to spend a lot of money on primary marketing research if the information they get isn't going to help them make at least twice as much money. We can give clients a lot of information from secondary sources – it's quicker if we do it because we know the sources and it's not an expensive service. If we do set up a survey for them, our policy is to do it quickly and in the most cost-effective way. For example, we recently sent a team of six researchers with a questionnaire into an airport mall for a day and got a mass of data which couldn't have been got in any other way.* 99

Collating information means organising and presenting it in a form which makes it easier to understand.

Collating information

Once marketing researchers have got the information they need – from primary or secondary sources – it needs to be collated. Quantitative data is often collated in the form of charts, tables and graphs. Qualitative data is usually collated in written reports. It is a lot easier to collate information if it has been collected in a suitable form in the first place, as the owner of the marketing research agency explains:

66 *People think that writing questionnaires is easy, but actually you have to think very carefully about the questions so you get the information in a form that's easy to analyse. If we're wanting mainly quantitative data, we try to ask closed questions with a 'Yes' or 'No' answer, or use a scoring system – for example, 'How good is the signposting in the airport, on a scale of 1 to 5?' Asking qualitative questions is harder, because you're trying to find out people's attitudes or feelings but you also want to collect as much precise data as you can. We are very experienced at collating this type of 'soft' data.* 99

Using the information

It's a waste of money collecting information that you can't use. For example, if you're selling rollerblades in Liverpool, information about the sale of rollerblades in Cornwall and Devon isn't much use. But if you know that sales in Manchester doubled in the last six months, you might use this information to double your order to the manufacturer.

A company manufacturing roller skates would be very interested to know about sales of rollerblades nationally. It might think seriously about launching its own rival product, or running an advertising campaign encouraging people to buy skates rather than blades.

Using marketing research for product innovation

Before launching a new product or service, organisations need to be sure that there are customers to buy it. So they use marketing research techniques to test and analyse new product or service ideas and opportunities.

There are two main ways of creating a new product or service:
- the organisation has an idea for a new product and service and uses marketing research to test people's response to the idea – this is product-led development
- the organisation asks the customers what new products or services they would like and then create a product or service to fit the customers' wants – this is market-led development

The aim of marketing research into possible product innovations is to find out if there's a sufficient number of potential customers to make it worth the development, production and launch costs of the new product or service.

219

ACTIVITY

Choose a leisure and recreation organisation in your area which provides products or services aimed at your age group (for example, a cinema or a nightclub). Plan and carry out marketing research, with the broad objective of identifying opportunities for the organisation to develop new products to appeal to your age group. Make sure that you cover the five steps described in this section:

■ set objectives

■ choose suitable research methods

■ carry out the research

■ collate the information

■ explain how the organisation could use the information.

ACTIVITY

The organisation you focused on for the activity above has asked you to present your marketing research findings in a report. Decide the best way to present the information you have collected – consider using tables, pie charts, bar charts and 3D bar charts – and prepare a report. Include a brief explanation of why you have chosen to present your findings in this way.

Using marketing research for product modification

No organisation can afford to be complacent about its products and services. Markets change, people's tastes change, competitors move in. Keeping up to date with changes is an important and ongoing aspect of marketing research. The information tells an organisation when it's time to update or modify their products and services so that they keep up with what the market wants.

The sales director of a theme park explains how their marketing research activities contributed to product modification:

66 *Our figures showed a drop in interest in the log-ride – where people travel along a rapid watercourse in hollowed-out logs. We conducted some on-the-spot interviews with customers who used the ride and customers who looked at it but moved on to other attractions. The general opinion was that you got too wet. So we did some tests and modified the logs to cut down the amount of spray thrown up as the logs went along.* 99

Presenting research findings

Organisations usually summarise and present marketing research findings in a report with figures and charts. The aim is to make data eye-catching, clear and interesting.

Presenting research findings

■ Decide on the best way to present the findings – usually in a report.

■ Think about who is going to read the report and what they want to do with the findings.

■ Think about the order in which the findings should be presented.

■ Write a summary of the research and how it was carried out.

■ Present any numerical data in graphs, charts or tables.

■ If there are a lot of figures, it may be a good idea to group them at the end of the report.

■ Summarise the research findings in a few sentences.

■ Suggest what the organisation should do next.

Key questions

1 What is the purpose of marketing research?

2 What are the differences between primary and secondary sources of marketing research data? Give three examples of each type.

3 What information can you get from:

– quantitative research?

– qualitative research?

4 Name five primary research methods.

5 What are some sources of secondary research?

6 What are the three main contact methods used in marketing research?

7 What steps are taken when planning a market research project?

8 How would you use marketing to decide whether or not to:

– introduce a new product or service?

– introduce changes to an existing product or service?

SECTION **4.4**

Marketing communications

All leisure and recreation enterprises need to make customers aware of their products and services in order to achieve their objectives. This section looks at the methods used by leisure and recreation organisations to communicate with their customers, and considers how organisations evaluate their marketing communications. It also takes a final look at marketing plans, so that you can see how organisations choose and prepare their methods of communication.

66 We have found that mailing lists are an excellent way of bringing people in to our concerts. So now we are building up our own database and we mail everyone on it every six months. This is definitely the most successful way of getting an audience. We have tried advertising but that isn't very successful. We've tried newspaper adverts and putting posters in music shops but it doesn't really work. The direct contact is much more effective. 99

leader of a band

66 Our income is from two sources: competitors' entry fees and sponsorship. Sponsors provide the prizes and cover the fixed overheads that we have to pay. Our first sponsor was a family shoe shop. The race gave them a chance to advertise themselves to families and young people. 99

organiser of a regatta

66 A marketing plan is written for the property every five years. We also have a shorter-term plan agreed every year at an annual meeting. 99

marketing manager of a leisure centre

4.4.1 Introduction

Marketing is all about understanding and communicating with customers – 'getting the message across' about the products and services on offer.

> Organisations communicate with customers in many different ways:
>
> - advertising – in newspapers, magazines, on television, on radio, at point of sale or point of delivery
> - direct marketing – direct mail, telemarketing, door-to-door distribution, direct response advertising
> - public relations – press releases, lobbying, community relations, corporate communication
> - sales promotion – to consumers and trade
> - sponsorship – schools, sports, arts and leisure events.

One of the challenges of marketing is choosing the right forms of communication for the target audience.

Communication is a vital part of successful marketing, and organisations need to say in their marketing plans how they intend to do it.

A leisure and recreation organisation may decide to use any number of these communication methods as part of a marketing campaign. A large organisation with a lot of money to spend on marketing may run a coordinated campaign using all five; a small, local company with a limited budget may just run a sales promotion, or concentrate on public relations. Whatever the organisation's size, their choice of method would be based on:

- the most effective ways of reaching their target audience
- the type of message they wanted to get across

DISCUSSION POINT

Publicity that works well stays in your mind for a long time. What publicity for a leisure and recreation facility or service can you remember best? Why has it stayed in your mind? See if other people remember the same things as you.

223

- the organisation's image
- how much money they have to spend.

They would also ensure that:
- the methods were complementary
- the activities were coordinated in a way that strengthened the message
- they could cope with the predicted levels of response the activities generated.

The following extract is taken from the quarterly marketing plan of a national hotel chain. One of its main problems is under-occupancy in winter, and it is planning a campaign to counteract this by promoting winter breaks.

This is our major campaign for 2000, and we should try to get our message across to the public in as many ways as possible:

- Advertising. We will place colour ads in style magazines, classified ads in broadsheet newspapers, and run a TV advertising campaign in early autumn. We will also update our winter breaks brochure.

- Public relations. We will aim to get at least two features in national newspapers/magazines; plus coverage on a TV holiday programme. To create goodwill, we will organise special Santa Breaks for under-privileged children at selected hotels.

- Sales promotion. We will offer three nights for the price of two during November, January and February. Guests will be able to enter a competition for a luxury week's summer break.

- Personal selling. All reception staff will be briefed on the winter break offers, and encouraged to tell guests about what's on offer.

- Direct communications. We will write to regular hotel guests, sending them a copy of the new winter breaks brochure and offering them a special rate if they book before the middle of October.

4.4.2 Advertising

Advertising is the process of publicising a product or service. It is used to raise awareness, to inform, to attract inquiries, to generate or increase sales, and to create an image.

Advertising is a powerful way to promote a product or service, but it can be expensive and most companies have to think carefully about what to advertise, when to do it, and where to place advertisements. It is crucially important that advertising is targeted at the right audience.

The media used for advertising include newspapers, magazines, television, radio, the Internet, posters, point-of-sale materials and brochures. Advertising in national newspapers, magazines and on television is much more expensive than advertising in the local media. If the market for a product or service is large, organisations will have more to spend on advertising. Some organisations use only one or two different media, either because that's what their budget will stretch to or because they have analysed them as being the most effective way of advertising their products and services. Some organisations – usually the larger ones – will put together an advertising campaign which uses a range of media.

A successful advertisement must:

- catch the attention of the public
- keep the interest of the reader, viewer or listener
- persuade the audience that they need or want the products or services advertised
- make the audience take action.

Newspaper advertising

There are three basic types of newspaper:

- national press, which report national and international news and items of national interest
- local press, which report mainly local news and items of local interest
- specialised press, which report on particular areas of industry, commerce or special interest.

Every newspaper aims itself at a particular type of reader. Many people have a favourite national newspaper which they always buy because its news-reporting style, coverage and feature articles appeal to them. Local papers are designed to appeal to people in the localities they cover. Specialised papers are read by people with an interest in the special area the paper covers.

Advertising is a source of income for newspapers because advertisers have to pay for the amount of space on a page they want to use. To make it worth the money, advertisers have to decide carefully what type of person they want to appeal to and interest and then advertise in the papers which that type of person would read. Or they may advertise in a range of papers but change the style of the advert to fit in with the style of the paper and the type of reader.

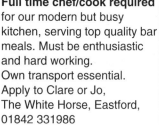

Classified advertisements

Classified ads are usually very short and don't cost much to buy. They are used to sell products or promote services, but give little information about quality.

Loot, *Exchange and Mart* and *Daltons Weekly* are papers which just have advertising – they contain no news items.

Display advertisements

Display ads give much more information about the product or service being offered. They make use of logos and headlines to catch the eye.

Full time chef/cook required
for our modern but busy kitchen, serving top quality bar meals. Must be enthusiastic and hard working.
Own transport essential.
Apply to Clare or Jo,
The White Horse, Eastford,
01842 331986

Hundreds of special offers in our Summer Sale.
Massive savings on a full range of sports equipment including: trainers, track suits, and swimwear.
Look out for our special 'HALF PRICE' blue stickers

KITALL
10 High Street, Cranfield, Essex

ACTIVITY

Make a collection of classified and display advertisements from national, regional and local newspapers that have been placed by leisure and recreation organisations to promote products or services. Do they catch attention, keep interest, persuade, and stimulate action?

What links can you see between the types of products/services being advertised and the people likely to read the newspapers?

Find out the cost of placing a classified advertisement and a display advertisement in your local newspaper.

Feel the trill of floating on the wind – drift through the valleys and get a view that will never be equalled. Our fully qualified training staff will take you through all the safety procedures and techniques to enable you to FLY solo after one week.
Call FREEPHONE Activity Now!

Magazine advertising

Like newspapers, magazines and journals all have different kinds of reader. Some cover quite specialised subjects, others are more general. Many magazines cover a particular leisure activity, and these are important places for suppliers of products or services to advertise. For example, a magazine on angling would be a good place for a supplier of fishing products to advertise.

Television advertising

Advertising on television is a very effective way of reaching large numbers of people. But it's very costly – particularly at peak viewing times between 6 and 11 p.m. – so only very large organisations can afford to do it.

Radio advertising

There is an increasing number of commercial national and local radio stations. Radio advertising is cheaper than television but audiences are smaller.

DISCUSSION POINT

Collect examples of five national magazines. Make sure they are very varied, e.g. a TV listings magazine, a women's issues magazine, plus one or two on leisure activities. What sorts of advertisement appear in these magazines? Why have the advertisers chosen these magazines?

ACTIVITY

Produce a list of leisure and recreation organisations which regularly advertise on radio and television.

If possible, record examples of their advertisements on video or audio cassette. How do they use radio and TV advertising to get their message across? What sort of images do they use? When do they advertise? (At what time of day? Near or during which sorts of programmes?)

Internet

Increasingly the World Wide Web is a used as an advertising channel. Many ISPs (internet service providers) are creating gateways or 'portals' for organisations who agree to conform to a standard of service. They provide an Internet presence for a wide range of goods and services. Next time you surf the Web, see how many advertisements you see for the leisure and recreation industry.

Posters

Posters are a particularly important way of advertising local events, activities, venues or services. Where they are positioned is important, and they need to include photographs or drawings that will stay in the public's mind for a long time.

The manager of a small concert hall talks about how he uses posters to promote a concert:

SYMPHONIA HALL
May 16th at 8pm
Tickets £12.50

The Four Seasons

66 *Sharp, attractive posters are very important for our concerts. We have a number of regular sites for posters: inside and outside the hall itself, but also in the local libraries, in selected shops (often music and bookshops), certain cafés and restaurants, notice-boards in nearby villages, and schools. We also have a number of display cases in sites around the town. When we print posters, we usually have smaller versions printed as handbills which can be left in places where we think people interested in coming to our concerts will see them.* 99

Most towns and cities also have a number of large poster or billboard sites. These are often very expensive and are used mainly by national organisations. Some people evade these costs by fly-posting their posters on, for example, bus shelters, the windows of empty shops or houses, or walls. Fly-posting simply means putting a poster in an unauthorised place and there are bylaws which make it an offence to do this.

Point-of-sale material

Think of the number of times you go into a record store not intending to buy a tape or CD, but come out having bought several. The atmosphere of the shop might have made you buy something, but there are also all the posters, special promotions and special offers. These are all materials which promote products at the point of sale.

Point-of-sale materials are aimed at the impulse buyer – the sort of person who sees something and buys it straight away, even though they hadn't thought of buying it before going into the shop. Some people take longer to make their minds up, but even they may be persuaded to buy something when there is a special discount, bright packaging, or a leaflet packed with useful information.

Brochures

Brochures aren't designed for the impulse buyer, but for customers who have already decided they might buy something but need more information before buying.

The brochure is particularly useful for promoting services: an exercise course at a sports centre is not like a piece of leisurewear – it cannot be bought off the shelf, taken home, tried on and returned if unsuitable.

Regulatory standards for advertising

The Advertising Standards Authority is the regulatory body for these advertising media:

- newspapers and magazines
- posters
- directing marketing
- sales promotion
- cinema
- video cassettes
- Teletext.

The ASA also regulate UK advertising on the Internet. (The ASA's codes for non-broadcast advertisements are avilable from *http://www.asa.org.uk*.) All advertisers using these media have to abide by the guidelines set out in the British Code of Advertising Practice. The key principles are that the adverts should be:

- legal, honest, decent and truthful
- prepared with a sense of responsibility to the consumers and to society
- within the generally accepted principles of fair competition in business.

Adverts appearing on television and cable are regulated by the Independent Television Commission (ITC). Its guidelines are called The Code of Advertising Standards and Practices. As well as placing a ban on using television to advertise certain products – such as cigarettes – the ITC also has strict rules about advertising aimed at children and adverts using child actors or models.

Advertising on radio is regulated by the Radio Authority.

The Trade Descriptions Act 1968

This Act stipulates that there be no misrepresentation in how products and services are described.

Two musicians from a red-hot young modern jazz group from France were injured in a road accident forcing an arts association to cancel a gig at short notice. The arts association books a well-known local group for a lower fee to replace the French group, offers full refunds on the door on the night and provides one free drink in the interval for those whose decide to stay and hear the replacement band.

The Consumer Protection Act 1987

The Act protects consumer rights against misleading information about things such as the price and type of goods or service and facilities.

> A fitness club offers discounted rates to new members taking out a year's subscription. The offer is very attractive in terms of price but it includes a number of add-ons, such as one-to-one swimming instruction. It wasn't clear in the promotional advertisements that these add-ons were not included in the discounted price so the club has to honour the advertised price when people joined accepting these services.

The Data Protection Act 1984, updated 1999

This Act requires organisations who hold information about customers in a computer database not to use that information without the customer's consent.

> A city-based arts and leisure centre has a large regional mailing list. The centre receives significant sponsorship from a major financial business interest. This business wishes to promote its financial services using the extensive postal and e-mail mailing list which the centre has built up. Under the Data Protection Act the centre has to get permission from everyone on its mailing list. They introduce a special promotion to an early evening performance of a popular London musical which is touring the regions. This promotion also includes a form seeking permission to send out details of other services.

4.4.3 **Direct marketing**

Organisations use direct marketing to sell directly to the general public, rather than through shops or agents. The main advantage of direct marketing is that it can be cheaper; for example, a tour operator selling directly to the public will not have to pay commission to agents. However, they may have to spend a lot more on promotion in order to make the same number of sales.

Direct mail

Promoting a product or service by post – direct mail – gives organisations an opportunity to target messages at a specific group of customers (for example, particular professions, geographical areas, or age groups). Direct mail is now a very popular way to promote leisure and recreation products and services,

ACTIVITY

Imagine you are the marketing manager of a country hotel. To try to improve occupancy rates in the winter, you decide to run a direct mail campaign targeting customers who have stayed at the hotel before.

Design a one-page leaflet and write a direct mail letter to send to the hotel's customers. How will you catch their attention? Will you offer them incentives to keep them interested?

and the number of promotional letters sent out to customers has increased dramatically over the years. Some organisations use direct mail as one of a range of promotional activities. Some use it as their only activity. Conversion rates (the number of sales produced from a mailshot) are low for direct mail but they can be increased by careful targeting. To keep people's interest, direct mail is often combined with other promotions, such as special offers, prize draws and discounts.

A direct mail manager describes how she increased the conversion rates of enquiries to sales for direct mail promotions:

66 *When I joined the company, their philosophy was the more people you mailed, the more likely you were to reach people who were interested. I had other ideas. My philosophy is: 'If you don't want it, it's junk mail; if you do want it, it's information,' and I wanted to concentrate on the people who did want to hear about us. I put a lot of work into analysing and updating our database and finding new markets for our product. It paid off – by carefully targeting the mailshots, the conversion rate of enquiries to sales increased from 25 enquiries to a sale to 14 to 1.* 99

Telemarketing

Telemarketing is similar to direct mail, but instead of sending information by post, the organisation uses the telephone to communicate with potential customers. Like direct mail, telemarketing works best if the calls are carefully targeted.

The telesales supervisor of an organisation specialising in sports and leisure clothes explains how they uses telemarketing as a follow up to sales campaigns:

66 *The sales team give the telemarketing team information on successful and unsuccessful sales leads and the telemarketers contact the people to ask them about their decisions to buy or not buy. The information we gather is useful for the sales team, who can concentrate on potential buyers. It's also useful for the marketing team. It helps them build up profiles of our likely customers and evaluate the success of their promotional activities.* 99

Media direct response promotions

Direct response promotions are carried out through the media – television, radio, newspapers and magazines – and also through direct mailing. As the name suggests, they aim to make people respond directly to the promotion by filling in a tear-off slip or order form, or phoning through or faxing an order.

Like advertising, the choice of media – TV, radio or publication – for a direct response campaign needs to be carefully considered and will depend on the target audience. These campaigns are normally run for a certain amount of time. The products or services are often available at a discount.

DISCUSSION POINT

Have you bought a product or service through direct response? If so, what benefits did you see in buying this way? If not, what put you off?

ACTIVITY

Find two examples of the leisure and recreation industry which are predominantly Internet-based services. How do they promote these services? Who are they aiming these services at?

Electronic shopping

Electronic media – televisions and computers – are no longer marketplaces of the future, but of today! Customers can look through catalogues and price lists, and can even walk through realistic shopping centres which are shown on screen.

The technology for electronic shopping is fast developing. It started with Teletext-style promotions and is now one the main attractions of the Internet. Shopping using digital television is now a reality.

The Internet and digital television have opened up new and exciting opportunities for suppliers of goods and service across all industries. Many small organisations see the World Wide Web as offering them the ability to compete for the first time with multinationals. The popular music industry is a prime example where technology is changing the structure of the industry.

ACTIVITY

Direct marketing is meant to reach you, the customer, and encourage you to try, or buy, the goods and services on offer. In your experience, which sorts of direct marketing work, and which don't work? Collect examples of the different types of direct marketing described above. These could be media direct response in journals or newspapers, catalogues or brochures, or a description of electronic shopping.

How successful do you think each one is? Does it reach its target audience and make an impact? Have you ever bought a leisure and recreation product as a result of direct marketing?

Personal selling

Product-oriented selling

In product-oriented personal selling, the technique is to persuade customers they want the product or service you have to sell. For example, a salesperson selling sportswear at a sports event aims to persuade people passing by that they need the product. This is a product-oriented approach.

Personal selling with a product orientation is used mainly for mass markets – goods which a lot of people will want to buy; for example, food and drink.

DISCUSSION POINT

Think of a time when a salesperson has used either a product-oriented approach or a customer-oriented approach to persuade you to buy. What techniques were used? What made you decide to buy or not buy?

Customer-oriented selling

In customer-oriented selling the technique is to find out what customers want then persuade them that your product or service fits their needs. For example, a fitness centre employee works with a client to find out their level of fitness and their preferences and develops a training programme to suit them.

Customer-oriented selling is used to sell goods or services to targeted people. Because it is expensive to target individuals in this way, the product or service being sold is often expensive, such as holidays or luxury goods.

Face-to-face sales

Most personal selling, whether product-oriented or customer-oriented, is carried out face to face. It is usually offered by trained sales staff – for example, the receptionist at a leisure centre, who talks to customers about facilities, classes and events, and encourages people to use or attend them.

Telesales

Personal selling may also be carried out over the phone. This can be either:

- when a customer is contacted 'cold' by a representative of an organisation
- when a customer contacts the organisation to talk about products or services they have seen advertised.

Many people think cold canvassing by phone is a nuisance, and salespeople expect a low success rate. On the other hand, if a customer makes contact with an organisation, the telephone conversation can play an important part in helping them make up their mind whether or not to buy.

> ### DISCUSSION POINT
>
> Think of examples when you have talked to salespeople, either face to face, or on the telephone. Have they tried to find out what sort of product or service would interest you or have they tried to sell you the product or service they want you to have? What did you think of their selling techniques?

4.4.4 Public relations

Public relations (PR) is now an important part of the marketing of leisure and recreation organisations. It is a way of making sure that the public hears or reads about what an organisation is doing. Larger organisations either employ their own PR officers or press officers, or bring in consultants to work on particular campaigns.

> **Examples of public relations activities**
>
> - sending out press releases
> - building relationships with sponsors
> - lobbying
> - developing community relations
> - promoting corporate communications
> - dealing with major problems

Organisations use public relations to deal with public criticisms, complaints or accidents to retain public confidence and customer loyalty.

THE LONDON EYE

The London Eye big wheel was due to be ready for the big Millennium celebrations in London. The plan was for a high profile ride on the London Eye on the evening of 31 December with government ministers and celebrities. In the weeks running up to the launch the developers of the London Eye identified a number of safety issues which led to the launch being delayed for several weeks. This resulted in loss of revenue as the Eye was to be an exciting new attraction over the New Year holiday period.

The promoters turned the problem into a marketing opportunity; they used the delay to reassure the public that health and safety was paramount and have successfully kept the Eye well profiled and created a high level of confidence and interest.

ACTIVITY

Imagine you work for a local leisure and recreation organisation. Write a press release giving information about an important event or activity which you are organising. Use your imagination to think of an interesting event to publicise. Make your press release punchy, but include all the information people will need. Remember to add details such as a contact name and phone number.

An **embargo** on a press release means that journalists cannot use the information until the date given.

Organisations use press releases to make sure that their events and activities are covered in newspapers and magazines, and on radio and TV. Press releases are a good way for organisations to promote themselves because, if successful, they result in free publicity.

A press release is usually sent out several days before an event or activity. This gives journalists time to plan how and when to cover the story. Ideally, a press release should contain enough information for a journalist to write an article without having to attend the event or activity. The owner of a drama centre talks about the press releases he writes:

66 *We take great care over press releases for new shows because we know that extracts from them may appear in the papers exactly as we wrote them, especially if the reviewers are too busy to come. This amounts to us writing our own previews or reviews! Brilliant!* 99

Press releases can cover a wide range of subjects, including the announcement of:

■ a new person taken on to work for the organisation
■ another company taking over the organisation
■ the launch of a new product or service
■ a large new contract being given to a company
■ forthcoming events and activities.

PRESS RELEASE   **ACTIVE SPORTS**   **PRESS RELEASE**

Date: 29 September 1999

Time: 12h00

Embargo until 06 October 1999

Active Sports to open new superstore

Active Sports will hold the Grand Opening for its new superstore branch on Thursday 6 October. The new store is located in the Castlewood Shopping Plaza on the city ring road.

This is a newly built location of three storeys which will include several departments such as sporting goods, fashion, outdoor camping equipment, and an extensive new shoe department specialising in sports footwear.

The Grand Opening will be hosted by guest celebrities from city and regional teams.

As part of its expansion programme, the company has appointed the advertising agency Brown, Patel and O'Reilly to manage the £100,000 advertising campaign.

For further information please contact Sajel Makwana, Press Officer.

Telephone: (0159) 111111   Fax: (0159) 111112

Lobbying

Lobbying is campaigning to influence politicians to take action.

Lobby groups represent particular interests. Charities lobby on behalf of their social or welfare interests. Businesses lobby on behalf of their commercial interests. Lobby groups have a range of aims – for example, more funding from government, a change of law or policy at national or local level, more public awareness. Sometimes, different lobby groups share a general interest or concern but more often they conflict with one another.

Community relations

Most organisations like to support the local community. Local people are more likely to buy goods or services from an organisation which has a positive image in the community. Community relations are particularly important for an organisation which depends on the local community for its staff and trade.

Corporate communications

Large organisations use 'corporate communications' as a type of PR for their staff. The aim is to provide information, bring everybody closer together and to create a good working atmosphere. Many produce in-house magazines or newsletters which give news about the company and its activities, employees – who has joined the company, who has retired, who has had a baby, and so on – and how well products and services are selling. Some use specialist PR organisations to advise on or produce corporate brochures and magazines.

4.4.5 **Sales promotion**

Sales promotion is an important part of the marketing mix. Leisure and recreation organisations target sales promotions at consumers (the general public), and at trade (other companies). In both cases, the aim is to:

- raise awareness of new products or services, so they start to sell well
- remind people of existing products and services, so that they go on to sell even better.

Consumer promotions

Sales promotions to consumers – the general public – include:

- Samples – may be given away in magazines, sent through the post, or be on display at point-of-sale.
- Coupons – offer customers money off their next purchase, and may be:
  - printed in newspapers and magazines
  - sent through the post
  - promoted at point-of-sale
  - included on packaging.

  Coupons can usually only be used for a limited period of time.
- Competitions – which customers can only enter if they buy a product or service. Many competitions include a 'tie-breaker', which asks people to think up a slogan. The company can then use this in future advertising campaigns.
- Special offers – are used to introduce new or improved products and services. A special offer will either offer more of the product (possibly for less money) or an extra service.
- Gifts – are usually offered at point-of-sale or on mail order, and may be free or at a specially reduced price. Customers usually have to prove they have bought the item before they receive the gift. Sometimes the gifts are themselves promotional material, e.g. sweatshirts, tea towels or baseball caps with the company's name or logo on.
- Loyalty incentives – are offered to customers who can show that they use a product or service regularly. They are then given a discount so that they continue to buy the product or service.

Trade promotions

Similar promotional activities are directed at customers within the trade. Organisations use trade promotions to provide incentives for trade customers to use products or services, or to encourage them to sell its goods.

- Discounts – are sometimes given to trade customers buying goods before, or at the time of, a special promotion. If an organisation is aiming a sales promotion at consumers, it may need to encourage the trade to buy in more stock so that there is enough for people to buy. In this case, the trade customers are usually offered a discount, which in turn encourages them to recommend the product to customers.

DISCUSSION POINT

Have you ever entered a competition connected to a product or service that you have bought? Would you have bought the product or service normally? Have you bought the product or service since? Did the competition make you think differently about the company? If so, how?

- Allowances – are sometimes given on trade sales, such as by making some further purchases free if a high enough level of sales is achieved.
- Free products – may be given to trade customers when a new product is being launched.
- Free gifts – may either be given to promote a brand name (e.g. kit bags or clothing), or may be offered if a shop sells more than expected.
- Trade exhibitions – let organisations in the trade see what new products or services are available. They are useful for seeing what competitors are offering and picking up sales leads. They also give organisations a chance to demonstrate products and services and get feedback from potential customers. Large annual events involving hundreds of exhibitors are held at venues such as the National Exhibition Centre in Birmingham or the Earl's Court Exhibition Centre in London.

4.4.6 **Sponsorship**

Organisations involved in sponsorship offer support – money, staff, facilities or equipment – to commercial or community activities. In doing this, they hope to attract people's attention and create a good public image for the company. Sponsorship doesn't necessarily make a direct contribution to profits.

In the leisure and recreation industry there are examples of:

- leisure and recreation organisations benefiting from the sponsorship of other organisations
- leisure and recreation organisations themselves sponsoring other activities.

The manager of a sports centre talks about this two-way sponsorship:

66 *We have a very good relationship with a local producer of bottled mineral water and other soft drinks. They have sponsored a number of events at the centre, including open days and competitions. In return we have sponsored them in other ways, by offering our facilities and staff at reduced rates for their events. We find it's a very profitable relationship – we work together very well, with our shared interest in health and well-being.* **99**

Examples of different sponsorship activity

- providing a minibus for a local community organisation
- paying for the printing of publicity material for a charity event
- providing staff for a fund-raising event
- running a special event for a charity
- donating products for fundraisers to use as prizes in a competition

Sponsors normally expect their name and logo to appear in any publicity material so that the public knows that they have given support.

ACTIVITY

Visit some local leisure and recreation outlets and facilities. Make a note of any examples you see of sponsorship. For example, posters for theatre and sports events will carry logos and brief details of any sponsor.

Examples of sponsorship

- McDonald's provides litter bins in town centres.
- Virgin sponsors the 'Tidy Britain' Campaign.
- BT sponsors an annual Swimathon.
- National Westminster Bank sponsors a national cricket knockout tournament.
- Army Careers sponsors Festivals of Support.
- Benson & Hedges sponsors the Masters snooker tournament.

4.4.7 The effectiveness of marketing communications

With so many different ways to communicate, it is important for organisations to pick those which will work for their target customers – to choose the right 'communications mix'.

4.4.7 The effectiveness of marketing communications

With so many different ways to communicate, it is important for organisations to pick those which will work for their target customers – to choose the right 'communications mix'.

To evaluate the effectiveness of marketing communications, you need to know:

- what the marketing objectives were
- how achievement of the objectives is to be measured
- who the targets were
- why the communications methods were chosen
- what the plan for implementation was (costs, timescales, resources).

Effectiveness can be measured in the following terms:

- how many sales are made (volume of sales)
- how many customers buy from you again (repeat business)
- how many customers buy your products and services in preference to similar ones offered by your competitors (brand loyalty)
- how many customers buy from you because they trust your reputation (customer loyalty)
- how many new customers you attract (new business)
- how many people have heard of you (public awareness)
- what proportion of the total number of customers for a product or service type buy from you (market share)
- whether the marketing activities kept within set budgets.

The sales and marketing departments in leisure and recreation organisations will evaluate the effectiveness of:

- all their promotional activities put together – for example, total promotional spending against total revenue raised through promotions
- individual promotional activities and projects – for example, expenditure on a single campaign and the revenue directly attributable to it.

ACTIVITY

Make a checklist of questions you would ask to evaluate the effectiveness of an organisation's marketing communications. Next, write a proposal for carrying out your evaluation which shows:

- how you would gather the information you needed
- who you would talk to at the organisation
- how you would present the information you gather.

239

Produce a report on how two leisure and recreation organisations market their products and services. You can either choose:

■ large national organisations (use information from brochures, newspaper advertisements, and so on)

■ local organisations (interview people involved in marketing).

You should choose one organisation from the leisure industry, and one from the recreation industry.

When producing your report, think about the following:

■ the objectives or purpose of each marketing activity

■ the marketing methods used

■ how well the activity works.

Important aspects to think about:

■ number of sales (or number of tickets sold, places booked, etc.)

■ repeat business – how many people come back to buy more, revisit, etc.

■ brand loyalty – do people buy the brand again because they think it is better than other brands?

■ customer loyalty – do people buy from the organisation rather than from another one selling similar products or services?

■ new business – are there many new customers?

■ public awareness – is the general public aware of the product or service?

■ increased market share – are more people buying the product or service? Are total sales high compared to other companies?

■ keeping within budget – does the company spend too much on marketing, or does it spend as much as it planned?

How can you work out the answers to these questions? How can you work out whether a promotion is successful or not?

Measuring the effectiveness of marketing

It is worth remembering that a change in sales may not be entirely down to promotional activity – sales may increase or decrease because of factors which have little or nothing to do with the organisation. For example, there is always an increase in the sale of tennis equipment and the use of tennis courts during and just after the Wimbledon Tennis Championships, and sales of some brands of equipment are affected by the sponsorship of leading players. Clearly, organisations offering tennis products and services do well because of Wimbledon, but they also have to work hard to make the most of the opportunity that the Championships provide.

4.4.8 Presenting a marketing plan

Timescales

The timescales of a marketing plan state the whens. The plan would have:

- a start date and an end date for the plan as a whole – the overall timescale
- start dates and end dates for the individual activities within the overall timescale
- start and end dates for the individual tasks of each activity.

For example, an organisation whose objective is to increase sales over the year would plan a series of promotional activities throughout the year. Each promotional activity would have a start and an end date and each task involved in the activity would have start and end dates.

Costs

It's very important to estimate the costs of a project before the work begins. Like timescales, costs need to be worked out and allocated:

- in total
- for each activity
- for each task.

Sometimes organisations set a budget for implementing the marketing plan and choose activities that fit into the budget. Sometimes they work out what they would like to do, then estimate the costs, then see whether they have the money to do it or whether they need to revise the plans.

Resources

Resources are equipment, space, information, materials and people. For example, a plan involving a direct mail campaign as part of a promotion for a new product would need:

- people to decide on the target customers, write the promotional literature, organise the design and print work
- access to information on customers
- office space and equipment
- mailing facilities
- paper for promotional literature
- envelopes
- telephones and faxes
- people to deal with the increase in customer enquiries and orders
- people to pack and send the product to customers
- sufficient supplies of the product to meet the predicted demand.

241

The Blue Marble is a small bookshop which specialises in children's books, situated in the centre of a large market town. During the first three years of operation it has built up a small but dedicated client base and is now thinking of ways to expand its market.

1 Organisational objectives:
   To grow at a rate of 15% a year, and make a return on investment of 30%

2 The marketing environment:
   Strengths – there are a lot of families with children in this town
   Weaknesses – customers are limited primarily to children and families
   Opportunities – teenage readers and educational institutions
   Threats – a large chain bookshop with a medium-sized children's department is situated on the other side of the town centre

3 Key marketing objectives:
   Look at the market needs of both existing and potential customers.
   Make sure that existing product meets needs of current market.
   Keep our product and service competitive.
   Make a greater profit through increased sales.
   Promote quality rather than price.

4 Marketing research methods:
   Secondary
   British Library Association statistics about young readers
   British Publishers Association reports and research
   Primary
   questionnaire survey of recent customers
   sending a mystery shopper to evaluate the service offered by the competitor

5 Marketing communication methods:
   Advertising
   in local newspaper

a leaflet and bookmarks which are handed out to customers at the till
Promotions
bags and T-shirts printed with store logo
Public relations
attend trade bookfairs in the UK and Europe
sponsor reading contents through the public library
Sales
send staff on training workshops to increase their selling skills

6 Implementation:
   Costs of marketing to be taken from existing budget.
   Research to be carried out within next three months.
   Campaign to run for six months (during winter period).

7 Evaluation techniques:
   Monitor sales figures for each month.
   Compare statistics with those published in book industry trade literature.
   Survey customers.
   Criteria for evaluation:
   Maintaining or increasing number of customers in store.
   Meeting target for new business from local schools.
   Meeting target for increased business from teenage readers.
   Marketing budget set and kept to.

The owner of the bookshop explains the importance of the marketing plan:

66 *The marketing plan details how we're going to achieve our business objectives. It's vital that it is based on thorough research of the markets and that all the resources needed for its implementation have been thought through. It's not a wish-list. It's a realistic plan of action and every member of the organisation will play a part in its success.* 99

Key questions

1   What are the five main methods of marketing communications?

2   What things does an organisation consider when choosing its marketing communication methods?

3   What is PR and why is it so important to an organisation?

4   What is an embargo on a press release?

5   What do organisations hope to achieve by sponsorship?

6   What steps can be taken to ensure that a marketing plan is implemented successfully?

Assignment

Prepare a marketing plan for one product or service in a leisure and recreation organisation of your choice.

The first step is to choose:

■ a leisure and recreation organisation for which you can prepare the plan – ideally, this should be an organisation that you know, but you can use a case study if it isn't possible to use a real organisation

■ a product or service – again, a real product or service would be ideal, but you can make up a product for your plan, even if the organisation is real

The marketing plan should include:

■ the organisation's mission and objectives

■ a SWOT analysis, which examines the organisation's internal business environment

■ a PEST analysis, which examines the organisation's external business environment

■ an analysis of any relevant competitor activity faced by the organisation

■ an analysis of the organisation which examines how it makes use of the marketing mix to meet the needs and expectations of its customers (is the organisation marketing the right product? at the right price? in the right place? with the right form of promotion?)

■ details of a market research plan which would identify opportunities for product development; include the objectives of the market research, the primary and/or secondary methods used to collect information, and how the research may affect the marketing mix

■ details of marketing communication methods to be used to promote the product.

KEY SKILLS

You can use the work you are doing for this part of your GNVQ to collect and develop evidence for the following key skills at level 3:

when you	you can collect evidence for
	communication
present your investigations into marketing to your peers	key skill C3.1b make a presentation about a complex subject, using at least one image to illustrate complex points
investigate and evaluate marketing within leisure and recreation	key skill C3.2 read and synthesise information from two extended documents about a complex subject; one of these documents should include at least one image
	information technology
investigate and evaluate marketing within leisure and recreation	key skill IT3.1 plan, and use different sources to search for, and select, information required for two different purposes
	working with others
conduct and gather market research	key skill WO3.1 agree realistic objectives and the action and resources needed to achieve them; provide information, based on appropriate evidence, to help agree responsibilities; agree suitable working arrangements with those involved
	key skill WO3.2 organise and carry out tasks in ways that help you to be effective and efficient in meeting your responsibilities; seek to establish and maintain cooperative working relationships, agreeing ways to overcome any difficulties; exchange accurate information on the extent to which work is meeting expected time-scales and quality, agreeing changes where necessary to achieve objectives
	key skill WO3.3 agree the extent to which the objectives have been met; identify factors that have influenced the outcome; agree ways the activity could have been done differently to enhance work with others
	improving own learning and performance
plan, undertake and review your research into marketing communications and the marketing mix	key skill LP3.1 seek information on ways to achieve what you want to do, and identify factors that might affect your plans; use this information to agree realistic targets with appropriate others; plan how you will manage your time to meet targets, including alternative action for overcoming possible problems and use of support from others
	key skill LP3.2 prioritise and manage your time effectively to complete tasks, making revisions to your plan as necessary; seek and actively use feedback and support from relevant sources to help you meet your targets; use different approaches to learning, drawing on learning from other tasks and adapting methods to meet new demands
	key skill LP3.3 provide information on quality of your learning and performance, identifying factors that have affected the outcome; identify targets you have met, seeking information from relevant sources to establish evidence of your achievements; exchange views with appropriate others to agree action for improving your performance

UNIT

4

UNIT 5

Customer service in leisure and recreation

247

About this unit

The leisure and recreation industry is highly competitive. Many organisations provide similar products or services and it is often the quality of customer service that distinguishes one organisation from another. It is important that all staff are aware of the part they play in giving customers the highest standards of service. Giving excellent customer service plays an important part in helping organisations keep existing customers and attract new ones. It is critical to commercial success.

In this unit you will learn why excellent customer service is important in leisure and recreation and the part that personal presentation and communication skills play in dealing successfully with customers. You will appreciate that different customers have different needs. You will learn how to deal properly with customer complaints and how to measure, monitor and evaluate customer service procedures and practices.

SECTION **5.1**

The importance of customer service

Customer service is a vital part of any leisure and recreation organisation. In this section you will learn why good customer service is important. You will also see the benefits that good customer service brings to an organisation.

---

66 This is a 24-hour-a day job because that's the kind of attention a business like this requires. In this sort of service industry you can't expect to lock up at 6.00 p.m. and put your feet up. The phone can go at any hour and I always have to know what's going on. The welfare of the horses and the riders is top priority. **99**

owner of a riding school

66 Most of our business comes from repeat business – if customers like us the first time they tend to come back. I'll go out of my way to make sure that a regular customer is well looked after. Sometimes it means taking special requests not listed on the menu, or preparing meals in a particular way, but it can mean the difference between keeping customers or seeing them go elsewhere. **99**

manager of a restaurant

66 The skills needed in this work are mainly to do with customer care – you have to know how to deal with all kinds of customers: parents and small children, people who want to do Aquafit, people who need coaching. You have to be very caring, but at times very firm about how things are run. **99**

swimming development officer

5.1.1 **Sales**

"Let us do the worrying for you"   *"Put your feet up and let us do the rest"*

"Let us take care of you"   **"For professional service and personal attention"**

"Personal service from a family business"   *"A better service, the best result"*

Leisure and recreation is one of the most competitive industries. This applies equally to the local gym, West End theatres and subsidised community events as to small specialist recreation businesses such as white water rafting.

Effective customer service is about caring for customers and meeting their needs and expectations. Succesful leisure and recreation organisations give good customer service a high priority. They understand that without customers, there would be no business!

As this keen swimmer explains, satisfying customers can be even more important than meeting their needs:

> ❝ *I go swimming every day, and was delighted when I heard a new pool was opening near my home. The pool is modern and large, and a big improvement on existing facilities. I went at the first opportunity, but left very disappointed. The pool was great, but there weren't enough staff on duty and I had to wait ten minutes to gain entrance, the changing rooms and toilet areas were dirty, and somehow the whole place was unwelcoming. I'm back at the old pool now – the facilities may not be as good, but it's very friendly and I feel safer there.* ❞

Excellent customer service brings a number of commercial benefits for leisure and recreation organisations, such as:

- increased sales
- new customers
- a better public image
- an edge over the competition
- a happier and more efficient workforce
- customer loyalty and repeat business.

DISCUSSION POINT

Think of the words people use to praise or complain about customer service. How much of it describes intangible things like feelings, perceptions and emotions? What pictures of an organisation come into your mind when someone tells you about good or bad experiences they've had as customers?

Over the next two weeks, make a note of every occasion that someone recommends a facility or product to you – for example, a shop, a CD, a restaurant, or a film. How many of these word-of-mouth recommendations do you act on? You will probably find that a large number of the things you choose to do have been influenced by other people's opinions.

DISCUSSION POINT

In their advertising, many leisure and recreation organisations try to create a positive image by talking about the quality of their customer service and their friendly, welcoming and efficient staff. Discuss how organisations create positive images in this way, giving examples from television, radio, newspapers and magazines.

Increased sales

Good customer service leads to an increase in an organisation's sales. In a commercial facility aiming to make a profit, more sales mean more profit.

The manager of a camping supplies shop describes how he sees the link between effective customer service and increased sales:

66 *A few months ago I decided to make sure that our customer service was really up to scratch. I invested in putting my staff on a training course in customer care. The shop now has a much friendlier atmosphere, and the staff feel much more confident about offering good service. When I checked sales figures last month, I was pleased to see that sales were up by over 20 per cent from three months ago.* 99

New customers

Satisfied customers not only return to an organisation, they also tend to bring new customers with them. Leisure and recreation organisations should never underestimate the power of word of mouth. Happy customers tell their friends, families and colleagues, and the general good reputation of the organisation attracts new customers.

Enhanced image

All leisure and recreation organisations want to present a good image. The way that they treat their customers is a crucial part of this. It would be pointless investing time and money in creating first-class products and services, only to put the customers off by treating them badly.

ACTIVITY

Think about the customer service you've had from leisure and recreation organisations.

■ Make a note of a service which particularly impressed you.

■ Make a note of a service which you thought was poor.

■ What was it about each of these services that gave you these impressions? Think about your needs and expectations at the time, and how they were met or exceeded.

■ Write two letters, one a letter of praise to the organisation which provided a good service, the other a letter of complaint, suggesting improvements which might be made to customer service. Make sure that you emphasise how the customer service you have received has affected your perception of, and attitude toward, the organisations.

The managing director of a fitness centre describes her organisation's view of customer care:

66 *We see customer care as an integral part of what we offer. We fulfil our customers' needs for fitness facilities through our gym equipment, exercise classes, swimming pool and squash courts. But the customer service we offer provides for their personal needs – the 'feelgood factor', the personal touch that makes the customers feel that they're seen as people not numbers. It makes people feel good about the organisation and trust it to fulfil their needs and expectations. Once we've given people the image, we work hard to make it a reality.* 99

Paul is one of the reception staff at the centre. He clearly recognises the effect that his attitude towards customers has on their perception of the organisation as a whole:

66 *Customers come here to relax and enjoy themselves. So they expect that to start happening from the moment they come in the door. I'm one of the first people they see. The way I treat them can colour their experience of our facilities. If I'm unwelcoming or off-hand, they'll feel irritated or disappointed. And no matter how brilliant our facilities are, that feeling will stay with them. So instead of enjoying themselves, they'll be thinking: 'He was rude. What sort of an organisation staffs its reception with people like that.'* 99

Many organisations use quotes from their satisfied customers in their promotional materials. These are known as **endorsements** and they help project a positive image of the organisation and their products and services. They also use pictures of people enjoying their products, services and facilities. The aim is to build up the expectations and trust of potential customers.

TOPSY TWISTER!!
Try it if you dare! These people did

"Brilliant! I can't wait to go again!" – John Wade, 18 yrs old.
"Wow! What an experience!" – Sue Older, 43 yrs old.
"Roller-coaster heaven!" – Kevin Healey, 25 yrs old.

An edge over the competition

Customer service is a form of 'added value' – it is what makes the difference between simply having your needs met as a customer, and feeling completely satisfied. Good customer service can be an important selling point for organisations, giving them an advantage over their competitors.

A customer explains how she felt about local fitness centres and gyms:

66 *I am lucky to live in large town. The are several fitness centres and gyms. Two belong to national chains, one is run by the local authority and the others by independents. The national ones are smart and modern; unfortunately the local ones are scruffy and over-crowded. I was automatically drawn to a small fitness centre which was bright and catered for busy executives. I am middle aged and haven't done much sport. I just felt I needed to change my lifestyle but I was nervous about going a gym. They took me seriously and offered a highly individual service and took the trouble to understand my concerns and personal preferences. There are lots of disadvantages, a tiny pool and a small range of exercise equipment. It gets very packed after work. Recently a big chain came here with an amazing array of equipment and exercise options. I was attracted to them but I won't change. My centre know me; I always get greeted by people I know and they know how to work with me. I wouldn't change it just because there are better facilities down the road.* 99

Employee satisfaction

All types of organisation, both large and small, use customer satisfaction information as an indicator of their employees' skills and use the data to set standards for improving motivation, skills and attitudes. Many organisations in this industry use their mission statements to communicate that customer satisfaction and their safety are at the top of their business objectives.

Repeat business and customer retention

Customers remember how they have been treated by an organisation. If they feel they have been treated well and leave satisfied, they are likely to return. If they feel unwelcome, have to wait too long or find that they are not getting what they expected, they are likely to go elsewhere.

Effective customer service can help organisations to:
- gain repeat business – by encouraging customers who have used a product or service to do so again
- keep customers – by encouraging customers to feel a sense of trust in the organisation, or loyalty to it, so that they come back again and again.

ACTIVITY

From your own experience, give three indicators of poor customer service. For each indicator, explain why this would affect staff moral and what can be done to improve customer satisfaction.

DISCUSSION POINT

Why do you choose to go to one leisure centre over another? Or to one restaurant rather than another?

Key questions

1 What are the results of good customer service?

2 How does good customer service affect an organisations workforce?

3 How does customer service affect an organisation's profitability?

SECTION **5.2**

Personal presentation

The way you present yourself to customers has a direct influence on their enjoyment, your job satisfaction and the future success of the organisation that employs you. This section covers the different aspects of personal presentation which contribute to good customer service.

❝ *It's important to give a good first impression by being smartly dressed. Most of our customers consider a night out at the theatre to be a special treat, and they have dressed up for the occasion. They expect the theatre staff to be dressed formally as well. Our staff don't wear uniforms but we do require professional business attire and a tidy, well-groomed appearance.* **❞**

manager of theatre

❝ *When I'm hiring staff, I look for one particular personality trait: enthusiasm. We want our customers to enjoy their time at the park, and they can only do this if the staff have the right attitude. If I'm presented with a choice between two candidates, one with lots of qualifications and training and one with a lot of enthusiasm, it's the second one who will get the job.* **❞**

manager of a theme park

5.2.1 **Making a good impression**

As soon as customers come into contact with a leisure and recreation organisation, they form first impressions. They notice:

- the decor and tidiness of the reception area
- how staff dress and how they present themselves
- whether there is a warm and friendly welcome
- the quality of the organisation's leaflets or brochures and the helpfulness of any information provided
- the service they receive on the first telephone conversation or when they receive a reply to an enquiry.

These first impressions can have a lasting effect on how a customer views an organisation.

In most organisations there are some staff who are usually the first point of contact with customers, such as receptionists, switchboard operators, box office staff, front-of-office staff or sales staff. These people are particularly well placed to create a good first impression. It means they have to communicate professionally and efficiently and be positive, whatever happens or is said. This may mean dealing with difficult questions, or even awkward customers, calmly and politely.

DISCUSSION POINT

You will have a lot of experience of being a customer of different leisure and recreation organisations, for example:

- going to a cinema or theatre
- using a sports or leisure centre
- finding information from an entertainment centre.

Think about your first impressions of these and similar leisure facilities you have used. What things helped form your impressions? Discuss your experiences of using these facilities with other students in your group.

How did the organisations and their staff communicate with you as a customer? Which of the organisations you discussed would you be most likely to visit or use again? Why?

5.2.2 **Presenting a positive image**

The personal image of staff can communicate strong messages about an organisation's attitude and image.

Whenever people meet for the first time, they assess each other according to their:

- appearance – dress, physical appearance
- actions – handshake, voice, body language
- attitudes – to other people, to situations.

This is why people dress up for interviews and greet and speak to the interviewer in a friendly manner – they are presenting a personal image that they hope will create a good impression.

Dress

Dress neatly and in appropriate fashion. In most cases it is appropriate to wear modest, professional styles which will not distract or offend the customer. Many leisure and recreation organisations require staff to wear a uniform which identifies them clearly to the customer.

Personal hygiene

When dealing with customers it is essential to present oneself in a clean and healthy fashion. Customers will notice if your hair is oily and uncombed, or your face or hands are dirty, and will take offence by it. A high standard of personal hygiene is particularly vital in restaurants or dining areas, and anywhere that food is prepared and served.

Personality

Your personality is a valuable part of the customer service you provide. It expresses your own individuality and allows the customer to feel that they are being treated personally. However, be aware of personality limitations that may interfere with the ability to serve customers. For example, a person who is rather shy would be ill-suited to act as a tour guide to large groups of people.

Attitude

Whatever your personality, your attitude will reveal more to the customer than anything else. A positive attitude means that you embrace the task of meeting the customer's needs and will make a sincere effort to do so. It will reflect a positive image of the organisation to the customer.

ACTIVITY

How does this employee's personal image play a part in the way the organisation provides customer service?

Key questions

1 Why is personal presentation an important part of customer service?

2 What sorts of things do customers notice when forming a first impression about an organisation or its staff?

3 In what ways can you present a positive public image?

SECTION **5.3**

Types of customer in leisure and recreation

Leisure and recreation products and services are used by all types of people, with differing sets of needs. One of the challenges for an industry as diverse as leisure and recreation is to provide good customer service to people of all ages, types and nationalities. In this section you will learn about the different types of customer you will be serving.

❝ I often conduct group tours around the museum, showing visitors the different exhibits and sharing information about particular pieces of artwork. Many of our visitors are from other countries, and their understanding of English may be limited so I must try to speak as clearly as possible and ensure that they are not excluded by a language barrier. We also host many groups of schoolchildren, who have particular kinds of needs – for example, to keep the tour at a brisk pace and to involve them as much as possible by asking questions. When I started this job I was sent on a training course which was specifically aimed at providing customer service to large groups of people. ❞

museum guide

❝ We're a residential pub and in the last ten years or so the neighborhood around us has changed a great deal. There has been a large increase in young families living in the immediate area, so we decided to redesign the beer garden to include a small play area. We also hired a chef to introduce a more extensive menu, including a children's menu, so that families in the area would consider us a good place to come for pub food. Business has been thriving and many of the families are regular customers. ❞

owner of a pub

5.3.1 **Types of customer**

UNIT

5

SECTION **5.3**

Individuals and groups

Leisure and recreation products and services are used by people of all ages, types and nationalities, including those with specific needs, such as people with disabilities or with young children. To provide excellent customer service, you will need to identify and meet the differing needs of a wide variety of customers, such as:

■ individuals

■ groups

■ people of different ages

■ people from different cultures

■ non-English speakers

■ people with specific needs, for example those needing wheelchair access, people with sensory disabilities and people with young children.

Individuals

Communication with individual customers gives staff in leisure and recreation organisations the best opportunity to find out what the customer needs and to explain to the customer how the organisation can meet those needs. It helps to build up good one-to-one relationships with customers. This is important – customers who feel they are valued and recognised as individuals are more likely to return.

A regular customer at a gym explains how the staff's skills in individual communication has gained them her customer loyalty:

❝ *I'd tried a number of different exercise programmes at a number of different gyms and fitness centres but I always ended up dropping out after the first session or two. The classes I'd tried seemed to be run on the principle of 'keep up or keep out'. The instructors didn't seem interested in helping you improve and one or two seemed to be there to show off how fit they were. When I first contacted my current gym by phone, I was amazed at how much information the receptionist gave me in response to my general enquiry. Right from the start I felt they made it their business to find out what I was looking for. And the individual treatment continued from there. I booked in for an assessment session with one of the instructors and from that he devised an exercise programme just for me. He made sure I knew how to do the exercises and how to use the equipment and he worked with me until I felt confident to do them on my own. At every session we would talk about how I was getting on and we'd work out any adjustments to the programme that we felt were necessary.* ❞

Groups

Many staff working in leisure and recreation organisations need to communicate with groups as well as individuals. Group communication can either be:

261

- face to face – for example, a fitness coach teaching an aerobics class, meetings
- written – for example, through signs, notices, promotional materials, memos, letters.

A guide in an art gallery explains some of the skills he uses in talking to groups:

66 *In an average day, I do between eight and ten gallery tours. I have to be fresh and enthusiastic for each one. Luckily for me, I love the gallery and the exhibits are all like old friends to me. So I think of the tour as a way of introducing people to things I love. I know a lot about the exhibits and the artists who created them. But I have to tailor the information to suit the groups I'm taking round. For example, knowledgeable art enthusiasts have different needs and interests from school parties. I've been on guided tours of galleries myself all around the world and quite often the guides treat you like a herd of sheep to be got through the gallery as quickly as possible. I like to make every group feel I'm doing the tour just for them. Talking to a group of people can be quite difficult. I make sure that everyone feels included in the group by looking around at the group members while I'm talking. I talk slightly more slowly than I would in normal conversation and take care to speak clearly. I always encourage people to ask questions and make their own comments on the exhibits. My proudest moment was when a woman came up to me after a tour and told me she now felt she knew the artists personally and that their work had really come alive for her.* 99

DISCUSSION POINT

If you ran a fitness centre, what would you identify as the characteristic needs for these age groups?

- the under-fives
- the over-60s
- 30- to 40-year-olds

Different age groups

Different age groups have different needs and tastes. Organisations will target services to cater for:

- a range of age groups (e.g. theatres, cinemas, theme parks)
- specific age groups at particular times (e.g. matinees for the under-14s or the over-60s)
- particular age groups (e.g. a youth music venue).

Different cultural backgrounds

Many leisure and recreation organisations have to cater for a wide range of cultural needs. Here are some examples:

- language
- diet
- religious observances
- dress codes
- social conventions.

ACTIVITY

Visit your nearest leisure or sports centre. Ask the staff there about the contact they have with people from different cultural backgrounds. Find out what the staff do to make sure that any special customer needs are met.

Non-English speakers

Many people have a first language which is different from the majority of the population (in the UK, this means people with English as a second or foreign language). There are many reasons why organisations need to make arrangements for people who do not speak English or for whom English is not their first language. These include catering for people from ethnic minorities who have not had the opportunity to learn English, students from other countries visiting the UK to learn English, newly arrived immigrants and visitors travelling to the UK as part of their holidays.

Specific needs

To provide good customer service, leisure and recreation organisations must make sure that everyone has the same opportunities to use their products and services. This means catering for customers with a range of specific needs, including people:

- with young children
- with difficulties in seeing (visual impairment)
- who have difficulty moving or getting about (restricted mobility) or who may need wheelchair access to facilities
- who have difficulty hearing (hearing impairment)
- who have problems with reading or using numbers (literacy or numeracy problems).

ACTIVITY

Ask the staff at your nearest library about the contact they have with people who are non-English speakers or people for whom English is not their first language. Find out what the staff do to make sure that any special customer needs are met.

HARRY'S BAR
MENU
STARTERS £3.50
Cream of vegetable soup   Avocado and prawn salad
Roll mop herrings with rye bread
Melon and parma ham
Smoked salmon pate with granary toast

MAIN COURSES £7.50
Beef stroganoff with rice   Half chicken roast
Pork schnitzel   Poached salmon   Grilled herby trout

VEGETARIAN £6.00
Stuffed baked red pepper
Spinach and ricotta cannelloni
'Everything' salad   Mushroom moussaka
Four cheese pizza

All served with a selection of fresh vegetables or
salad with a choice of potato dishes

DESSERT & COFFEE £2.50
Brandy walnut cheesecake   Chocolate mousse
Fresh fruit salad   Flambé banana surprise

What specific needs are these organisations meeting?

ACTIVITY

The schools liaison officer of an art gallery has been asked to prepare for a visit from a school party. To make sure that she provides good customer service, she sends out a questionnaire in advance to find out more about the students' needs and wants. She finds out that one is in a wheelchair, and another has hearing difficulties. Over half don't speak English as their first language and 25 don't eat meat.

She asks your advice on how to provide good customer service. Write a short memo summarising different points she needs to bear in mind when planning the visit.

What would have been the repercussions if she hadn't found out in advance about her customers' special needs?

Key questions

1 Name six different types of customer who may have specific customer service needs.

2 How can leisure and recreation organisations and their staff provide good service to people from different cultures?

3 How can you offer good service to customers who don't speak English?

SECTION **5.4**

Dealing with customers

This section explores the topic of communicating well when dealing with customers. To provide good customer service, you will need to communicate effectively, whether orally or in writing, to individuals or groups, face-to-face or over the telephone.

❝ We get a lot of business over the telephone so it's essential that staff are trained in telephone etiquette. They receive it as part of their initial training when they start working here, and we often review it at staff meetings. ❞

manager of a bookstore

❝ My job involves coordinating plans and schedules with a variety of people every day. I would say that about 80% of my job involves communication. Often I'll make arrangements with somebody by telephone, and then send a letter or an e-mail afterwards to confirm the details in writing. ❞

community event organiser

5.4.1 Effective communication in customer service

Effective communication means giving:

- the right message
- to the right people
- at the right time
- in the right way.

Customer service is all about meeting customers' needs and matching – or better still, exceeding – their expectations. To do these, you need to be absolutely sure that you know what the customer wants. The best way to find out is by talking to them and listening to them. So effective communication is crucial to good customer service for both external and internal customers.

Dealing with customers face to face

Face-to-face communication brings customers and staff members into direct and personal contact. In this situation, making a good impression and presenting a positive image of the organisation all rely on your personal skills. A face-to-face encounter with a customer gives you many advantages. For example:

- the communication between you is two-way
- you can see your customer's reaction
- you can check on the spot that you have understood the customer.

When dealing with customers face to face, you need to be aware of the messages you send through your body language. This includes:

Body language means the non-verbal signals you give out through your posture, facial expressions, gestures and eye contact.

- facial expressions – frowning, smiling and so on
- eye contact – keeping or avoiding it
- body position – sitting or standing close to people, or moving away from them
- body posture – sitting or standing upright, slumping, leaning back
- gestures – pointing, shrugging, nodding and so on.

Your body language should be in tune with your verbal message. For example, in making a customer feel welcome, you'd give your greeting with a smile.

Without speaking to these people, what can you tell about their attitudes?

267

Carry out research into body language. You may find it helpful to look in books on communication, or psychology textbooks. Make a chart listing as many types of positive and negative body language as you can. Think about your own behaviour – is your body language good?

Using the results of your research, produce a set of guidelines for receptionists on how to use positive body language when dealing with customers face to face.

Talking to customers on the phone

Telephones are a vital communication method in any organisation. They mean that people can contact each other quickly and directly and they allow immediate two-way communication. Although most people use telephones in their daily lives, using a telephone effectively for business communication needs a certain level of thought and skill. A trainer who runs training courses in telephone skills explains why:

66 *As with other forms of business communication, telephone calls should be conducted in an efficient and professional way. A sloppy approach can damage an organisation's image. When customers contact an organisation by phone, they expect the same courtesy and helpfulness as they would face to face. They expect the person who answers the phone to greet them in a friendly but business-like way, give them the information they need or put them through to the person who can help them. It's all part of providing a customer service that meets the customers' needs.* **99**

Written communications

Visit any leisure and recreation organisation and you'll see a lot of written information. Some will be for external customers and some will be for internal purposes. Here are a few examples:

- letters
- memos
- reports
- forms
- staff handbooks
- instruction manuals

- signs
- notices
- leaflets
- brochures
- posters.

Whatever the format, written communication should:
- be easy to understand
- be clearly laid out
- use accurate language, grammar and spelling
- include all the right information
- give details of who to contact with queries or for more information.

DISCUSSION POINT

Here's the experience of a potential customer ringing to find out about the classes run at a dance centre:

RECEPTIONIST:	Hello?
CUSTOMER:	Hello. Is that Julienne's Dance Studio?
RECEPTIONIST:	Yes.
CUSTOMER:	I wonder if you can help me. I'd like to know what sort of classes you run, the times and the prices.
RECEPTIONIST:	Classes, times and what, dear?
CUSTOMER:	Classes, times and prices.
RECEPTIONIST:	Classes, times and prices. Hang on, I'll put you through to someone who'll tell you. Now, what's her extension? 62. Oh no, that's the wrong one – 63, that's it.

(a minute of silence)

RECEPTIONIST:	Hello? Caller, are you still there?
CUSTOMER:	Yes.
RECEPTIONIST:	Oh, hello dear. I was trying to put you through but I can't find her. Hold on . . . Janice, where's Julie? Oh, is she? Are you taking the post down? Take these letters for me – I'm on the phone. Thanks. Hello, Caller?
CUSTOMER:	Yes?
RECEPTIONIST:	Hello dear, yes . . . um . . . the person you need to speak to has just popped out. Can you call back in about – ooh, I don't know – 10 minutes or so?
CUSTOMER:	Um, well, yes, but couldn't you, er–
RECEPTIONIST:	Thank you, dear. Goodbye.

What sort of impression has the receptionist given of the organisation? What sort of customer service has the receptionist provided? If you were the customer, would you call back? What should the receptionist have said and done?

THE
Fleetwood
FACTORY

37 Garvington Lane Groton Suffolk Telephone 01787 0100055

MEMO MEMO MEMO MEMO

ALL STAFF,

PLEASE BE AWARE THAT THERE IS A COMPULSORY FIRE SAFETY COURSE
TAKING PLACE FOR ALL EMPLOYEES ON THE 19TH MAY 2000, AT 2.00PM.

PLEASE MAKE THE NECESSARY ARRANGEMENTS TO MAKE
YOURSELVES AVAILABLE.

THANKS.

Hugh

HUGH

ACTIVITY

Here is an extract from a notice in a hotel, explaining what customers should do if the fire alarm goes off. How well does it work as a piece of written communication? Write an improved version.

NOTICE TO CUSTOMERS

On hearing the fire alarm being sounded, the correct procedure to follow is to pass with all necessary haste to the nearest emergency fire exit which can be found at either end of all corridors. The lifts must never be used in the course of an evacuation procedure. Personal belongings should not be collected before making an exit from the building. Having vacated the premises, customers should make their way to the assembly point which can be found situated in the car park to the fore of the hotel where hotel staff should be reported to for names to be recorded.

What sort of communication would you use for each of these?

- a customer whose squash court has been double-booked
- health and safety information for swimming pool customers
- information for hotel reception staff on room charges
- confirmation of theatre tickets

Verbal and non-verbal communication

All the methods and forms of communication described so far break down into two types:

- verbal – using words
- non-verbal – not using words.

Some communication uses only one type. For example:

- a telephone conversation uses only spoken words (vocal communication)
- a letter uses only written words
- road signs use symbols to direct or warn drivers (visual communication).

More often, communication is a combination of the two types. For example:

- a face-to-face conversation would be a combination of spoken words and body language signals
- a brochure would be a combination of written words and pictures or photographs.

Whichever type is used, the important thing is that it is the appropriate and most effective way of communicating with the customer.

ACTIVITY

Draw up a list of examples of how the staff of a leisure centre can communicate well with customers in a way that promotes good customer service. Your list should include examples of communication that are:

- verbal
- non-verbal
- by telephone
- face to face

- written
- with individuals
- with groups.

5.4.2   The benefits of effective communication

Effective communication creates good relationships with customers – both internal and external. It also creates a happy working environment and satisfied staff. When communication is good, the organisation becomes:

■ more efficient – because everyone has the information they need
■ more effective – because information is getting to the right people, in the right way at the right time.

Here are some quotes from customers and staff in the leisure and recreation industry which illustrate the importance of effective communication.

A customer at a gym:

❝ *The staff at the gym I go to always treat me in a friendly way. They greet me by name when I arrive which always makes me feel special. They have all the information about the facilities at their fingertips. And the instructors take a lot of time to show me how to use the gym equipment and work out exercise programmes to suit me personally. I wouldn't go anywhere else.* **❞**

The managing director of a water-sports centre:

❝ *Through our staff appraisal system, we realised that staff morale was low. The heart of the problem was poor communication. People felt they weren't being given enough information about the important things like product information, how well they were doing and the company's future plans, and was spending too much time bogged down in masses of paperwork and meetings. So we got everyone to think of themselves as internal customers and suppliers and to suggest improvements for our communication systems and procedures based on their needs. As a result, we developed more efficient and realistic ways of communicating, staff morale is high and productivity is up.* **❞**

The marketing manager of a seaside marina:

❝ *Our direct mail campaigns weren't pulling in as much business as we'd hoped. We needed to improve their effectiveness but we weren't sure how to go about it. We bought in some outside help from a corporate communications consultant. It was money well spent. Having an outsider's view helped us to recognise that we'd slipped into set patterns of thinking – about the organisation's image and our customers – and it was costing us business. We analysed our target customers more closely and carefully defined their information needs. Then we created promotional materials to match those needs. The result was an instant improvement in business – and a lesson that being effective means keeping in touch with the customers' needs.* **❞**

Good communication increases:

■ customer satisfaction
■ staff satisfaction
■ organisational efficiency
■ organisational effectiveness

ACTIVITY

Devise a booklet and accompanying poster for staff in a leisure and recreation organisation you know about that would help them to understand the role of good communication in customer service.

271

Key questions

1 What are the advantages of face-to-face communication when providing customer service?

2 Name five aspects of body language which can affect the image you present when dealing with customers.

3 Describe how good customer service can be offered over the telephone.

4 What are some guidelines for preparing good written communication?

5 Give examples of verbal and non-verbal communication.

SECTION **5.5**

Selling skills

Selling is part of customer service. People expect to pay for the goods and services they receive and selling is one of the ways for staff to meet their needs. Many jobs in leisure and recreation involve selling even if it's not their main function. In this section you'll look at the different steps in selling products and services.

❝ I'm always selling to people, really. I talk with customers about the music, and about the latest news and gossip in different bands. I ask them what they think about new releases and I give them recommendations of the different albums I like myself. It's what I like most about the job – being able to go away from a customer knowing you've made a sale and there's an opportunity for more business later. ❞

sales clerk in a record store

❝ I don't think of what we do as selling. Our aim is to give the people who come here a high standard of food and to get the atmosphere right for them to relax and enjoy their meal. That's why I put so much into the look of the place. I think if customers come in and feel at home straight away they are much more likely to enjoy themselves. In a way I suppose that is selling, but it comes naturally to me! ❞

owner of a restaurant

5.5.1 The functions and objectives of selling

Selling is the most important role of some leisure and recreation employees. For others, selling is not their main role, but it is still important:

- wardens at a country house open to the public are there to help people visiting the house, but may also become involved in selling guidebooks, postcards and other souvenirs
- reception staff at a leisure centre deal mainly with enquiries and bookings, but are well placed to sell other services, such as subscriptions, party bookings or the centre's restaurant facilities
- museum staff are there to help customers by providing information and dealing with problems but they may encourage customers to visit special exhibitions for which there is an entry fee.

The functions of selling

In simple terms, 'selling' means persuading a customer to part with their money for a product or service. In practice, this can involve:

- giving customers information about products or services
- creating and keeping good relationships with customers
- dealing with customers' queries or problems
- dealing with customers' complaints.

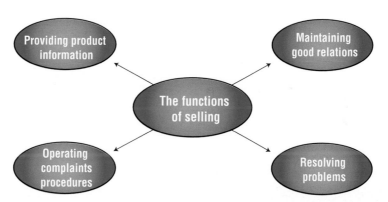

The objectives of selling

Selling lies at the heart of customer service. The objectives of selling are very similar to those of giving good customer service.

Objectives of selling are:

- securing repeat business – encouraging existing customers to continue dealing with the organisation
- increasing sales – finding new customers and encouraging existing customers to buy more
- achieving customer satisfaction – making sure that customers are happy with their purchases and the service they receive
- increasing profitability – finding cost-effective ways of maximising income
- securing competitive advantage – keeping ahead of the competition.

ACTIVITY

Make a chart showing the different ways in which the organisation's sales methods help it to achieve its sales objectives of:

- securing repeat business
- increasing sales
- achieving customer satisfaction
- increasing profitability
- securing competitive advantage.

A telephone booking person working for a theme park describes selling roles in his company:

66 Our customers come to us after seeing ads on the TV or in papers and magazines. All tickets are sold over the telephone, so it is the telesales staff who do most of the selling. We have to create a good impression and show that we will do anything to ensure they can visit when they want to and to answer the queries about facilities for children and parking. I try to get on well with my customers, so that they know they have all the information. I don't want them to go elsewhere because they feel unconfident about our service and facilities. You have to judge the best way to do this from listening to their voices and from the little clues you get from what they tell you.

Of course, everyone in the organisation has their own part to play in selling. For example, the facilities and parking staff have to deal constantly with queries – although if a customer rings me direct with a problem, I like to try to deal with it for them. Details of customers are passed to the administration staff who then make sure they go on the mailing list and get our leaflets, plus details of special offers and stuff like that. That's an important part of selling, too, as it keeps us in people's minds. 99

5.5.2 Sales techniques

Selling requires knowledge, skills and techniques. People whose jobs involve a lot of selling usually receive training from their employers in these skills and techniques, but they can also be useful for people working in jobs where selling is only a small part of their responsibilities.

Preparing for a sales interview

When a salesperson and a customer talk, it is not like an ordinary conversation that takes place between friends. In this situation (sometimes called a sales interview), both people have their own aims. The person selling has the main aim of making a sale – persuading the customer that buying a particular product or service is the right thing to do. Customers may want to find out information, but don't want to agree to buy the product or service until they are quite sure about it.

Preparing well for sales interviews can help employees to meet their aims and make a sale. A travel agent provides these four golden rules for sales clerks before opening for the day:

- Be ready to make a good impression on everyone who walks in the door – think about your appearance and attitude.
- Make sure you're up to date on destinations, offers, flights, insurance and so on.
- Have brochures, leaflets and other information to hand, and switch your computer on.

- Decide with other members of staff who will answer phone enquiries if you are busy. An unanswered phone can put off both the customer in the shop, and the one on the other end of the line.

Approaching the customer

How customers meet sales staff depends on the type of product or service being offered. At one extreme are the timeshare touts in holiday resorts, pestering people to show them an apartment or new holiday complex. At the other extreme are the fans of a rock band who queue up for hours to buy tickets for a concert.

As these examples show, it can be either the customer who approaches the person selling, or vice versa. It is often easier for the sellers when customers make the first move, as they know they are dealing with people who are already interested in the product, and should be willing to buy, provided the product or service is right.

When the person selling makes the first move, they need care and sensitivity to make sure they don't put the customer off. A sales assistant working in a museum shop describes how she approaches customers:

66 *Working in a shop, I've quickly learnt to tell what customers want and what they expect me to do. It's never a good idea to pounce on customers – that would put most of them off – but some do want you to take the lead, perhaps because they're not sure what they want or don't know where to find something. I try to use body language rather than approaching them too enthusiastically – I make eye contact and give them a welcoming smile to attract their attention. If they smile back, I usually give a friendly greeting to make verbal contact. Sometimes a queue builds up at the till in the summer, and I'm too busy to help a customer immediately. When this happens, I make sure I let the customer know I've seen them by explaining that someone will be with them as soon as possible.* 99

Investigate customer needs

Leisure and recreation organisations use marketing research to find out in general which products and services to sell. Members of staff involved in selling then need to find out, and meet, the specific needs of individual customers.

This is straightforward if customers know what they want: a simple 'I would like' or 'Do you have?' tells a salesperson straightaway what a customer's needs are. If customers don't know what they want, or don't understand exactly what products or services are, then selling skills are needed.

A leisure complex operator realised that it wasn't making the most of the potential to sell the range of its facilities to visitors through its information staff. As it was difficult to organise sales training with staff who were often part-time and worked different shifts, it produced a set of guidelines for them to follow. The extract on the left gives advice on how to identify customers' needs.

Identifying customer needs will probably involve asking two types of question:

■ closed questions, which restrict the answers that can be given to 'yes', 'no', or one of a limited number of answers

■ open questions, which give the customer the chance to give views, opinions or preferences.

1 Give the customer your full attention.
2 Use good communication skills, friendly body language and a welcoming approach.
3 Ask the customer a few questions to find out about their needs and expectations.
   • who is the customer?
   • what type of activity are they interested in? (educational, fun for their children) etc.)
   • when might they want to go do these things?
   • where might they want to go to?
   • why do they want to go – is it something they definitely want to do, or just a possibility? You may also need to find out how much the customer is prepared to pay.
4 Listen carefully to the customer.
5 From the customer's answers, decide what activities would best meet the customer's needs. A customer may have several needs – you may have to find out which one(s) the customer considers most important.
6 Summarise the customers' needs to make sure that you have understood them all.

Sales negotiating

For a product or service to be sold, the buyer and seller have to agree on price and the conditions of the sale. Not all selling situations are simple:

- a customer buying in bulk or paying a large amount of cash may ask for a discount.
- services may not be available at the time required
- the make or model of a product may not be available and other similar products need to be considered.

The manager of a hotel reports on how he filled rooms when business has been slow:

66 *During the recession of the early 1990s, we knew that we had to be flexible about room prices. People were spending less money on leisure and taking fewer holidays, and customers became precious! Many customers realised this and tried to get a cheaper price for a hotel room, especially if they were offering cash. If we had refused to negotiate, then they would have looked elsewhere. As far as I was concerned, an occupied room at a cheap rate was better than an empty room!* 99

Not all the staff within an organisation are allowed to negotiate like this. If a customer tries to haggle with sales staff who don't have the authority, they should fetch a more senior member of staff for the customer to speak to.

If a customer wants to negotiate about price or conditions, staff members should:

- keep within the limits of their authority
- find out how far they can negotiate – lowest price they can accept, for example
- make offers confidently
- never be grudging or rude when agreeing to a reduction or different conditions
- be prepared to be assertive and to say 'no', but always do so politely.

Overcoming objections

Customers usually make objections when they are uncertain whether or not to buy a product or service. They may not be sure whether the goods or services on offer actually meet their needs, or they may be unsure about the price or about some of the conditions of the sale.

The seller needs to find out why the customer is making objections and work out how serious they are. Customers may make objections as a way of saying that they have changed their mind and don't want to buy a product or service any more.

If customers have a real concern, the seller needs to find a solution, e.g. by suggesting another similar product or by finding a way of changing the service to suit the customer.

When there is no suitable solution, it is better to tell customers that and stop selling, rather than try to persuade them to accept something that would be unsuitable. That is much more likely to make an impression of good customer service, and may make the customer come back to the organisation at a later date.

Closing the sale

When a customer agrees to buy a product or service, the seller is said to 'close the sale'.

There are situations where customers can't or won't make up their minds on the spot. They may need to consult others or spend a bit more time thinking. Some customers may simply need a little reassurance or some gentle persuasion to make a decision – good sellers are able to provide it, without putting too much pressure on the customer.

Before actually agreeing to buy a product or service, many customers show that they are ready to buy in other ways:

- through positive, open body language
- by asking further questions ('How can I pay?' 'Can I pay in instalments?')
- by speaking positively about products or services ('Yes, I really would like to try that')
- by inviting the seller to reassure them ('So you think my children would really enjoy this?').

AIDA

In sales situations you will need to apply the AIDA technique:

- Attention – direct the customer's attention to the product
- Interest – whet their interest in the product
- Desire – pitch the product to increase their desire for it
- Action – take action by negotiating a sale

Key questions

1 What are the objectives of selling?

2 In what ways can you establish rapport with a customer?

3 What open and closed questions would you ask to establish a customer's needs?

4 What are the five guidelines you should follow when negotiating a sale with a customer?

5 What are the four steps of the AIDA sales technique?

SECTION **5.6**

Delivering customer service

In the diverse leisure and recreation industry, there are many types of customer service situations. Whatever the situation, it is essential to communicate well and respond to the customer's needs. This section looks more closely at how to deliver good customer service.

" We get a variety of questions from our customers, such as when to sow different seeds and how to cultivate particular plants. They also need information about the products and tools we sell and how to use them. Often we are asked for advice about how to deal with weeds or how to keep a garden free of pests such as bugs or rodents. We also provide assistance to customers by helping them carry their purchases to their cars – many customers buy large trays of starter plants or heavy bags of compost, and they appreciate the help. "

assistant in a garden centre

" My job is to look after guests in whatever way is necessary, and that covers an endless variety of situations. No two days are ever the same. I make reservations and call taxis, pass on messages, hunt down missing luggage, arrange dry cleaning, and much more. We often host large receptions in our ballrooms – weddings and business luncheons for example – and there are a million different things that might come up. Whatever happens, we do our best to provide the highest level of service. "

hotel concierge

5.6.1 Considering customer needs

THE FIRST RULE OF CUSTOMER SERVICE

The customer comes first! Look at who your customer is, and evaluate their particular needs and concerns so you can provide an appropriate service.

The first step in delivering customer service is to consider the customer. The extract on the left is taken from a theme park booklet issued to all staff.

Is it an internal customer?
- Make sure service is appropriate for the level of customer. (Is the customer your manager? Or a colleague?)
- Should you take a formal approach to customer service (e.g write a memo)?

What is the customer's cultural background?
- Is your customer's first language English? If not, seek help with translation/ use leaflets in different languages.
- Does your customer have different dietary needs?

Are you dealing with a group?
- How many people are you catering for?
- Are there any individual specific needs within the group?
- Do we offer any concessions which apply to the group?

Is your customer an individual?
- Are there any special facilities we can provide for individual customers?

How old is the customer?
- Does your customer have special needs because of age? (e.g children's menus and play facilities)?
- Do we offer any concessions likely to be of interest to the customer (e.g mid-week breaks for pensioners)?

Does the customer have specific needs?
- Does your customer have difficulty seeing (visual impairment)?
- Does you customer have difficulties moving about (restricted mobility)?
- Does your customer have hearing difficulties?
- If the answer is yes to any of these questions, provide appropriate service.
- Is your customer vegetarian?

Prioritising customer needs

Delivering good customer service to customers with more than one need involves:

- identifying the different needs
- prioritising them
- dealing with them in order of priority.

ACTIVITY

What sort of information and service do these customers need, and how should it be presented?

- a first-time customer in a fitness class
- a customer ringing to find out about the availability of vegetarian food at a music venue
- a party of people with hearing difficulties on a guided tour of a museum
- a customer who's just had their wallet stolen
- a blind customer who wants to use the swimming pool

5.6.2 **Situations requiring customer service**

There are many different ways of providing customer service. Some of the situations which require customer service include:

- providing information
- giving advice
- receiving or passing on messages
- keeping records
- providing assistance
- dealing with problems
- dealing with dissatisfied customers
- products
- security and safety.

Providing information

Customers often need information. For example:

- someone in the audience at a theatre asks the person selling programmes for directions to the toilets
- a visitor to an art gallery asks an attendant for information about a picture
- someone joining a sports centre asks about opening hours.

Leisure and recreation employees are representatives of the organisations they work for. They need to know about:

- the products and services available
- prices and features of products
- health, safety and security at the organisation
- the organisational structure.

It's also helpful for leisure and recreation employees to have a wider understanding of the industry as a whole. For example:

- a shop assistant in a record shop should know about trends in the music industry
- a hotelier should know about different types of reservation systems available.

Most people in leisure and recreation work in a particular geographical area. They should know about the region they work in, so they can answer customers' questions about facilities in the area.

Some facilities are regularly visited by people from across the UK and overseas – theme parks, national monuments and national parks. People working in these facilities may need to know about:

- transport links and travel distances
- the geography of the UK
- facilities in other parts of the country.

> **DISCUSSION POINT**
>
> Think of a time when an employee gave you the wrong information about products and their prices. What were the results of the mistake?

ACTIVITY

Interview a member of staff who works in a leisure and recreation facility. Ask them:

- what type of help they give customers
- what type of advice they give
- what type of information they give.

If they're not sure of the difference between help, advice and information, explain it to them using examples. Using the information you have collected, write a short leaflet to help someone new to the job do these three things well.

Giving advice

Customers using facilities often ask staff for advice, to make sure they enjoy activities in safety and to the full. For example:

- asking a lifeguard if a pool is safe for a beginning swimmer
- asking the waiter what's good on a menu
- making sure from a member of staff whether a particular ride at a theme park is safe and suitable for young children.

Organisations need to make sure that their staff:

- know enough about the area they work in to give good advice
- are trained how to give it clearly and politely
- know that if they can't offer sound advice, they should ask someone with more experience – passing a question on to someone else may take longer but it's a whole lot better than giving bad advice.

Receiving or passing on messages

It may be necessary to receive or pass on messages when dealing with customers. Remember two important things when taking or leaving messages:

- Communicate the message clearly and entirely. Do not leave room for confusion about what the content of the message actually is.
- Communicate the message promptly. Do not leave it as something that could be forgotten or until it is too late to be of any use.

Keeping records

Most facilities keep records of sales and customers every day, including:

- receipts
- booking forms
- membership listings
- registering.

Facilities may also keep records of individual customers' preferences and special requirements.

In the past, most of these records were kept manually, in written books and sheets. Now, most travel and tourism facilities have put their recording systems on to computer, which:

- improves speed
- enables a lot of information to be stored in a small space.

ACTIVITY

Collect examples of different records kept by one leisure and recreation organisation. Use the records to produce a simple leaflet explaining the way in which the organisation keeps sales records.

Providing assistance

Customers using leisure and recreation facilities often rely on an organisation's staff for practical help. For example:

- helping a hotel guest find a parking space and carrying their luggage
- an assistant in a bookshop holding open the door for a customer with a pushchair
- showing a theatre audience member to a seat in the dark.

Leisure and recreation organisations need to:

- identify the different types of help their customers might need
- make sure staff are trained, equipped and available to provide it.

Dealing with problems

Things sometimes go wrong in any organisation. It is the responsibility of staff to address any problems that customers bring to their attention. The best way to deal with problems is to tackle them immediately and constructively. It won't help to blame someone else or to avoid the problem at hand. Compare the following remarks from diners at a restaurant. Who do you think received better customer service?

66 I ordered a filet of steak, medium-rare, but what I got was burnt to a crisp! When I pointed this out to the waitress, she responded by complaining that they were understaffed and implied that I should just accept the meal I'd been served. When I insisted upon sending it back to the kitchen, it took another 35 minutes before I received the correct order. By then my companions had all finished their meals and had to wait for me. 99

66 I accidentally knocked over the bottle of wine that the waiter had just delivered to our table, breaking the glass and spilling red wine all over the table. I was so embarrassed! It was an awful mess. The waiter returned to the table instantly and offered to reseat us at the next table over, then he brought another bottle of wine at no extra charge. He even smoothed over the awkwardness of the situation, by saying that he enjoyed a little unexpected excitement once in a while and getting me to laugh with him about it. 99

Dealing with dissatisfied customers

Occasionally you will be presented with customers who are displeased with some aspect of the products or services that they have received.

If customers do complain, employees should be patient, considerate and offer practical solutions.

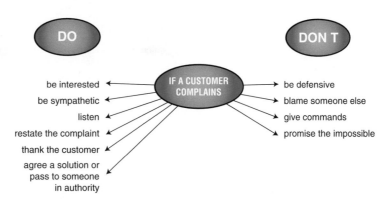

DO — IF A CUSTOMER COMPLAINS — **DON T**

be interested
be sympathetic
listen
restate the complaint
thank the customer
agree a solution or pass to someone in authority

be defensive
blame someone else
give commands
promise the impossible

DISCUSSION POINT

Think of a time when you, or someone you know, complained to a salesperson.

■ How did they handle the complaint?

■ Did you, or the other person, feel pleased with the outcome and use the facility again, or come away feeling dissatisfied and determined not to return?

■ What would you have done differently?

DISCUSSION POINT

Have these people received good customer service?

■ a swimmer whose handbag goes missing when she leaves it by the side of the pool

■ a restaurant customer who suffers food poisoning after not choosing what a waiter suggested from the menu

Security and safety

People nowadays are very conscious of security and safety. Customers want to be sure that they and others around them will be safe when using a facility, and that their belongings will be secure. Making sure that this is the case is an important part of good customer service.

It means:
■ giving information and advice to customers – how to use a piece of equipment properly, what to do with personal belongings
■ making sure that staff follow health, safety and hygiene regulations
■ checking that staff know how to use equipment safely.

Key questions

1 What is the first step in delivering customer service?

2 Why is it important to know how to prioritise a customers various needs?

3 Why is communcation important in customer service?

4 How does an organisation's staff meet customers' needs?

5 What are two important things to remember when receiving or passing on messages for customers?

6 Give an example of a way to provide assistance to a customer.

7 What is the best way to deal with a customer's problem?

SECTION **5.7**

Handling complaints

In customer service situations you may find that you need to handle complaints. In this section you will learn how to deal with customer complaints in a positive and effective manner.

> 66 Every complaint is an opportunity for a new sale. A customer whose complaints have been dealt with well feels very positive towards you, and is more likely to come back. 99
>
> *manager of a theme park*

> 66 The worst possible thing you can do with a complaining customer is to argue and be defensive. It doesn't matter if you are in the right and they are wrong – being right is often a great disadvantage because you put them on the defensive too. 99
>
> *receptionist at a leisure centre*

> 66 We don't generally have to deal with complaints – this would be more the job of the front-of-house manager. But we listen to what people have to say, try to get it sorted out, and apologise if there is a problem. Our general attitude is that we want people to go away happy and there is a lot we can learn from customers who aren't happy for any reason. 99
>
> *press and publicity officer at an entertainments venue*

5.7.1 Handling complaints

The complaints an organisation receives are the tip of a large iceberg. Only 5% of dissatisfied customers complain about the goods or services they receive. This means that 95% of dissatisfied customers don't bother to complain. So what do they do instead? They remain dissatisfied, but rather than try to get their money back via a formal complaint, they are likely to take their custom elsewhere.

This means that if a company receives only five formal complaints in a year, there could be 95 dissatisfied customers who do not return. These customers may tell their friends about the poor service they received. Their friends may also take their business elsewhere.

The best way to handle complaints is to avoid them in the first place. The most common reasons for customer complaints are:

- they are unhappy with a product or quality of service – customers who are given bad service when buying a product are more likely to buy something which doesn't meet their needs
- they have been kept waiting – the longer customers have to wait for service and attention, the more likely they are to complain. If waits are likely, organisations can help to relieve frustration by providing entertainment such as TVs or video screens
- they have been patronised – employees must take care not to adopt a superior attitude, or to assume that customers don't know what they're talking about.

How to deal with complaints

When dealing with complaints it is essential to respect what the customer has to say, and then find a solution to the problem which meets the approval of the customer. Keep in mind the following guidelines:

- listen carefully to the customer
- apologise in general terms for any inconvenience caused
- let the customer know that the matter will be fully investigated and put right
- try to see the problem from the customer's point of view
- keep calm and do not argue with the customer
- find a solution to the problem
- agree upon the solution with the customer
- make sure that what you promised to do gets done.

Now consider this example.

A couple booked expensive front row seats for a musical as part of a long-awaited trip to London. When they arrived they found that their seats were taken by two people who also had tickets. Here is the conversation that took place between the couple and an employee of the theatre.

Customer: Look, I wonder if you could help me here. We've booked front row seats for tonight's performance, and . . .

Employee: (interrupting) I'm sorry, sir, but I'm very busy seating people at the moment. Could you go and ask the woman over there?

Customer: No I can't. I've already spoken to her and she sent me over to you. We booked these seats six months in advance, we've been looking forward to it for ages, and now we get here only to find someone else sitting in our seats. It's really not–

Employee: (interrupting) These things happen occasionally. It's not my fault, the ticket office staff sometimes double up on bookings.

Customer: (angry) I don't care whose fault it is, or how it happened, I just want my seats.

Employee: Look, if you wait over there, by the toilets, I'll see if there are any spare seats just before the performance starts.

Customer: (furious) You must be joking! If you think we're going to spend the evening hanging around toilets and then being seated behind a pillar, you're wrong. Come on, we're going. I've made a note of your name, and I'll be taking this further.

ACTIVITY

With a friend, roleplay the situation again. Try to find better ways to handle the complaint.

ACTIVITY

For this activity you will need a partner. Think of a situation in which you have a complaint about a product or service provided by a travel or tourism organisation. The complaint can be real or you can make it up. Each write a letter complaining to the organisation, and give it to the other person.

Each of you should now reply in writing to the complaint, as if you are a customer service assistant for the organisation concerned.

At the end of the activity, discuss how well you handled each other's complaints. As the person complaining, did you feel your complaint was handled well? Would the service you received make you more likely to use the organisation again?

Key questions

1 Why is it important for leisure and recreation organisations to take customer complaints seriously?

2 How should you respond to a customer's complaint?

SECTION **5.8**

Assessing the quality and effectiveness of customer service

How do leisure and recreation organisations know whether they are meeting their customers' needs and whether their customers are receiving good service? In this section you will look at the ways in which organisations evaluate and monitor the quality of the customer service they provide.

❝ At the end of our workshops we ask customers to fill in a short questionaire about various aspects of the service we offer. Most people are happy to fill it in and quite a few want to talk about what they like most or how they think we could improve the service. I listen carefully to them and add the information to a list that I make from reading the questionaires. It takes time but I think it's worth it to find out what our customers think. ❞

manager of an arts and crafts centre

❝ We have guides stationed in many rooms of the museum to supervise the displays and to answer visitors' questions about individual pieces. The guides often overhear people's comments to one another about the layout of the exhibits, convenience of the facilities, or service they have received. There is a notebook in the staff lounge where they can record any customer feedback they hear, both positive or negative. ❞

administrator of a large art museum

5.8.1 **Feedback loop**

Good communication often depends on having a good system for getting feedback:

■ from external customers – through direct or indirect comments, letters of praise or complaint, customer surveys or questionnaires

■ from internal customers – information from other departments (e.g. data about number of sales, occupancy or usage figures from the sales department, summaries of customer feedback from the customer services department)

■ on the spot to check that information given orally has been understood.

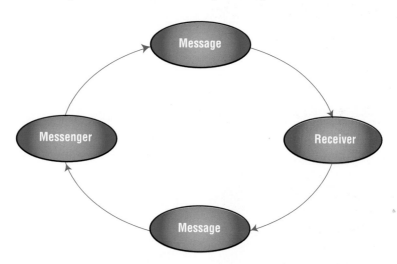

Customer feedback can help an organisation improve customer service by telling it what it is doing well, and how it could improve its performance. The marketing officer of a concert hall explains:

66 *The box office assistants have direct contact with customers. If the prices for a particular concert are more than we normally charge, the box office manager may tell me at our weekly meeting that people are booking seats for the lower-priced tickets and not booking the better, more expensive seats. I would have to think about doing a special promotion in the local paper, or advertising the concert more widely. I would also know for the next time that I should keep the ticket prices at the normal rate. We also give out a simple questionnaire with every ticket asking customers for their comments on the venue, its facilities and the concert programmes.* **99**

QUESTIONNAIRE

Name ....

Address ....

Male/Female ....

Single/Married/Partnered/Divorced/Separated ....

Profession ....

Do you have any children? If so, how
many and what ages? ....

Have you been to the Devere Concert
Hall before? ....

If so, which performance/s?
– name up to three. ....

On average, how many times a season
would you expect to come to the Hall? ....

Would you normally book for yourself
only, come with a friend, or with a group? ....

Do you normally reserve the same seats?
If so, which ones? ....

Is this decision based on who is playing,
ticket price or a combination
of both? ....

Do you ever take advantage of our
multiple booking discounts? ....

How far in advance do you usually
reserve your seats? ....

What form of payment do you usually
use to pay for your reservations? ....

In general, do you think that the price of
seats is fair? ....

Do you use the Concert Hall Restaurant
prior to a concert? If so, how often? ....

Do you use the Concert Hall Bar? ....

Do you pre-order interval refreshments? ....

On-the-spot feedback can help you check that your listener has understood what you've said. An assistant in a tourist information office explains how he uses questions to check that customers have understood the information he's providing:

> " Nearly all my customers are visitors to the area, many from abroad and I have to make sure that they understand all the information I give – details about tourist attractions, events, places of historical interest, route directions, places to stay and so on. I ask questions such as 'Would you like me to go over that again?' or 'Is there anything you're not sure about?' to check that I've made myself clear. "

The manager of an arts centre explains what he means by customer service:

> " We aim to show our customers that we care for them and are aware of their needs and wants. We conduct regular surveys asking them what they have liked, what they would like to see more of, and what sort of activities they want us to hold here. We have a very good idea of what most people want and need, and we try to satisfy that with the events and activities we put on. Safety and security are important when events are attended by the public. We follow health and safety standards carefully, make sure that qualified first aiders are always on hand, and offer facilities such as a staffed cloakroom to keep customers' possessions safe.
>
> Internally, we realise the importance of maintaining a good working atmosphere by providing a good service to each other. We hold regular staff meetings to check that all is running smoothly, and try to solve any problems or communication breakdowns as quickly as possible.
>
> Overall, we make sure that the customer service we provide is consistently high – in the box office, the restaurant, the cloakroom – in everything we do. Basically, we are trying to meet customer expectations, if not exceed them. Quality service is our aim. "

DISCUSSION POINT

Customer service can be broken down into a number of components:

- caring for customers (internal and external)
- meeting customer needs
- achieving customer satisfaction
- meeting customer expectations
- maintaining security
- maintaining safety.

Give one example of how the arts centre manager provides each of these components of customer service. Then for each example, suggest one way he could assess the quality of the customer service provided (e.g. he might assess the quality of fire safety procedures by asking for advice from the local fire prevention officer).

5.8.2 Service guarantee

Many organisations claim that they provide a quality customer service. But how can they be sure that what they are providing is of a high quality?

Some leisure and recreation organisations set standards of customer service quality, 'benchmarks', which they aim to achieve. They then give these standards to customers – often in a leaflet or on a notice-board in the reception area – so that customers know what sort of service to expect.

The manager of the arts centre decided that it would be a good idea to give customers a 'Service Guarantee' leaflet, listing the quality of service customers can expect (see next page).

Establishing quality standards – often known as 'quality criteria' – is the first step in assessing the quality of customer service. Once standards are in place, it is important to be able to measure how well the organisation is achieving them.

- Quality criteria for direct contact with customers need to be measured by asking customers whether standards are being met – customer feedback.
- Quality criteria which are not directly related to customer contact need to be assessed in another way, such as staff appraisal or regular internal reviewer observation.

The arts centre manager realised he needed to find ways to assess how well the organisation was meeting the different quality standards it had set in its 'Service Guarantee' document. After talking to other staff at the centre, he drew up the following list.

ACTIVITY

Look at the arts centre's 'Service Guarantee' leaflet. List the individual quality criteria in each area of customer service, and make notes on exactly how you think the manager could measure whether they are being achieved. For example, how could the manager use observation and staff checks to ensure that public toilets are kept clean and equipment is checked regularly?

Write a customer survey questionnaire which the centre could use to assess whether it is meeting the different service standards it has set.

Area of customer service	Method of assessment
Reliability of service	Employee and customer surveys
Health and safety levels	Observation, staff checks, number of accident reports
Accessibility	Observation
Consistency of service delivery	Observation and customer survey
Price	Monitoring pricing system; comparison with centres in other areas
Staffing levels	Internal review
Qualities of staff (appearance, knowledge, behaviour, judgement)	Staff appraisal, customer survey
Timing of service	Internal review
Value for money	Customer survey
Enjoyment of experience	Customer survey
Provision of individual needs	Customer survey
Service levels	Observation, customer survey

JUBILEE ARTS CENTRE SERVICE GUARANTEE

Customers are entitled to expect the following service standards from the Jubilee Arts Centre.
We will assess these standards regularly, to ensure they are being met and to see whether they need revising. If you have any comments
or complaints, please fill in a customer response form (available from the box office).

Reliability of service

All telephone calls to the box office will be answered within 45 seconds.
All customer letters will be answered within five working days.
Seats will never be overbooked – if customers buy tickets, they will get the seat they want.

Health and safety

The centre will be clean, safe and comfortable at all times.
Public toilet facilities will be inspected hourly.
Health and safety checks on all equipment will be made weekly.
Fire safety standards will be adhered to at all times.
Catering facilities will meet health and safety standards

Accessibility

Wheelchair access will be provided.
Six free wheelchair spaces will be available for registered disabled.
Car parking spaces will be available for 50 cars.

Availability

The box office will always be open at the hours stated.
500 seats will be available for every performance.
Customers will be able to choose where they would like to sit within each price bracket.
If their chosen position is not available, they will be offered an alternative.

Consistency

Staff will treat all customers with equal courtesy and care.
Customers can expect the same reliable service whenever they contact the Arts Centre.
All staff will be trained in every aspect of the Arts Centre's events, so they can all help equally well with customer enquiries and problems.

Price

Seats will always be available in at least three different price brackets.
Concessions will be offered to pensioners, students and the unemployed.
Seats for matinees will be offered to children at half price.

Staffing levels

At least ten members of staff will be on duty whenever the Arts Centre is open.
There will always be three people helping in the box office in the hour before a performance, to keep queuing to a minimum.

Qualities of staff

All staff will be polite, helpful, efficient and fair.
All staff will wear Arts Centre T-shirts or sweatshirts and name badges, so they are easy for customers to identify.
All staff will receive regular training, to ensure they have up-to-date knowledge on every aspect of the centre.

Timing of service

All telephone calls will be answered within 45 seconds.
All letters will be answered within five working days.
The box office ticket booking service will be open from 9.30 to 6.00 on weekdays, and 10.00 to 5.00 at weekends.

Value for money

The Arts Centre will endeavour to keep ticket prices as low as possible.
Some tickets for every performance will cost under £6.
Concessions will be offered, as listed.

Enjoyment of experience

The Jubilee Arts Centre aims to ensure all customers enjoy their visits to the centre. If you are disappointed,
please let us know so we can endeavour to improve our service in the future.
All customers should feel relaxed, safe and able to enjoy the event.

Provision for individual needs

Wheelchair access will be provided.
Disabled people and people with visual impairment who need to bring a companion to assist them
will be entitled to two seats for the price of one.
Audio links will be provided for people with hearing impairments.
Events programmes will be printed in English, French, German and Japanese.

Service levels

Customers can expect a high level of service at all times – whether they visit the centre at 11 am, or 11 pm.
Service levels will be high in every area of the centre; from box office to bar.

More and more leisure and recreation organisations are now required to achieve levels of performance based on national, European and international standards. For example, a growing number of organisations are assessed to BS EN 9000 – the quality systems standard. To reach the standard required, an organisation must set down how all its systems operate and prove that it is running according to these prescribed systems at all times.

5.8.3 Appraising customer service quality criteria

It is very easy for leisure and recreation organisations to decide what customer service quality criteria to set without really considering the needs and concerns of those involved – the customers. Before setting customer service quality criteria, organisations should spend time:

- talking to customers to find out what aspects of service are most important to them
- analysing the customer service provided by other organisations.

When appraising their quality service criteria, leisure and recreation organisations need to consider:

- the perceived importance of different aspects of service to customers
- how the customers would rank different customer service quality criteria.

Perceived importance to the customer

All customers are different, and their ideas on quality of service can vary considerably depending on:

- their attitude, which is often influenced by other people's opinions
- their personal needs
- their past experiences of a product or service.

What represents quality from a departmental manager's perspective may not correspond with the customer's view. Organisations need to carry out regular customer surveys to find out what is most important to customers and what they would like to see changed or improved.

The manager of a fast-food restaurant explains how a customer survey helped the organisation understand what customers saw as quality service:

66 We're a 'fast-food restaurant', and as our name suggests our overall aim has always been to provide food fast. In the past we saw this as the most important part of our quality service – once a customer reached the serving counter, they should have their meal in front of them within one minute. But a recent customer survey showed us that although customers wanted quick service, ours was so quick that it had become completely impersonal. They would rather it took a little longer and that they were treated with more care and respect. So we changed our approach to match. Waiting time is now two minutes, and the staff have time to talk to customers and make them feel welcome. 99

Ranking based on customer perceptions

Once a leisure and recreation organisation has found out what aspects of service are most important to customers, it needs to rank them in order to decide which are top priority.

DISCUSSION POINT

Look back at the Jubilee Arts Centre's 'Service Guarantee' leaflet. Do you think that the manager has thought carefully enough about what is most important to customers? Can you think of any aspects of service which are important to you that aren't covered by the leaflet? What customer service quality criteria from the leaflet do you think would be most important to a teacher wanting to bring a party of children with disabilities to the centre?

Choose a local leisure and recreation facility that you use regularly, for example your local cinema, leisure centre or swimming pool. What do you think its customer service quality criteria should be?

Look again at the Jubilee Arts Centre's 'Service Guarantee' leaflet, and produce a chart with the same headings for different areas of customer service. Under each heading, list two or three customer service quality criteria which would be important to you as a customer. From these criteria, choose the five which you feel are most important and rank them in order of importance.

Visit the facility, and using your criteria as a checklist appraise how well the organisation is meeting the customer service standards you have set.

The Millennium Dome was built at a cost of approximately £750 million. Greenwich was chosen as the site because the concept of a central time was invented there – hence Greenwich Mean Time (GMT). Time in other countries is expressed as the number of hours that it is behind or ahead of GMT. The Royal Observatory, Greenwich, hosts the meridian line which divides western and eastern hemispheres.

From the start of the project, the Millennium Dome had enthusiastic supporters, and equally passionate opponents. You can find out a lot more about the Millennium Dome by visiting the web site: *http://www.londonnet.co.uk/ln/guide/about/dome.html.*

The reactions of some visitors shows that some were happy with their visit, and others felt that customer service could be improved.

'It's definitely worth the money and there's plenty to look at. It's mind-boggling.' Mark Sitchett

'I've been to places like Alton Towers, and places like that are more like fun fairs aren't they? They're for having fun, but this is more about information, though there is a little fun too.' Daniel Calladine, 15

'Everybody wants to see the Body Zone.' Gemma Riley, 15

'I would also recommend they tell you when you get into a queue how much time it will take you to get through the line.' Judith Louria, 62

'At one point we were told we would be waiting for an hour and a half. We've been here two hours now and we are ready to leave. For the money we spent, that's not good.' Anne Watson, 49.

5.8.4 **Analysing the quality of customer service**

Analysing the quality of customer service can be difficult for organisations. Staff who realise that they are being observed and assessed are unlikely to behave normally and provide the usual level of customer service.

As a result, many organisations monitor their customer service quality by carrying out:

■ spot checks – staff don't know in advance that service is to be assessed, and don't have time to make any special preparations (for example, a hotel receptionist who doesn't know about a spot check won't have time to spend longer than usual tidying up)

■ checks by mystery customers – the organisation hires someone to visit the facility as a mystery customer, and report back to the management on their findings.

Incognito inspections

Inspections are also carried out by outside organisations to produce guidebooks and handbooks. For example, the Automobile Association (AA) uses inspectors to visit hotels all round the country and sample the services on offer. The service which they receive is then graded, and this grading is published in the annual members' handbook.

The manager of the Jubilee Arts Centre was finding it difficult to make a fair assessment of whether the centre was meeting its customer service quality criteria. Although a system was in place for internal reviews and checks, he felt that some staff were getting complacent and only meeting quality criteria when they knew they were being observed.

To counteract this, he decided to hire customer care consultant Jessica Palmer. She agreed to be a 'mystery customer' so she could visit the centre and observe customer service. He asked Jessica to focus on the quality criteria for:

■ health and safety levels

■ consistency of service delivery and staff

■ qualities of staff.

He also asked her to comment in general on the quality of customer service at the arts centre, in particular how well she felt that it:

■ cared for customers

■ met customer needs

■ achieved customer satisfaction

■ met customer expectations

■ maintained security and safety.

After visiting the centre twice to observe customer service and talk to fellow customers, Jessica submitted the following report to the manager.

ASSESSING CUSTOMER SERVICE AT THE JUBILEE ARTS CENTRE

I was asked to assess the quality of the customer service at the Jubilee Arts Centre using the following criteria:

Health and safety

- The centre will be clean, safe and comfortable at all times.
- Public toilet facilities will be inspected hourly.
- Fire safety standards will be adhered to at all times.
- Catering facilities will meet health and safety standards.

Consistency

- Staff will treat all customers with equal courtesy and care.
- Customers can expect the same reliable service whenever they contact the Arts Centre.
- All staff will be trained in every aspect of the Arts Centre's events, so they can all help equally well with customer enquiries and problems.

Qualities of staff

- All staff will be polite, helpful, efficient and fair.
- All staff will wear Arts Centre T-shirts or sweatshirts and name badges, so they are easy for customers to identify.
- All staff will receive regularly training, to ensure that they have up-to-date knowledge on every aspect of the centre.

The quality criteria in relation to the actual level of service

The following chart summarises the quality criteria I was checking, and the actual level of service I observed.

Quality criteria	Actual level of service
Cleanliness, safety and comfort	On my first visit all areas of the centre were clean and comfortable. On the second occasion the centre seemed short staffed, and cleanliness had suffered. Rubbish was under seats in the auditorium and the reception area was untidy.
Public toilet facilities inspected hourly	Again, the first time this had been done (a chart on the wall monitoring checks was up to date, and facilities were spotless). But on my second visit the toilets hadn't been checked for three hours and were dirty.
Fire safety standards adhered to	As far as I could see, all was well. Fire exits were well signposted and kept clear, extinguishers in place.

Catering meeting health and safety standards	As far as I could see catering met health and safety standards. Food preparation and serving areas looked clean and hygienic, staff were smart and wearing clean overalls with hair off their faces.
Treating customers with equal courtesy and care	I was extremely impressed by the attitude of staff. They seemed relaxed, happy and had time for every customer. I played the difficult customer on a couple of occasions, and was treated with care and respect each time. I observed staff dealing with children, elderly people, disabled and large groups of visitors, and felt that they treated everyone with the same courtesy.
Reliability of service	I felt this suffered at times because of low staffing levels. The second time I visited the centre I had to queue for ten minutes to pick up my tickets. I tried ringing the centre a few times, and the response time for answering the telephone was unreliable – ranging from two seconds to two minutes.
Knowledge of staff	This seemed good. I asked several awkward questions about facilities, forthcoming productions and current events, and the staff were able to answer knowledgeably in each case. On the one occasion when the member of staff didn't know the answer, she called her manager over.
Politeness and efficiency of staff	On the whole excellent – although a little more fraught on my second visit due to pressures of low staffing, I presume.
Appearance of staff	This left a little to be desired. Not all the staff were wearing their Arts Centre tops, and were hard to identify. I only saw one member of staff wearing a name badge. This is an area where I think there is room for improvement.

Overall, I feel the Jubilee Arts Centre is providing a good quality of customer service. It seems to care about its customers, and staff go out of their way to make people feel welcome and at ease. There seemed a good rapport between staff, so presumably internal customer care is working well.

The quality criteria in relation to customers' expectations
Talking to customers and observing audience reaction, the centre appears to be meeting customer needs and expectations. The programme of events is varied and the people I spoke to were all satisfied by the service and return to the centre regularly. Security and safety procedures seem adequate, but the centre needs to take care that they are not compromised by pressures of staffing.

ACTIVITY

Now its your turn to pose as a mystery customer. Make a list of leisure and recreation organisations in your area which you could visit without being recognised. You will need to be able to test their services against prescribed quality standards, so contact the organisations to find out whether they publish a leaflet or charter.

How will you work out whether these standards are being met? Think of ways that you can test the organisation's quality criteria promises. Consider the areas that are not easily measurable, as well as those that are.

Visit the organisation on two or three occasions and make observations and checks. Then following the format of Jessica's report on the Jubilee Arts Centre, write a report analysing the quality of customer service provided by the organisation.

Analysing customer service in related markets

As well as analysing their own customer service, many leisure and recreation organisations find it helpful to analyse other organisations' customer service in order to review and improve their own. This is often called benchmarking and may include considering:

- direct competitors
- other organisations in the same business
- related service organisations
- unrelated service organisations.

> **Benchmarking** is comparing what you do as an organisation with the market leaders in your sector field and setting business performance standards so you try to do at least as well – and preferably better.

Direct competitors

All organisations need to know what their competitors are doing.

The managing director of a company which organises walking tours in the Lake District carried out an appraisal of the customer service offered by other companies offering similar holidays:

66 *I wanted to see what sort of customer care was being offered on walking holidays elsewhere in the country and other kinds of holidays in the Lake District, such as riding and cycling tours. I looked at things like standards of accommodation and meals, picking-up arrangements, insurance, refunds – the sorts of things that can make one operator just that bit better and more attractive than another. I learnt quite a lot. I know now where I can get excellent lunchtime meals and snacks which are real value for money, and I learnt from a company in Wales how I can manage cancellations and refunds. The service we offer now has definitely improved and our regular customers have commented on it.* 99

DISCUSSION POINT

How do you think an organisation's customer service quality criteria should be influenced by the customer service provided by its competitors? Give examples.

DISCUSSION POINT

Can you think of any examples of good customer service which could be borrowed and introduced by leisure and recreation organisations?

ACTIVITY

Look back at the analysis of the quality of customer service in one leisure and recreation organisation which you carried out at the end of the last section. Make a list of organisations which you could use to draw a comparison of customer service practice. These might be:

■ direct competitors

■ other organisations in the same business

■ related service organisations.

Again, find out if they have published customer service quality criteria. Assess their services against the standards. Are the quality criteria being met?

Other organisations in the same business

It can be useful to analyse the services offered by organisations who are in the same business but not in direct competition. There may be things to learn. For example, a heritage site could look at the facilities like shops, cafés and carparks in heritage sites around the country to check that the facilities it offers are up to the same standards.

Related service organisations

Related service organisations can learn from one another. The manager of a sports centre explains how they looked at the reservations and customer information services offered by a large hotel to help them improve their own services in those areas:

66 *We were planning on expanding our premises and offering more facilities. This would mean more customers and we needed to expand our customer services to match. We needed to upgrade our computerised reservations system and we wanted produce a better range of leaflets and brochures about our new facilities. I contacted the manager of a nearby hotel and asked for her advice. She was only too happy to help and invited us to spend a morning at the hotel talking to the right people. We were shown their reservations system and we also talked to the publicity manager about cost-effective ways of producing and distributing leaflets and brochures. During the visit, I noticed the closed circuit TV system they used to keep an eye on the public areas of the hotel and the lifts, stairs and corridors. It struck me that a similar system could be useful at our centre and I'm going back to the hotel next week to talk to their security officer.* 99

Unrelated service organisations

Leisure and recreation organisations can also draw on good customer service practice from unrelated business organisations. For example, banks and building societies introduced 'hole-in-the-wall' cash and information machines to cut down queues and provide a more efficient customer service. Leisure and recreation organisations could also use this technology to improve their customer service: for example, many cinemas now provide tickets which have been booked earlier over the telephone by machine.

Comparing analyses

In comparing the customer services of different organisations, you need to ensure that your comparisons and contrasts are fair. It helps to have one set of criteria that can be used as a measure for all the organisations you are looking at. Sometimes you may want to draw parallels with unrelated organisations because you think there are ideas and practices which could be useful for the leisure and recreation organisations you are investigating. In these cases, you need to be sure that it is realistic and practicable for the examples you give to be adapted from one industry sector to another.

Here are the criteria used by Jessica Palmer (see page 302) to assess the customer service offered by the Jubilee Arts Centre:

Health and safety

■ The centre will be clean, safe and comfortable at all times.

■ Public toilet facilities will be inspected hourly.

■ Fire safety standards will be adhered to at all times.

■ Catering facilities will meet health and safety standards.

Consistency

■ Staff will treat all customers with equal courtesy and care.

■ Customers can expect the same reliable service whenever they contact the Arts Centre.

■ All staff will be trained in every aspect of the Arts Centre's events, so they can all help equally well with customer enquiries and problems.

Qualities of staff

■ All staff will be polite, helpful, efficient and fair.

■ All staff will wear Arts Centre T-shirts or sweatshirts and name badges, so they are easy for customers to identify.

■ All staff will receive regularly training, to ensure they have up-to-date knowledge on every aspect of the centre.

What types of organisation would you suggest she used to provide the centre's manager with the sort of comparisons he'd find useful?

In section 5.8.2, there is copy of a leaflet called 'Service Guarantee' issued to customers of an arts centre. The leaflet sets out the standards of services customers can expect. In 5.8.4 there is a case study describing how the manager of the arts centre hired customer care consultant Jessica Palmer to act as a mystery customer to check whether the centre was meeting its standards for customer service. The report Jessica produced highlighted the strengths and weaknesses of the centre's customer service as measured by its own quality criteria. The manager thought it would be useful to find out how the centre's standards of customer service compared with that of other organisations. But he wanted to make sure that the findings of the comparison would be relevant to the business he was in:

66 *As a result of the mystery customer exercise, I now have a good idea of how well the centre is doing from three angles: measured against our own criteria, measured against our customers' perceptions, and from Jessica's direct experience. I could see that there was room for improvement in places, but before deciding what to do, I thought some broader comparisons would be useful. I was very interested in how we compared with our direct competitors and also with organisations in similar lines of business but not actually in competition with us. I was also interested in any tips or models of good practice from organisations outside the leisure and recreation industry – so long as they were applicable to our circumstances. The reason I decided to produce the Service Guarantee leaflet for our customers in the first place was because I'd read the Customer Charter leaflet produced by the Post Office to explain their customer care standards and thought a similar thing would be useful to my customers.* **99**

Use the results of the analyses you did on pages 301 and 305 to make comparisons between the organisations you investigated. Make sure that:

■ you use the same criteria for all related organisations so that your comparisons are fair

■ any examples from organisations outside the leisure and recreation industry can be realistically adapted.

Write a report summarising your comparisons.

5.8.5 **Recommendations for improving customer service**

Organisations committed to good customer service are always on the lookout for ways to improve their standards. They will actively encourage comments and suggestions from customers and staff and have all sorts of ways for gathering feedback. Staff members may be given a 'watching brief' to look out for new ideas they come across in other organisations, the media, publications, conferences, and so on. They may buy in outside help such as consultants, and training programmes to help staff develop and update their customer care skills will also be a high priority.

Any recommendations for improvements would need to be considered carefully. The organisation would want evidence that the improvements suggested would be:
■ practical
■ realistic
■ cost-effective.

The organisation would expect the recommendations to:
■ be professionally presented
■ be based on a thorough analysis of its existing service
■ describe benefits the improvements would achieve.

Section 5.8.4 gives quotes and examples from an assessment of the customer service offered by the Jubilee Arts Centre carried out by customer care consultant Jessica Palmer. Following the assessment, Jessica presented a report to the centre's manager and staff outlining recommendations for improving customer service. Here's the manager's response to some of the recommendations she made:

❝ *Overall, Jessica felt that the centre offered a very high standard of customer service. This pleased me as my staff and I believe in good customer care and we work hard to please our customers. By mentioning what we were doing well at the start of her report, Jessica got us in the right frame of mind for responding positively to her suggestions for improvements. Some of the things she mentioned we agreed with and resolved to take action on immediately – for example, always wearing the Art Centre tops and our name badges. Jessica had a slight concern that we were understaffed from time to time. She suggested increasing staff numbers and reviewing the rota system. I think we do need more staff but our funds are being squeezed at the moment. I decided I needed to think further about this recommendation but we could definitely review the rota.*

In her comparisons with other organisations, again Jessica felt we did well. She'd looked at the customer services offered by another arts centre, a sports centre, a museum and a restaurant. She felt we matched and in many cases bettered various aspects of comparable service. One area she criticised was our facilities for children. She felt we could attract more customers by providing a few more family-friendly services. For example, the sports centre she'd visited offered a crèche and the arts centre's restaurant offered a children's menu. We

Making recommendations

Recommendations must be:

- explained
- practicable
- realistic
- justified.

could certainly do a children's menu but I felt a crèche would be beyond our financial means at the moment. But when Jessica was talking about the museum, she mentioned that they had special exhibitions for children. This gave me an idea. When we run exhibitions which mainly appeal to adults, we could put on some children's events at the same time in different areas of the centre. That way, parents could relax and enjoy the exhibitions designed for them while their children enjoyed events designed for them. We could afford one-off supervised events for children even though we couldn't afford permanent facilities like a crèche. **99**

ACTIVITY

Add a section to the report you did on page 307 which makes recommendations for improvements the organisation could make to its customer service. Think carefully about the recommendations you want to suggest. Make sure they are realistic, practicable and suitable for the organisation you have been investigating. To give your report a professional look, produce it on a DTP system and present it in some kind of binder or cover.

Key questions

1 What is the feedback loop and how is it used to assess customer service?

2 What are customer service quality criteria?

3 What are two important things an organisation should consider when setting its customer service criteria?

4 What is the purpose of evaluation methods such as spot checks and mystery shoppers?

5 What is benchmarking?

6 What should you bear in mind when making recommendations for improvements?

Assignment

Part 1

Part of your evidence for this unit is to present the results of an investigation into the effectiveness of customer service delivery in two leisure and recreation organisations of your choice.

Make a list of possible organisations you could use. For each suggestion, how easy will it be to get information about the organisation? If it is a local organisation, will you be able to visit it? Could it be an organisation where you do a work placement or some part-time or voluntary work? You may need to do some research to start with, e.g. telephoning or visiting the organisation to find out how helpful they would be – their responses may give you an idea of how good their customer service is.

When you have considered the list of possibilities, choose two of these organisations. Decide how you will present your conclusions. You could write up a report or you may prefer to give a presentation. If you give a presentation, you should also prepare some handouts summarising the information you have found.

Your report or presentation should include examples of any 'good' or 'poor' customer service which you noticed. It should also examine the aspects of customer service given below.

Personal presentation

Consider each of the two organisations you have chosen to investigate in respect to customer service. How do the members of these organisations present themselves?

Describe your first impression of each organisation, or of the individuals with whom you made initial contact. In what context did you form your first impression – did you meet staff in person, speak with someone by telephone, or receive something in writing? What details of the employee's personal presentation made an impression with you?

Types of customer

What types of customer do the organisations serve? Do they have any provisions for particular types of customer, for instance wheelchair access to the facility or a nappy-changing area for customers with small children?

Dealing with customers

In what ways do the organisations communicate with their customers? Where possible, collect examples of written communication and describe examples of other sorts of communication.

Selling skills

What sales skills are used by staff selling the organisations' goods and services? Think about how you will find these out. You may be able to discuss techniques with sales staff or even have the opportunity to watch sales staff in action. If so, draw up a checklist of sales techniques to look out for.

Customer service situations

What kinds of customer service situation do the organisations experience? If possible, observe staff members in action and take notes on the various types of situation they dealt with. How did they respond to these situations? How did their response reflect either good or poor customer service?

Handling complaints

Find out from the management or from staff members if there is a company policy regarding the handling of complaints. Has the organisation ever received a written complaint? How did they respond?

Assessing the quality and effectiveness of customer service

How do the organisations ensure that their service is meeting the needs of customers? What are the key customer service quality criteria used by each organisation? What procedures and practices are used by managers and staff to achieve the quality criteria? How do the organisations evaluate the effectiveness of their customer service delivery?

In addition to these areas, your report or presentation should include:
- an analysis of the quality of the service provided by each organisation
- an explanation of the criteria you used to assess the quality
- a comparison between your two chosen organisations in respect to the quality of service being offered
- recommendations for improvements each organisation could make to its customer service.

Part 2

Your tutor will arrange for you to deliver customer service in four different situations. Your performance will be assessed. Design a form that you can use to keep notes on what you did in each situation and how well you think you performed against the evaluation objectives and criteria.

Prepare and give a presentation on the customer service situations you were given. The presentation should include:
- a description of the evaluation objectives and customer service quality criteria for each
- your evaluation of your own performance

- a comparison between your evaluation of your performance and the evaluations made by other people
- recommendations for improvements
- an explanation of how you are going to make improvements.

KEY SKILLS

You can use the work you are doing for this part of your GNVQ to collect and develop evidence for the following key skills at level 3.

when you	you can collect evidence for
	communication
provide customer service in a range of situations	key skill C3.1a contribute to a group discussion about a complex subject
investigate and evaluate the customer service in two different organisations	key skill C3.1b make a presentation about a complex subject, using at least one image to illustrate complex points
	key skill C3.2 read and synthesise information from two extended documents about a complex subject
	working with others
evaluate the effectiveness of customer service delivery	key skill WO3.1 agree realistic objectives and the action and resources needed to achieve them; provide information, based on appropriate evidence, to help agree responsibilities; agree suitable working arrangements with those involved
	key skill WO3.2 organise and carry out tasks in ways that help you to be effective and efficient in meeting your responsibilities; seek to establish and maintain cooperative working relationships, agreeing ways to overcome any difficulties; exchange accurate information on the extent to which work is meeting expected timescales and quality, agreeing changes where necessary to achieve objectives
	key skill WO3.3 agree the extent to which the objectives have been met; identify factors that have influenced the outcome; agree ways the activity could have been done differently to enhance work with others
	improving own learning and performance
prepare for your involvement in a variety of customer service and selling situations	key skill LP3.1 seek information on ways to achieve what you want to do, and identify factors that might affect your plans; use this information to agree realistic targets with appropriate others; plan how you will manage your time to meet targets, including alternative action for overcoming possible problems and use of support from others
	key skill LP3.2 prioritise and manage your time effectively to complete tasks, making revisions to your plan as necessary; seek and actively use feedback and support from relevant sources to help you meet your targets; use different approaches to learning, drawing on learning from other tasks and adapting methods to meet new demands
	key skill LP3.3 provide information on quality of your learning and performance, identifying factors that have affected the outcome; identify targets you have met, seeking information from relevant sources to establish evidence of your achievements; exchange views with appropriate others to agree action for improving your performance

UNIT **6**

Leisure and recreation in action

About this unit

This unit gives you the opportunity to work as part of a team to plan, carry out and evaluate a real project that is of interest to you. The project can be an event or a business project, but it must be related to leisure and recreation. Your tutor will give you advice and ideas about what your team could do. To complete the unit successfully, you will need to use what you learn in many of the other compulsory and key skills units. This unit gives you the chance to develop essential business skills. You will produce a business plan for your chosen project before it takes place. You will also keep a log of your involvement in the project, as well as contributing to an evaluation to discover what went well and what could have worked better.

SECTION **6.1**

Feasibility of the project

The first step in planning for your project is to draw up a business plan. Your business plan will cover a number of issues, all of which must be discussed by your team in order to determine your project's feasibility. In this section, you will examine the various points which should be addressed in your team's business plan.

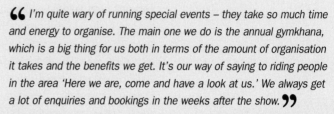

66 I'm quite wary of running special events – they take so much time and energy to organise. The main one we do is the annual gymkhana, which is a big thing for us both in terms of the amount of organisation it takes and the benefits we get. It's our way of saying to riding people in the area 'Here we are, come and have a look at us.' We always get a lot of enquiries and bookings in the weeks after the show. 99

owner of a riding school

66 Every project I take on has its own separate file, covering every aspect of the event at every stage of planning – outlines, correspondence, booking confirmations, budget plans, receipts, staff and service contracts, and much more. It's amazing how much planning goes into preparation for any single event. 99

special events officer in a city council

The objectives of the project

Working in the leisure and recreation industry will bring you into many situations where you need to practise teamwork with your colleagues in order to meet the needs of the customer and the organisation. Your GNVQ team will be planning and carrying out a project – either a business project or an event – in order to experience working within a team. The main difference between a business project and an event is that an event is a one-off occasion while a business project may be ongoing.

> Common objectives of leisure and recreation projects are:
> ■ to attract new customers
> ■ to promote the organisation, its products or services
> ■ to create a favourable image for the organisation, its products or services
> ■ to unify the organisation
> ■ to bring benefits to a community.

Attracting new customers

Organisations need to think of ways to attract new customers in order to increase their profitability. Projects and events can be a good way to do this:
■ Gyms and sports clubs often hold open days when people can come and try out facilities. If they are impressed by what they see and do, they will join.
■ Libraries hold special events for children to encourage them to read books.
■ Night clubs run themed nights, such as 70s and 80s nights, to attract a different range of customers to the club.

Promotion

Events can play an important part in promotion, and are often included in an organisation's overall marketing strategy.

The marketing manager of a museum of Victorian living explains:

66 *We carry out regular promotional activities in order to maintain public interest in the museum, including placing advertisements in local and national newspapers, sending direct mailshots to schools, and issuing press releases. But every now and then we decide we need to do something really special, and organise a major event. The aim is to make it as attention-grabbing as possible, and to tie it in with whatever promotional campaign we're currently running. So last year, to tie in with an exhibition, we organised a Victorian Christmas festival in the town. This year we are focusing on the theme of Victorian children, and are organising a performance of Nicholas Nickleby at the theatre, using children from local schools.* 99

Feel the thrill of floating on the wind – drift through the valleys
and get a view that will never be equalled. Our fully qualified
training staff will take you through all the safety proceedures
and techniques to enable you to FLY solo after one week.
Call FREEPHONE Activity Now!

Creating a favourable image

Projects and events can help leisure and recreation organisations create a
favourable image among the general public. Organisations are particularly
keen to create a positive image when they:

■ are new

■ are launching a new product or service

■ have received bad publicity.

Unifying the organisation

Most of the objectives of leisure and recreation events are linked to
customers – raising the profile of products and services, presenting a good
image to the public, and promoting sales. But projects and events can also
achieve objectives within the organisation itself, giving staff:

■ an opportunity to work together to achieve challenging goals

■ a chance to develop teamworking skills

■ a clearer vision of the organisation and what it hopes to achieve

■ the opportunity to enjoy working in a different and stimulating
environment.

All of these can combine to improve staff efficiency, motivation, and
teamwork.

A receptionist at a swimming pool describes her experience when they held a swimming marathon to raise money for a local hospice:

66 *We were all involved in some way in arranging and running the event. I was working closely with people I don't usually work with and I really enjoyed it. I feel I know my colleagues much better now. As part of the event, the three directors agreed to be thrown into the pool if staff pledged £5 each. We all did and in they went! I used to be a bit scared of them but having seen them join in with the fun and the hard work, I feel more at ease with them now.* 99

DISCUSSION POINT

Do you think that working as a team towards a goal always increases motivation and improves teamwork skills? What has been your own experience of working as part of a team?

ACTIVITY

A sportswear company is opening a new shop in a shopping centre. To mark the opening, the company decides to hold a fashion show in aid of local charities at the nearby leisure centre. What do you think are the objectives of the event? Make a list of as many as you can think of, and explain how the event would achieve them.

Providing benefits to a community

The main aim of some leisure and recreation projects is to bring benefits to a community, rather than to promote an organisation and its products or services. For example, an organisation might aim to:

■ support community initiatives and activities by running projects for youth groups, children or elderly people
■ stage events which raise funds for charities or organisations in the community.

Profit-making leisure and recreation organisations often stage events to raise funds for charity, with the secondary aim of creating a positive image of the company being concerned about community issues. In this way, as well as helping people, they attract new customers to the facility. Events like these still benefit the community, but they are also public relations exercises for the organisation.

ACTIVITY

Most of your work for this unit will involve planning and running a project with the rest of your GNVQ leisure and recreation team. Hold an initial planning meeting, and talk about what you want to achieve through your project. Look through the different objectives explained in this section, then begin your business plan by identifying your team's objectives:

■ decide what your aims are going to be
■ list your objectives in order of importance (you will probably have more than three)
■ keep a record of the objectives, so you can refer to them as you plan, run and then evaluate your project.

Leisure and recreation organisations identify their target market according to different market segments which describe particular types of customer. Market segments are divided by:

■ age

■ sex

■ ethnicity

■ socio-economic class

■ geographic location

■ lifestyle.

DISCUSSION POINT

Can you think of other possible costs and benefits to customers attending a leisure and recreation event? Have you ever been to a leisure and recreation event where you felt the cost of attending outweighed the benefits of going? How did this make you feel? Would you go to a similar event again?

ACTIVITY

With your GNVQ project planning team, hold a meeting to determine who your customers will be, what their needs may be, and how your project will address those needs. Keep a list of anticipated customer needs, and check items from the list as your team makes decisions about how the project will meet those needs. Include this list in your business plan.

When planning a project, you must prepare to meet the needs of customers. This can be done by identifying:

■ who your customers will be

■ what you expect their needs to be

■ how your project will meet their needs.

Who your customers will be

First you need to decide who your project will be aimed at and who your customers will be. This is your target market.

For example, if you have chosen to organise a leisure and recreation exhibition at your school or college, your customers will be your classmates, and possibly also other students and teachers.

Your customers' needs

In order to determine your customers' needs, imagine that you are a customer who is participating in your project or attending your event. As a customer, what would you expect from this experience?

For instance, will your customers be arriving by car? They will need access to a car park or convenient street parking. Will your project be taking place indoors, during colder months of the year? Your customers may need a secure place to put their coats. Will you be serving food and drink? Your customers will need a choice of options, particularly if they have special dietary needs.

In general, customers need to feel that the cost of taking part in a project or event doesn't outweigh the benefits gained, or they will feel dissatisfied and won't support future projects.

Possible costs to customers include:

■ entrance fees

■ time and money spent travelling to the event

■ time spent at the event

■ money spent on products and services at the event

■ threats to health and safety (e.g. food poisoning, sporting accidents).

Possible benefits to customers include:

■ enjoyment

■ education

■ special offers on products and services

■ finding out about products and services which will be useful to them in the future.

How your project will meet your customers' needs

When you have determined the expected needs of your customers, you must consider how your project will meet those needs.

6.1.3 Marketing the project

Once you have determined who your customers will be, you must find ways to market your project. You can use the marketing mix as a guideline.

Marketing mix:
- product
- place
- price
- promotion

Product

Identify your product. This will depend on what type of project you choose to do. For example, if you are planning a class trip to a local heritage site, your product will be the trip – how you get there, and what you do while you are there. If you are planning to stage an event, your product may be a form of entertainment, or the food and drink being served.

Place

Identify your place. Where is your project going to take place? Is it convenient for your customers? Is it a suitable venue for an event? You will examine this more closely in section 6.1.4 Physical resources.

Price

Will your project involve a charge to your customers? If you are staging an event, what will you charge as an admission fee? Will the price simply cover the cost of the project, or will you be charging extra in order to gain a profit? This subject is examined more closely in section 6.1.5 Financial aspects of the project.

Promotion

You will need to find ways to promote your project, particularly if you are staging an event which happens at a specific place and time. Your customers will need to know when and where to attend the event. This is done through advertising.

Advertising is also used to encourage as many people as possible to attend, therefore it should promote the event in such a way that it will appeal to potential customers.

There are several forms of advertising that can be used to publicise events:
- newspapers
- magazines
- radio
- television
- posters
- leaflets and brochures.

Local news media – newspapers, radio, television – often cover student events as features. Posters and leaflets are another good way to promote your project. They can be distributed in a variety of places where people will see them. Libraries, tourist information centres, local advice and information centres, even post offices and shops with public notice-boards will often be happy to put up posters or leaflets for student activities.

6.1.4 **Physical resources**

Resources required and their sources

Resources are a key factor for most projects – without them many projects, especially events, wouldn't be able to take place at all. Imagine a disco without a sound system and lights, or a rounders match without bat and balls.

Teams need to identify the resources needed for a project at an early stage, and build into their business plan:
- a list of resources needed
- time to find the resources
- money to hire or buy them.

If teams do need to hire or borrow equipment, they need to consider arrangements for payment and loan return.

Materials and equipment

Almost all leisure and recreation projects need:
- materials – e.g. posters, leaflets, stationery, menus
- equipment – e.g. sound equipment, sports equipment, lighting, seating.

Some equipment may involve:
- hire costs
- health and safety precautions
- specialist skills for use
- insurance
- storage.

Planning teams should estimate the materials and equipment needed for a project at an early stage so that they can:
- find, borrow and hire equipment
- get materials produced, printed and distributed (this can take several weeks).

Estimating resources also enables teams to work out whether an idea for a project is feasible. For example, if a team is staging an event which needs a marquee for 500 people, and finds out that there are no large marquees available on the necessary date, then plans will have to change.

> DISCUSSION POINT
>
> Can you think of any leisure and recreation projects for which resources aren't a key factor?

ACTIVITY

Estimate the materials and equipment needed for each of the following projects:

■ a Christmas party for 100 infant school children, to be held in a school hall

■ a sponsored swim for charity

■ a conference for 50 delegates from the catering industry.

Choose one of the projects to look at in more detail. Write a breakdown of what materials and equipment you would need, and where you could get it from. With a large enough budget, do you think it would be feasible for your GNVQ team to carry out the project?

Premises

Many leisure and recreation projects need premises where they can take place:

■ a football tournament needs football pitches, spectator areas and changing rooms

■ a party needs a room or space large enough to hold the number of people invited

■ a sailing competition needs a clubhouse, cordoned-off area of water, and viewing space for spectators.

Is this the right venue for this event?

Often, premises are in demand, and need to be booked well in advance. When working out the type of premises needed for a project, you must consider:

- how many people will be participating in the project
- what types of activity will be taking place
- what facilities are needed (e.g. a bar, food preparation area, dance floor)
- whether there is disabled access
- how far people will travel to attend
- how much money it costs to hire different venues.

Once the team has decided where to stage a project, it needs to work out how the premises should be used. Often this is straightforward – if a children's party is to be held at a hall with a kitchen area attached, it is obvious that entertainment and games should take place in the hall, and catering in the kitchen. Sometimes it is more complicated – at a college open day, different departments need to decide where they will stage exhibitions and demonstrations.

A coach at an athletics club organising its club championship explains why it is important to allocate space sensibly:

66 *In athletics, you have to be very careful that the track and field areas are used in the best way possible. You couldn't have javelin, shot-put and discus all taking place at the same time – it would be chaos, and very dangerous. Instead, we spend a lot of time deciding which areas to use for which events, and when they should be held. This year we used two separate jump pits – one for long jump, and one for triple jump. As the long jump tends to be the more popular event, we put this in the pit by the finishing line. We realised that we were going to be tight on time to get the throwing events finished, so we moved the discus to a training ground by the side of the track. It's a case of finding the best compromise to make good use of the space.* 99

6.1.5 Financial aspects of the project

DISCUSSION POINT

If you were the finance coordinator for an event, which of the following would you say was an efficient use of money?

- Spending £100 on printing 300 posters which would be ready a day before an event takes place.

- Ringing five equipment hire companies to find out about costs, and using the one who gives the lowest quote.

- Going to a wholesalers to buy food and drink, rather than to the local supermarket.

- Bulk-buying 500 cans of drink at a cheap rate for an event for 100 people.

Your team will need to consider the financial aspects of running your project, such as:

- budget
- start-up costs
- income
- handling payments.

Budget

The team's treasurer or finance coordinator is responsible for working out the overall budget for the project. They look at the amount of money that team members want to spend on different areas of the project, and work out whether there is enough money available. If there isn't enough money in the budget, they can:

- check whether all the spending is really necessary
- organise extra fund-raising or sponsorship to finance the project
- ask team members to cut back on the amount they spend.

ACTIVITY

A new gardening centre is opening in a large town, and is organising a special event. It has decided that it needs to attract lots of people, and that promotion will be a key factor in the success of the event. The planning team has appointed a publicity officer, and given her a budget of £800 to spend on promoting the event. It has asked her to produce and print posters, place an advertisement in local newspapers, and try to get an article about the event printed in the local press.

Advise the publicity officer how to spend her £800 budget. Carry out research into the cost of different promotional items to make sure that your plan is realistic.

Start-up costs

Start-up costs are what you initially pay to purchase materials for your project, as well as other resources such as staff and services if necessary. Ideally your start-up costs will be reimbursed through the income you earn from your project or event.

Leisure and recreation facilities often account for project start-up costs in their budgets. The money is earmarked in advance to be used for events and campaigns. Any income earned goes first to cover start-up costs; any additional income is profit.

Anticipated income

Anticipated income is the amount of money a team hopes to make from the project. This will vary depending on its targets:

- if a team is aiming to raise money, success depends on income, and anticipated income is a key target

ACTIVITY

Your tutor should be able to outline the options available to you for start-up costs for your GNVQ leisure and recreation project. Set aside time during a team meeting to discuss your budget as well as the resource materials which will constitute your team's start-up costs. Include your decisions in your business plan.

- if a team has a large enough budget to cover its costs, and isn't aiming to make a profit, then anticipated income isn't a key target.

If the success of a project does depend on the money it makes, then the team needs to build anticipated income into plans from an early stage. This means identifying where income is going to come from, estimating how much it will be, and changing plans if it becomes clear that the income isn't going to be enough.

Handling payments

The team must determine how to handle payments for the project. Some key considerations are:

- How much will you charge for participation in your project or event?
- Do you have a safe place to store money?
- What forms of payment will be accepted?
- Who in the team will be responsible for taking payments?

6.1.6 **Staffing for the project**

People are the single most important factor in the success of any project. Without the right staff, a project will fail.

All projects need staff who:

- are available to plan and run the project
- have the skills needed to make sure that the project runs smoothly
- have enough time to participate.

To make the most of staff, people need to be given jobs which match their skills and the amount of time they have to spare. It would be senseless to put a trained chef behind the bar while a waiter does the cooking. Similarly, there's no point giving someone a responsible, time-consuming job if they don't have enough free time to do it well.

DISCUSSION POINT

Sometimes leisure and recreation organisations don't have enough staff with the right skills for an event, and have to hire extra people. A busy hotel is organising a New Year's Eve party for 100 guests. It needs:

- one chef
- three kitchen assistants
- five waitresses
- a pianist for during the meal
- someone to run the disco afterwards.

The hotel could provide a chef, two kitchen assistants and three waitresses. But no more regular hotel kitchen staff or waitresses were available, and no one at the hotel could play the piano or run the disco.

It would cost the hotel:

- £45 to hire a waitress for the evening
- £40 to hire a kitchen assistant
- £75 to hire a pianist
- £125 to hire someone to run the disco.

The hotel has £280 to spend on extra staff. What do you think it should do?

Providers of services

As well as resources, many leisure and recreation projects depend on services in order to succeed. These might include:

- catering
- entertainment
- first aid.

What providers of services would be needed for an event like this?

If a team planning a project identifies services as a key factor, it needs to make sure that it plans where to get them from well in advance, and makes sure that the services on offer are of a high enough quality. Here's what can happen if services aren't planned carefully enough:

❝ We left everything much too late when planning my daughter's wedding reception, and were generally disorganised. The day was a near-disaster – we just hope the guests saw the funny side. We didn't book a photographer early enough, and in the end we just asked everyone to take snaps. I popped into the florists in town the week before the wedding, but by then she was already doing three weddings that day. I ended up having to use a florist ten miles away, which was much more expensive. Worst of all, we didn't book catering services early enough, and ended up having to use a new firm that nobody knew anything about. The food was cold, bland and badly presented. I've certainly learnt the importance of organising services well in advance! **❞**

ACTIVITY

At a meeting of your GNVQ project team, decide how to allocate resources. Look back to the lists of resources you made at earlier planning stages, and think about:

■ how to spend your budget

■ who needs equipment, where and when

■ who needs materials, where and when

■ how to organise space within the premises

■ how to organise staff to make sure that you make the best use of their skills, time and availability.

6.1.7 Administration systems

Project and sales administration systems used in leisure and recreation organisations include:

- booking forms
- tickets
- customer records
- membership lists.

UNIT

6

SECTION **6.1**

All of these help make the selling of goods and services a smoother process.

Booking forms

All sorts of leisure and recreation organisations use booking forms. For example:

- theatres – to book seats for a performance
- restaurants – to book meal reservations
- sports centres – to book sports facilities.

Booking forms show details of the product or service the customer wants and help the organisation to make the necessary arrangements and to keep records.

Tickets

Tickets have two main purposes:

- they allow the customer the right to enter and use a facility or service
- they act as records of bookings or sales for an organisation.

Computer-based and paper-based systems

In the past, project and sales administration systems meant a lot of paperwork, but today more and more administration is being done on a computer.

In practice, information is often processed on a computer, and then given to customers on paper. For example:

- Customers' records are often stored on a database so that when a customer buys something or has a query, the record can be updated by staff. If necessary, a paper-based account can then be printed out regularly for the customer.

- Clients of holiday companies are often asked to fill out a booking form in a brochure, but the details on the form are then transferred to a computer database. Queries can be dealt with quickly, as any staff member can call up the details of the booking on their computer screen.
- Membership lists can be created either as a separate list in a computer file or by combining individual customer records. Membership cards can then be printed for customers from these computer-based lists.
- Many venues operate computerised ticketing systems, where tickets are printed out by the computer operator. In a venue with numbered seating, for example, the computer will automatically update the seating plan as tickets are sold so that staff can quickly see which seats are sold and which are still for sale.

The box office manager of a concert hall with 1,200 seats remembers how they used to sell tickets:

66 *Before the computerised ticketing system, selling tickets was pretty laborious. Because all seats are numbered we had to use large diagrams of the auditorium, on card, with a complete plan of all the seats. When seats were sold, these were crossed off using one colour of pencil – we had different colours representing sales, reservations, complimentary seats, reserved seats and so on. Because we had three staff selling seats, they often had to pass the plans across to each other and if two customers at different windows wanted to buy tickets for the same concert, one had to wait.* 99

DISCUSSION POINT

Security of information is an important consideration for leisure and recreation organisations. Lost or damaged sales information can be expensive in terms of time, money and customer goodwill. How can organisations ensure the security of computer-based information? And of paper-based information?

6.1.8 **Project timescales**

Time is always a major factor in planning projects, especially events in which everything must be ready by the time the event starts. Because of this, teams need to set a project timescale with a range of deadlines for different tasks. When planning a timescale, keep in mind that delays can have serious effects on the plan as a whole.

DISCUSSION POINT

How reliant will you be on your team colleagues' abilities to keep to deadlines? Who will be affected by your deadlines?

A publicity coordinator for a theatre group planning a charity event in June explains how dates and deadlines affected her tasks:

66 *Before I could plan designs for publicity materials, I had to know who was booked to perform. The deadline for bookings was the end of February. That meant my start date for the design stage of publicity materials was the beginning of March. Tickets were to go on sale on 1 May so the publicity materials all had to be distributed by then. So my end date was 26 April, the previous Friday. I scheduled everything from design briefings to delivery of printed material to fit into those deadlines. If the bookings deadline was missed, not only I would have to reschedule my activities and tasks, but I would also have had my overall time cut by the extra time taken to complete the bookings.* 99

Legal aspects of the project

Health and safety measures

Health and safety is a key factor of almost all projects, in particular those involving the general public, sporting activities and food. Teams organising an event need to be especially aware of health and safety. If they don't plan health and safety measures at an early enough stage, their event may be illegal and not allowed to go ahead.

Teams need to check:

- whether their event is affected by any health and safety laws (e.g. number of people allowed to attend, fire regulations, food preparation laws, licences)
- that they have permission to stage the event (e.g. from the site owner, police, local authorities, school or college)
- buildings and equipment, to make sure that all is in safe working order
- the layout of the event
- that they have organised enough first-aid support
- that everyone involved in running the event understands and follows health and safety routines.

ACTIVITY

A team running a disco for 200 people in a school hall has asked for your advice on health and safety. It wants the disco to go on until 1 a.m., and is organising a buffet and the sale of non-alcoholic drinks. Carry out research, and write a memo advising them on the health and safety factors it needs to consider.

Security measures

Security is also a key factor in all events. Teams need to make sure that:

- the site for the event is secure, arranging security staff when necessary
- equipment is stored safely and can be locked away when the site is empty
- the public's well-being and personal belongings are safeguarded (this may mean employing security guards or asking for police support).

DISCUSSION POINT

What part does insurance play in security at events? If you were organising a pop concert at a large indoor arena, what aspects of the event do you think you would need to insure?

6.1.10 Contingency plans

Sometimes projects are disrupted by circumstances completely beyond the organisers' control. Although teams can't cater for all eventualities, they should try to anticipate possible problems and plan what to do if things do go wrong. This is called a contingency plan.

To draw up a contingency plan, teams need to:
- anticipate what might go wrong
- plan how to prevent these problems
- have back-up measures in case problems do occur.

Teams organising events make contingency plans for two main types of problems:
- emergencies (such as fire, or a serious accident)
- foreseeable non-emergency deviation (such as bad weather, or equipment breaking down).

Contingency plans for emergencies

An emergency is the most serious type of problem an event might face. Possible emergencies include:
- fire
- a bomb threat
- a major accident
- a health emergency (such as a heart attack).

Teams need to appoint a health and safety officer to take responsibility for:
- organising contingency plans for these types of emergencies
- making sure that plans are put into practice efficiently if there is an emergency.

The Fire Precautions Act of 1971 requires some leisure and recreation facilities to get a fire certificate from the local fire authority before they can stage events. To be sure of safety, planning teams should contact the local fire officer for more information on fire regulations and safety.

Fire precautions

All teams planning an event should follow these guidelines:
- practise a fire drill, so staff know how to evacuate the building
- restrict the number of people allowed in the venue – never allow more people in than is allowed by law or the fire officer
- make sure that fire escapes are clearly signposted and not obstructed
- have people on hand who are trained in fire safety.

In case of fire or a bomb threat, health and safety officers need to make sure that plans are in place for evacuating the site. Even quite small events should make sure that there are:

- access routes for emergency vehicles
- emergency exits signposted
- meeting points clearly marked
- procedures for calling the emergency services
- stewards who know what to do if there is an emergency, and who are briefed fully on evacuation procedures.

Procedures should also be in place for calling the emergency services and organising access for vehicles in case of a serious accident or health emergency. All events should have first-aid equipment and a trained first-aider on standby, who could provide on-the-spot care if necessary.

Contingency plans for foreseeable non-emergency deviations

Foreseeable non-emergency deviations can occur at any time, and although they're not life-threatening, they can severely disrupt an event. Teams need to anticipate all the things that could go wrong, and make contingency plans to minimise the effects of such problems.

A team organising a garden party explains its contingency plans for the event:

❝ We appointed a health and safety officer who made sure that plans were in place in case of emergencies such as fire or accidents. But we also realised there were lots of other, less serious problems which could threaten the success of our event. Knowing the weather in the UK, rain was the most likely problem. We considered transferring the party to an indoor venue if it rained, but decided this would completely destroy the garden party theme. Instead, we managed to borrow a marquee which we had on stand-by in case of pouring rain on the day of the event, and erected canopies in case of showers. We did consider taking out an insurance policy against bad weather, but it was going to be too expensive. We also drew up a detailed action plan for alternative procedures on the day if one of the event team was ill, the musicians didn't turn up, catering equipment broke down. We even thought about how we'd be affected by a power cut! ❞

ACTIVITY

Make a list of the foreseeable non-emergency deviations that could happen if you were organising a tennis tournament. What contingency plans would you make?

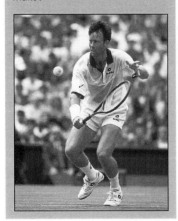

ACTIVITY

What contingency plans do you need to draw up for your project? Make two lists, one of plans for emergencies, the other of plans for foreseeable non-emergency deviations.

6.1.11 Deciding how the project will be reviewed and evaluated

Evaluation criteria are the things against which the project is evaluated. They can be quantitative, such as the number of people participating, or qualitative, such as how much customers enjoyed an event.

Evaluating a project means agreeing what worked and didn't work, and assessing whether the project was a success or a failure. Evaluation can only be completed after a project is finished, when all the facts are available.

To be able to evaluate a project, teams need to decide what to evaluate – their evaluation criteria. It is important that evaluation criteria are clear, specific and easy to measure, as the organiser of a beach party explains:

66 *One of our evaluation criteria was based on our main objective – to provide enjoyable family entertainment. Although the whole team felt that the families who came had enjoyed themselves, we didn't keep any record of customer satisfaction. As it was, we could only report that we thought people had a good time, perhaps because it was a lovely hot day, or because the entertainment was good value – we just don't know! If we'd wanted to use such a vague evaluation criterion, we should have planned how to measure it in advance.* 99

DISCUSSION POINT

How could the beach party organisers have measured whether they provided enjoyable family entertainment?

Evaluation criteria

- Did we meet our objectives?
- Were key deadlines met?
- Did our planning promote effective performance?
- Was the project effective/successful?
- What went well and what went badly for you individually?
- How well did the team work as a whole?
- How did working as part of a team help or hinder you?

DISCUSSION POINT

Why do you think it is important to have evaluation criteria, rather than just having a general chat about whether or not you think a project succeeded?

Key questions

1 What things should be included in your project's business plan?

2 What are the most common objectives of leisure and recreation projects?

3 What are three things you should consider when preparing to meet the needs of your customers?

4 What resources need to be considered when planning a project?

5 What are four financial aspects that must be considered when planning your project?

6 What kinds of service staff are necessary in projects and events?

7 Describe two examples of administration systems used in projects and events.

8 What aspects of health, safety and security must be considered when planning a project or event?

9 What is the purpose of a contigency plan?

10 Give some examples of useful evaluation criteria for projects and events.

UNIT

6

SECTION **6.1**

SECTION **6.2**

Teamwork

Developing effective teamwork skills is an important part of your leisure and recreation project. Many event planning teams find it helpful to have a team plan which sets out the responsibilities of each member of the team. This section explores the principles of teamwork and highlights the team skills your project will require. It also gives you the chance to construct your own team plan.

❝ When we plan our annual pantomime we start by making sure that it includes stars who will appeal to all the different age groups. We generally have a meeting between the marketing manager, myself and the distribution people at which ideas are shared. We start advertising in early summer and send out customised letters to each particular group – whether it's cubs and scouts or old people. We then start our poster campaign and distribute leaflets throughout the area so that we gradually build up interest. Nearer the date we have a major launch for the pantomime: we invite the press, have a big photocall and give interviews. **❞**

press and publicity officer at an entertainments venue

❝ I have overall responsibility and I organised everything the first year. Now there is a team of six who became involved in 1997. All have expertise; one is an accountant, one has computer knowledge and skills, the local rowing club provide a couple of their top people to advise and one person from that club organises qualified umpires and marshals. Operational roles are quite clearly defined and documented. We have at least three planning meetings. We have milestones that have to be reached by certain dates. **❞**

organiser of a regatta

The purpose of your team

DISCUSSION POINT

How do you think individual team members' targets would be affected by these team targets? Do you think it is more sensible to set team targets and then individual targets, or the other way around?

As you saw in section 6.1.1, deciding your team's objectives is an important stage in planning your project. Once a project has been chosen, these objectives need to be broken down into more specific targets.

There are two main types of target in planning your project:
- individual targets – to be achieved by individual team members
- team targets – to be achieved by the team as a whole.

Planning teams usually hold a special meeting to set the targets for a project.

Individual targets

Individual team members usually have two types of target when organising a project:
- personal development targets – e.g. 'to develop my leadership skills', 'to play an active part in meetings'
- targets related to their role in the team – e.g. a secretary might set himself the targets 'to circulate information efficiently', and 'to make sure that all correspondence is professionally presented'.

Team members usually draw up their own individual targets, and then talk them through with the chairperson or the rest of the team to make sure that they fit in with everyone else's goals, timescales and use of resources.

Team targets

Team targets are the team's specific goals in organising a project. They should be clear and simple, so that the team can evaluate at the end of the project whether it has succeeded in meeting its targets.

A GNVQ project team planning an all-night comedy marathon got together to set its team targets. After spending a lot of time talking about what it wanted to achieve, the team held a brainstorming session and came up with some key words, such as 'cost' and 'fun'. From these, the team put together the following list of targets:
- to plan an all-night comedy marathon to raise money for Comic Relief
- to make sure that everyone gives their services free of charge, including performers
- to keep entrance costs down as much as possible
- to make sure that the venue is suitable for the event and complies with health and safety regulations
- to make sure that the event runs according to plan
- to list a detailed running order of performers on the night
- to produce a clear contingency plan
- to make sure that everyone has fun!
- to make the donation as soon as possible after the event.

ACTIVITY

Hold a meeting of your GNVQ planning team and set your team targets for your project. Look back at your original objectives, and break these down into clear, detailed goals which you will be able to use at the end of the event to evaluate its success.

Make sure that every team member has a copy of these targets so they can monitor progress towards achieving them.

Working on your own, start setting your individual targets for the project. Section 6.2.2 will address the subject of people's roles within the team. If you already know what role you are going to play in the team (e.g. secretary, promotions manager), you will be able to set detailed targets. If you don't know your role yet, you can set general targets (such as 'to develop my teamwork skills'), and then fill in more specific targets at a later stage.

Roles and responsibilities of team members

For people to work well as a team, they need to know what they are responsible for. If everyone tried to do everything, nothing would get done efficiently.

Teams organising a project need to:

- decide the different functions needed (e.g. event coordinator, health and safety coordinator, finance coordinator)
- decide who should be responsible for each of these functions
- establish a structure for the team (e.g. who reports to whom, who is in charge of making final decisions).

Functions

The exact functions, or roles, within a team will depend on the project being organised. However, most teams organising a leisure and recreation project include some or all of the following:

- project coordinator – responsible for producing an overall plan for the project, coordinating activities, and chairing team meetings
- secretary – responsible for communication within the team, producing minutes for meetings, and circulating action lists and planning sheets
- finance coordinator – responsible for working out and allocating budgets and keeping accounts for the project
- resources coordinator – responsible for ensuring that the team has all the materials, equipment and staff it needs
- promotions coordinator – responsible for public relations, and for preparing and producing publicity materials
- health and safety coordinator – responsible for all aspects of health and safety for the project
- security coordinator – responsible for all security aspects of project.

The project coordinator should also have a deputy coordinator, who keeps up to date with progress and would be able to take overall responsibility if the coordinator was absent.

A good coordinator:

- is well organised
- has good communication skills
- gets on well with people – other team members, people in authority, people from different organisations
- is able to tell people what to do, when necessary
- has time to do the job
- is enthusiastic about the project.

ACTIVITY

In your project planning team:

■ agree the different roles needed

■ carry out a skills audit, and decide who should do what

■ prepare an organisational chart for the team.

Before allocating roles and responsibilities, teams often carry out a skills audit. Each team member lists:

■ their skills (e.g. being able to drive, typing)

■ things they are good at (e.g. communication, art)

■ things they don't like doing (e.g. maths)

■ skills which they would like to improve (e.g. research)

■ aspects of the project they are particularly interested in (e.g. promotion).

The team can then use these lists to ensure that:

■ the project makes the most of team members' skills

■ people are given jobs they will enjoy and be good at.

DISCUSSION POINT

A GNVQ leisure and recreation team is planning a fund-raising barbecue. One of the team members says that she is skilled at wordprocessing, hates using numbers, and quite enjoys public speaking. What role in the team would suit her best?

Preparing briefings for roles

Each team member's role should be explained in a briefing – a written description of their job. Role briefings should include lists of:

■ the main tasks the team member has to carry out

■ the outcomes they should achieve

■ their responsibilities

■ contingency arrangements they need to know about

■ resources they need and are responsible for.

ACTIVITY

In a team meeting, talk about what different roles involve. After the meeting, write a briefing for your own role, and show it to the rest of the team.

6.2.3 Team structure

People in a project-planning team need to understand:

■ their role in the team

■ how their responsibilities relate to other people's roles.

For example:

■ a promotional coordinator will need to talk to the treasurer regularly about the budget for producing and printing materials

■ a secretary will need to talk to the chairperson about the agenda for meetings when preparing meeting notes.

Most project planning teams find it useful to produce a chart showing:

■ the structure of the team

■ lines of authority

■ who different people report to.

The more people there are in a team, the more helpful an organisational structure is.

Ten people were involved in planning the all-night comedy marathon mentioned in section 6.2.1. They decided that areas of responsibility should be divided up as follows:

■ event manager (responsible for coordinating the team and event)

■ finance manager (responsible for the budget and ticket sales)

■ secretary (responsible for communications within the team)

■ catering manager (responsible for organising catering for the event, with one bar manager)

■ stage manager (responsible for organising and booking the acts, and for coordinating the work of lighting and sound specialists)

■ promotions manager (responsible for publicising the event)

■ health, safety and security manager (responsible for coordinating health, safety and security, with the help of extra security staff).

The team's organisational chart looked like this.

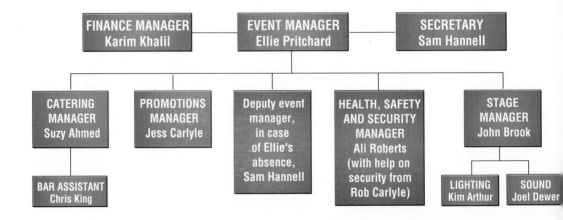

6.2.4 Team-building and interaction

Accomplishing a project requires all team members to interact well together. Without cooperation, preparations will be disorganised, and the project is likely to fail.

Team interaction takes place on many levels:

- in meetings of the whole team
- when team members work together in smaller groups to achieve specific targets
- on a one-to-one basis between team members.

Although team members have particular responsibilities, they must always remember that they are contributing to a team effort, and focus on the overall team plan as well as their own role and targets.

Checklist for team interaction

- Be aware at all times of the team's plan and schedule.
- Don't treat your own area of work as more important than any other. It might seem so to you, but it is only one part of the overall plan.
- Be willing to help other team members when you are less busy.
- Follow established procedures for reporting information about progress, problems, tasks achieved, etc.
- Go to meetings and make an active contribution to them wherever possible.
- If problems arise, share them with others. They are generally easier to solve as a team.

DISCUSSION POINT

Have you ever experienced uncooperative behaviour when working in a team? What happened? How did you feel? How did the lack of cooperation affect the overall success of the team?

Factors influencing teamwork

There are several factors which may influence how well the team works. These are:

- communication
- leadership
- personality clashes
- access to resources
- the working environment.

Communication

Often, good communication is the key to a successful project. If team members communicate and get on with each other, they will probably work well together.

This is especially true in team meetings, which involve a range of people with different personalities and ideas. Unless people are flexible and willing to listen, meetings can quickly become arguments with no-one agreeing on anything. Successful meetings depend on people focusing on the purpose of the meeting, and working hard to cooperate with each other.

ACTIVITY

Write this list of communication skills in the notebook you use for your project meetings, and try to follow the guidelines at the next meeting. Think about your own behaviour in meetings. Are there any extra reminders you'd like to add to the list?

Communication skills

- Listen carefully to what people are saying.
- Be brief and concise in what you say.
- Keep focused on the purpose of the meeting.
- Keep your remarks to the point.
- Don't interrupt other people.
- Don't dominate the group.
- Don't let yourself be dominated.
- Use positive body language (e.g. don't yawn or slump in your seat).

Leadership

The role of the project coordinator is to guide the team, motivate them and help them to resolve any conflicts that may get in the way of the project aims.

The success of the project can be hindered if the team leader is:

- dominating – takes control and won't allow others to contribute
- ineffective – unwilling to take responsibility and make decisions.

A good team leader is someone who can:

- make decisions which will benefit the whole team
- listen to what other team members have to say
- respect the skills and ideas that other team members offer the project
- address problems straight on and not avoid them
- motivate team members to do their best.

DISCUSSION POINT

Can you name a person who you think provides excellent leadership? (It can be a public figure or someone you know personally.) What qualities or skills do they have which make them a successful leader?

Personality clashes

The success of a project can be damaged by personality clashes and personal conflicts. When team members are not getting along for personal reasons, this can create tension among the entire team. Sometimes personality clashes get in the way of the project's aims and objectives.

If there is a personality clash among your team members, it is important to remember that you can't force people to like each other. But it also shouldn't interfere with the purpose of the team, which is to carry out your project as successfully as possible. Here are some important tips to keep in mind:

- Be honest about it if there is a problem between any of the team members. If you avoid the issue or try to take sides, it will never get resolved.
- Show respect to everyone in your team, even if personally you don't like them.
- Be willing to negotiate solutions to any conflicts. Don't be stubborn or hold a grudge.

Access to resources

Your project may be affected if you have trouble gaining access to the necessary resources.

The resources you will be most concerned with in your GNVQ project are:

- time – you will need enough time to plan and prepare for your project or event
- space – you will need space in which to hold your planning meetings, as well as a venue
- money – in some cases you will need access to money to provide for your start-up costs
- work materials – this will depend on what you choose to do for your project
- materials for events – if your team is planning an event, you may need quite a few materials to set it up.

If your team is having trouble with access to any of these types of resources, you may need to consult with your tutor in order to find a solution.

ACTIVITY

At a meeting with your GNVQ project planning team, go through the above list item by item and determine if there are any problems accessing the necessary resources.

The working environment

Another factor which can affect the success of your project is your team's working environment. You will need a quiet space which is large enough to fit your team comfortably and where everyone can see and hear each other clearly. If you are trying to hold your meetings in a space which is crowded or noisy, you will not be able to focus adequately on the team objectives.

❝ *We held our first meeting at Michael's house. There were ten of us squeezed into his bedroom, sitting on the floor and in corners, and holding our notebooks in our laps. He's got three younger brothers who were running about in the rest of the house, up and down the stairs, and shouting at one another. And his older sister was in the room across the hall, playing music at a deafening volume. Needless to say, we didn't get anything accomplished at that first meeting. It was so disorganised that we ended up just drinking cups of coffee and chatting with one another. We held our next meeting in the college library, in a room that is set aside for seminars and group discussions. There's a large table and a chalkboard at the front of the room. It felt much more professional and organised, and I think we were all motivated by the atmosphere. We made real headway at that second meeting, and arranged to book the room twice a week for the rest of the term.* **❞**

Key questions

1 What is the difference between individual targets and team targets? How do they relate to one another?

2 What five things are considered in a skills audit?

3 What should be included in a role briefing?

4 Why do teams need a team structure?

5 On what levels does team interaction occur?

6 Name four useful communication skills.

7 What qualities does a good team leader possess?

8 How does your working environment affect how well your team works?

SECTION **6.3**

Carrying out the project

Running a leisure and recreation project can be stressful and exhausting, even if all the planning has been done properly in advance. It can also be tremendously rewarding. The chances of things going well are increased if all the people involved are clear about their roles and cooperate with each other. In this section you'll be looking at how to work with the whole team when carrying out your project.

66 There is so much to do on the day that you don't realise how quickly time is passing. We start with a final meeting in the morning, four hours before the regatta starts. We make sure that the arrangements for teams arriving are all in place – they start to arrive mid-morning. Spectators tend to arrive around one o'clock for a two o'clock start, so the stewards and people in the refreshment tent are all in place by midday. 99

organiser of a regatta

66 Things can go wrong unexpectedly. The first year we ran the fête the weather was perfect and all the stallholders were really happy. The next year it started off fine but half way through the afternoon there was a tremendous rainstorm. It turned into a washout, literally. So from then on we organised a marquee in case of rain and encouraged all the stallholders to bring awnings and coverings. 99

organiser of a summer fête

6.3.1 Carrying out the project

ACTIVITY

Look at the role briefing you prepared for your own role in planning a project (see section 6.2.2). Make sure you read it through again before the project takes place.

Completing your tasks

Carrying out a project can be a complicated, stressful and nerve-racking job – especially if the team hasn't prepared well enough.

To make sure that everything runs smoothly, team members need to know what they have to do, when and how. This information should be set out clearly in their role briefings (see page 343). If role briefings are prepared carefully and everyone follows them, all should go according to plan.

A GNVQ project team has organised a leisure and recreation luncheon at their college, to which three guest speakers from the leisure and recreation industry have been invited. The catering coordinator for the luncheon explained how her role briefing helped her make sure that her part of the project went smoothly:

❝ *We wrote role briefings two months before the event, at an early planning meeting. My role briefing – for catering – covered all aspects of my job, from preparation through to actually running the luncheon:*

Objectives
Making sure that food and drink is bought and prepared in time for the event.
Making sure that there is enough food and drink for all the participants.
Making sure that food and drink are bought within budget.
Making sure that the kitchen is clean and tidy after use.

Tasks
Decide the menu for the luncheon (food and drink).
Check out food wholesalers to get the best deal.
Work out a budget for food and drink.
Organise five volunteers to help with preparing and serving food.
Buy the food and drink within budget.
Find out from the college administration where food could be prepared and served.
Work out how much crockery and cutlery is needed, and tell the resources coordinator.

Prepare food and drink.
Serve food and drink.
Organise washing up after the event.
Distribute any leftover food and drink among the project team.

Contingency plans
Two reserve helpers in case any of the volunteers can't make it on the day.
20 spare sets of crockery and cutlery.
Mops, cloths and washing up liquid, in case of spillage.

Resources needed
Money for buying food and drink.
Food and drink, trestle tables for food, cutlery, crockery, washing up liquid, cloths, mops.
A kitchen area for preparing food.
An area for laying out food.
A sink and draining board for washing up.
Five volunteers to help with preparing and serving food.

I referred to a copy of my role briefing at every stage of planning and running the luncheon. I put my tasks into chronological order, ticked them off as I completed them, and looked at what I had to do next. I checked my list of responsibilities and the resources I needed regularly, to make sure all was going according to plan. And the contingency plans helped out on the day, when some of the crockery got broken and one of my volunteer helpers phoned in sick. After the event, I looked back at the objectives given in my briefing, and was pleased to see that I had achieved them. ❞

Dealing politely with customers, other members of your team and any other people involved with the project

Projects can be very busy and stressful for the people running them. It is essential that you remain calm and polite with your fellow team members and classmates, your customers, and any other people involved with the project. Getting upset or behaving rudely can spoil its success, and can distract your team members or staff from performing well at their tasks.

Supporting other team members

Supporting your fellow team members is very important throughout the project, particularly on the day of an event. The best-laid plans can go astray if team members don't work well – with each other and with their customers.

The team plan sets out people's roles and responsibilities for the project, and good teamwork is needed to make sure that it is followed. Individual team members are responsible for working together in line with the team plan, their team structure, and their roles within it.

Reacting quickly and confidently to problems

If any problems do occur during your project or on the day of an event, you should respond immediately. Ignoring a problem or delaying before you attend to it could make it even worse.

DISCUSSION POINT

What should each of the following people do to support their team members during a leisure and recreation event?

- A promotions manager who doesn't have much to do, but sees that the catering staff are rushed off their feet.

- A catering manager who has to pop to a nearby shop to buy some more orange squash.

- An event coordinator who realises that an event is going to overrun and that the team will be working later than expected.

How can team members support one another?

- By being flexible and helping other team members as needed.
- By making sure that other team members know what they're doing, so everyone's up to date with progress.
- By reporting regularly to their manager.
- By being tolerant with each other.
- By making constructive criticism, not personal attacks.
- By communicating well with each other.

ACTIVITY

How good are you at cooperating with people? Write a list of different ways in which you can support your team members, customers and other staff during the course of your project.

A member of a GNVQ team which planned a local primary school's sports day explains how his team reacted when a problem occurred:

Everything went really well except for an accident which occurred: a little boy tripped over in the egg and spoon race, and had to be taken to hospital with a broken arm. Margaret was supervising the race and she reacted at once. She stopped the race and asked people to move back, and she sent for Adam who is the health and safety officer of our team. He's got a first-aid certificate, and he went immediately to this little boy's aid. Meanwhile I called an ambulance to the scene, and other team members organised the kids into other activities so that there wasn't a crowd milling about while this one little boy was tended. The whole team reacted as quickly and efficiently as possible.

Keeping to any agreed timelines

Very few leisure and recreation projects take place without any disruptions at all. Keep in mind however that disruptions can be annoying, confusing or even dangerous for customers. Project teams need to act quickly to recognise and solve any problems in order to keep to agreed timelines.

To help them do this, they try to anticipate disruptions in advance by preparing contingency plans (see section 6.1.10).

Knowing when to get help and advice from others

Throughout your project and especially during an event you will need to know when to get help or advice from someone else. Sometimes it is difficult to make the decision to seek assistance, especially if everyone else seems busy already. But it may be very important to get help or advice, even if the timing seems inconvenient, as this theme park assistant explains:

On my first day at this job, the park was especially busy and the queues for the rides were very long. One family had been waiting in line for half an hour, and when they got to the front they asked me whether the ride was safe for their four-year old. I wasn't sure, but my supervisor wasn't around. I very nearly just said oh yes, it's fine, but I knew that I should get some advice. So I apologised to them and explained that I would have to find out, and that it would be several minutes. They were fairly exasperated about that, and even when I'd gone to find my supervisor I wondered if I was just wasting their time. But my supervisor came to speak to them, and it turned out that the ride was for children aged five and over. She gave them some free tickets for other rides as an apology for the inconvenience, and she told me that I had done the right thing to come and find her. If I'd let their child on the ride it would have been unsafe and I could have got into a great deal of trouble for allowing it.

DISCUSSION POINT

The team in charge of a village fête is in a state of complete panic. It's 2.20 and the official opening was supposed to be at 2.00. The mayor hasn't arrived, the brass band is awful, a little girl has just been thrown off during a pony ride, now the heavens have opened, and people are already wandering home.

Should the team have contingency plans for these disruptions? What should be their priority now?

Key questions

1 How can you use your role briefing to help you complete your tasks?

2 How can team members support one another?

3 How should you respond if a problem occurs during your project or event?

SECTION **6.4**

Evaluating the project

Once the project is finished, it is important to evaluate what happened and to gather feedback. You will need to determine whether or not the objectives set by your team at the outset have been achieved. In this section you will learn ways of giving and receiving feedback. You will also see how the evaluation process improves both individual and team performance.

66 We measure the success of our summer play-scheme by the numbers of children being reached, calculating this using half-day sessions. We also ask the children themselves in some of the sessions to say what they thought, by circling cartoon faces looking happy or glum. 99

community play officer in a city council

66 After the festival we discussed how it went and in particular what went wrong. Most of the discussion was on the musical side, but we also discussed the acoustics of the venue, the helpfulness of the staff and other things like the temperature. 99

leader of a band

66 We have a 'wash-up' meeting on the day after the event where we pick up litter, then meet. We count the money, check that all the bills will be paid, and set a meeting for deciding what to do with the profit from the event if there is money left in the pot. Every one of the key people evaluates what they did and decides which bits need to be changed for next year. 99

organiser of a town's annual heritage festival

6.4.1 **Evaluating the project**

After your project is completed and the team has gathered feedback from a range of sources, it should hold an evaluation meeting. To start the discussion, look back at your business plan and your list of evaluation criteria.

Providing evaluation feedback to other team members

It is only useful to comment on other team members' performance if the feedback is constructive. Constructive feedback is both negative and positive – it picks up on problems and weaknesses, but suggests ways to improve in the future.

> **Points to remember when giving feedback**
> - Take time to think about whether you would like to hear what you are going to say. For example, would you like to be told that your ideas were boring? Would it improve your performance in the future?
> - Try not to accuse people. What's the point of saying 'You're always aggressive', or 'You never think about other people'?
> - Include yourself in the feedback statement when possible. For example, 'I sometimes thought you dominated the team, and even though I realised we'd got stuck that made me feel like I didn't have anything to offer.'
> - Be clear and honest about what you think. For example, don't say to someone that they're multi-talented in all aspects of teamwork if you have felt throughout the project that they have interfered and caused disruption. Try to find a constructive way to say what you think and feel.

Before your team's evaluation meeting, think carefully about the feedback you want to give to other team members. Make notes in each case, taking particular care when you want to make a constructive criticism. It's worth taking time in advance to make sure that you voice your feedback in a constructive way.

Responding to evaluation feedback

Receiving feedback can be difficult. People are sensitive about being criticised, even if, like this financial coordinator, they realise they need an evaluation of their performance:

❝ I wasn't absolutely sure about my ability as financial coordinator on this project, and was very worried about whether people would think I was useless and criticise me during our evaluation meeting. But at the same time, I knew that I needed someone to look at what I had done and say 'this aspect of what you did was good, but you could have tried this here' – constructive criticism, I suppose. In the end, I quite enjoyed the evaluation meeting and found it incredibly useful. Even when people pointed out ways I could improve my performance, at least I knew where I stood. ❞

To get the most out of a feedback session, team members need to:

- be open to criticism
- ask questions about areas of their performance where they lacked confidence
- react honestly
- listen carefully and make sure they understand what is being said
- remain calm and take time to reflect on what has been said.

Feedback from team colleagues

Feedback from colleagues can be particularly difficult for team members to accept. Before responding, they should ask themselves:

- Are the criticisms fair?
- Do I deserve the praise?
- What can I learn from this feedback?

As one project coordinator found out, if you can accept criticism from your colleagues, it can be extremely useful:

66 *It never occurred to me that the team thought I was trying to take over. I really did think they were grateful that I offered to take responsibility – at least it seemed to get things moving. It was only during a feedback session at a late planning meeting that I was made aware of how my behaviour was affecting other members of the team. I was cross to start off with, you know – if only so and so had done this or that then I wouldn't have had to run everything. But after I'd calmed down I realised that actually they were right, that I always wanted to do things my way. It was awful to realise that even though I went on and on about democracy, I wasn't being very democratic!* 99

Feedback from customers

Customers are on the receiving end of products, services and activities, so can give some of the best feedback.

Team members often receive feedback informally from customers during an event. For example, customers might:

- compliment a catering assistant on the range of food on sale
- complain about the long wait to get in
- comment on the programme design.

Team members need to keep records of this feedback so that they can respond to it constructively and share it with other team members.

Feedback from teachers and tutors

Teachers and tutors are in a good position to give GNVQ team members evaluation on their performance. They:

- have monitored the project from its earliest stages, so they have a good overview
- understand the constraints which the team was working under
- aren't directly involved, so they can give balanced feedback.

Key questions

1 What is constructive feedback?

2 What are four important points to remember when giving feedback?

3 How should team members respond to feedback?

Assignment

Part 1

Hold a team meeting to propose possible projects and select the most feasible one to implement. At the meeting, each team member should make a presentation which:

- describes three event options which meet the project objectives
- gives brief details of the objectives and timescales, necessary resources, and legal aspects of each project option
- explains which of the three they favour and why.

When everyone has made their presentations, hold a vote to select the best one.

After the meeting, write an account explaining what happened at the meeting and the reasons why the selected option was thought to be the best. Prepare a business plan for the project which summarises the details of the project that has been chosen. It should include:

- objectives and timescales for the project
- description of the project
- resource needs (physical, human and financial)
- legal aspects of the project (health and safety, security, insurance)
- methods to be used to evaluate the project.

Part 2

For the project you are planning, draw up a team plan which describes:

- team objectives
- team structure
- role allocations and briefings.

Make notes on how you contributed to the plan.

Discuss and agree how you will record your contributions to the project – for example, observation sheets, audio recordings, logs. Prepare any documentation you want to use to record observations.

Part 3

Keep a log of your own and the team's contributions to the project you are organising and running. Make sure that you include details of:

- the task(s) you were allocated
- your role in the project
- any problems that arose and how you reacted
- any time deadlines you were given and whether you kept to them
- the effectiveness of the team in achieving the project objectives.

Make sure that you include all your contributions, even if they weren't directly part of your team role. Arrange to have your log confirmed, for example by:

- your tutor
- other team members
- a video recording.

Part 4

Working as a team, decide and then implement an evaluation process for the project you organised and ran. Your evaluation process must be agreed as a team and should include:

- agreed criteria
- feedback from appropriate sources
- feedback from team members
- self-evaluation.

Identify any factors which affected the project and explain their effect. Then identify improvements to team and individual performances that you would implement if you conducted a similar project in the future.

Prepare and give a team presentation on the findings of your evaluation and the improvements you identified through the evaluation process.

Keep notes and other documentation on how you carried out the evaluation and prepared for the presentation.

Arrange to have your tutor present as an observer at any meetings you have:

- as part of the evaluation process
- in preparation for the presentation.

KEY SKILLS

You can use the work you are doing for this part of your GNVQ to collect and develop evidence for the following key skills at level 3

when you	you can collect evidence for
	communication
discuss the complexities of business planning with your peers	key skill C3.1a contribute to a group discussion about a complex subject
presenting your business plan with supporting OHTs	key skill C3.1b make a presentation about a complex subject, using at least one image to illustrate complex points
	key skill C3.3 write two different types of documents about complex subjects; one piece of writing should be an extended document and include at least one image
	working with others
plan your event or project	key skill WO3.1 plan the activity with others, agreeing objectives, responsibilities and working arrangements
work on your event or project	key skill WO3.2 work towards achieving the agreed objectives seeking to establish and maintain cooperative working relationships in meeting responsibilities
evaluate your event or project	key skill WO3.3 review the activity with others against the agreed objective and agree ways of enhancing collaborative work
	improving own learning and performance
plan your event or project	key skill LP3.1 agree targets and plan how these will be met, using support from appropriate others
work on your event or project	key skill LP3.2 use the plan, seeking and using feedback and support from relevant sources to help meet the targets, and use different ways of learning to meet new demands
evaluate your event or project	key skill LP3.3 review progress in meeting targets, establishing evidence of achievements, and agree action for improving performance using support from appropriate others
	problem-solving
plan and work on your event or project	key skill PS3.1 recognise, explore and describe two problems, and agree the standards for their solution
	key skill PS3.2 generate and compare at least two options which could be used to solve each of two problems, and select the best options for taking forward
	key skill PS3.3 plan and implement at least one option for solving each of two problems, and review progress towards their solution
	key skill PS3.4 agree and apply methods to check whether the problem has been solved, describe the results and review the approach taken